G000058256

Peer-to-Peer with VB .NET

MATTHEW MACDONALD

Peer-to-Peer with VB .NET
Copyright ©2003 by Matthew MacDonald

All rights reserved. No part of this work may be reproduced or transmitted in any form or by any means, electronic or mechanical, including photocopying, recording, or by any information storage or retrieval system, without the prior written permission of the copyright owner and the publisher.

ISBN (pbk): 1-59059-105-4

Printed and bound in the United States of America 12345678910

Trademarked names may appear in this book. Rather than use a trademark symbol with every occurrence of a trademarked name, we use the names only in an editorial fashion and to the benefit of the trademark owner, with no intention of infringement of the trademark.

Technical Reviewer: Ron Miller

Editorial Board: Dan Appleman, Craig Berry, Gary Cornell, Tony Davis, Steven Rycroft, Julian Skinner, Martin Streicher, Jim Sumser, Karen Watterson, Gavin Wright, John Zukowski

Assistant Publisher: Grace Wong

Project Manager: Beth Christmas

Copy Editor: Mark Nigara

Production Manager: Kari Brooks

Production Editor: Lori Bring

Compositor and Proofreader: Kinetic Publishing Services, LLC

Indexer: Kevin Broccoli

Cover Designer: Kurt Krames

Manufacturing Manager: Tom Debolski

Distributed to the book trade in the United States by Springer-Verlag New York, Inc., 175 Fifth Avenue, New York, NY, 10010 and outside the United States by Springer-Verlag GmbH & Co. KG, Tiergartenstr. 17, 69112 Heidelberg, Germany.

In the United States: phone 1-800-SPRINGER, email orders@springer-ny.com, or visit http://www.springer-ny.com. Outside the United States: fax +49 6221 345229, email orders@springer.de, or visit http://www.springer.de.

For information on translations, please contact Apress directly at 2560 Ninth Street, Suite 219, Berkeley, CA 94710. Phone 510-549-5930, fax 510-549-5939, email info@apress.com, or visit http://www.apress.com.

The information in this book is distributed on an "as is" basis, without warranty. Although every precaution has been taken in the preparation of this work, neither the author(s) nor Apress shall have any liability to any person or entity with respect to any loss or damage caused or alleged to be caused directly or indirectly by the information contained in this work.

The source code for this book is available to readers at http://www.apress.com in the Downloads section.

For my loving wife, Faria

Contents at a Glance

Contents

About the Author

MATTHEW MACDONALD is an author, educator, and MCSD developer. He's a regular contributor to programming journals such as *Inside Visual Basic* and *Hardcore Visual Basic*, and the author of several books about .NET programming, including *The Book of VB .NET* (No Starch), *ASP.NET: The Complete Reference* (Osborne/McGraw-Hill), and *Microsoft .NET Distributed Applications* (Microsoft Press). In a dimly remembered past life, he studied English literature and theoretical physics.

About the Technical Reviewer

RON MILLER works as a Senior Engineer at Pitney Bowes developing new shipping systems. He has been in the IT industry for over 20 years and has developed a variety of solutions from Distributed Asset Management systems to those providing daily sales figures to handhelds. Ron can be found searching for that "better solution" to the problem at hand. In his spare time, Ron takes pleasure in restoring older Lancias and BMWs.

Acknowledgments

No AUTHOR COULD COMPLETE A BOOK without a small army of helpful individuals. I'm deeply indebted to the whole Apress team, including Beth Christmas and Lori Bring, who helped everything move swiftly and smoothly; Ron Miller, who performed the tech review; Mark Nigara, who performed the copy edit (and discussed the countless ways to capitalize "web services"); and many other individuals who worked behind the scenes indexing pages, drawing figures, and proofreading the final copy. I owe a special thanks to Gary Cornell, who always offers invaluable advice about projects and the publishing world. He's helped to build a truly unique company with Apress.

In writing the code for this book, I've had the help of articles, sample code, and in-depth presentations from the best .NET developers. In particular, I should thank Lance Olson, whose sample formed the basis for the pinging code used to test peer connectivity, and Jason Thomas (the creator of the Gnutella client Swapper.NET—see http://www.revolutionarystuff.com/swapper for more information). Peer-to-peer is still evolving and changing crazily, and I hope to have the chance to update this book sometime in the future with the next round of developer tools and technologies.

Finally, I'd never write *any* book without the support of my wife and these special individuals: Nora, Razia, Paul, and Hamid. Thanks everyone!

Introduction

LIKE ALL NEW DEVELOPMENT MODELS, peer-to-peer programming has been praised, denounced, and often confused in the programming community. Peer-to-peer proponents claim that their technology holds the key to building virtual supercomputers that can share vast pools of knowledge and create self-sufficient communities on the Internet. Peer-to-peer critics claim it's little more than an interesting novelty—suitable for some applications, but useless in the business world.

This book takes a practical look at peer-to-peer programming, without the hype. You'll explore how peer-to-peer designs work, learn fundamental peer-to-peer concepts, and master the .NET technologies you'll need to implement them. You'll also see that while some aspects of .NET are ideally suited for the peer-to-peer world, other high-level features haven't materialized yet. The emphasis in this book is on *integrating* peer-to-peer designs into your applications. This means that you'll focus on "hybrid" peer-to-peer designs that combine traditional solutions and peer-to-peer concepts to create new features such as instant messaging, resource sharing, and distributed computing.

This book is organized into four parts. The first part explores peer-to-peer design concepts and architecture. The second and third parts lead you through the process of creating several hybrid peer-to-peer applications that are most at home on local area networks and in the enterprise environment. The fourth part introduces advanced peer-to-peer issues, including security and decentralized designs. In this part you'll explore how to use third-party platforms to meet challenges such as firewalls and network address translation and take your peer-to-peer designs to the Internet.

About This Book

This book is designed for experienced programmers who are familiar with the .NET platform and the VB .NET language and want to extend their skills to peer-to-peer programming. It doesn't assume any knowledge of peer-to-peer concepts, or of the distributed technologies that you can use to build a peer-to-peer solution (such as .NET networking or Remoting).

What This Book Teaches You

This book provides the following information:

- A detailed description of the .NET technologies that can be used for peer-to-peer programming, including Remoting, networking, web services, and encryption.

- A thorough explanation of peer-to-peer conceptions such as peer discovery, communication, and the role of a central lookup or coordination server.

- Examples of common peer-to-peer applications such as chat servers, file-sharing services, and distributed work managers.

- An explanation of some third-party tools that can help simplify peer-to-peer programming in .NET, such as Groove and the Intel Peer-to-Peer Accelerator Kit.

What This Book Doesn't Teach You

Of course, it's just as important to point out what this book *doesn't* contain:

- A description of core .NET concepts such as namespaces, assemblies, exception handling, and types.

- A primer on object-oriented design. No .NET programmer can progress very far without a solid understanding of classes, interfaces, and other .NET types. In this book, many examples will rely on these basics, using objects to encapsulate, organize, and transfer information.

- The "everything from scratch" decentralized peer-to-peer application. Some parts of peer-to-peer technology (such as firewall traversal and adaptive bandwidth management) are quite complex and extremely difficult to implement correctly. This book assumes that you don't want to code this infrastructure from scratch. Instead, you'll look at hybrid peer-to-peer designs and the emerging third-party technologies that can handle the lower-level plumbing for you.

If you haven't learned the .NET fundamentals, you probably won't be able to work through this book. Start with a more general book about the .NET Framework and the VB .NET language.

Peer-to-Peer and .NET

In the past, Microsoft programmers have been left behind in the peer-to-peer debate. While they were struggling with COM and multitier design, a new type of software architecture appeared, one that seems more at home in open-source languages and the world of the Internet. The .NET platform presents a platform that embraces the Internet.

That said, it's important to note that .NET still lacks some higher-level tools that will be needed to standardize and extend large-scale peer-to-peer applications. Some other programming platforms, such as JXTA (a Sun-led initiative for peer-to-peer programming that focuses on Java), currently offer more than .NET in this respect. However, as the .NET platform matures, support for peer-to-peer networking will only improve, either through .NET Framework updates or optional add-ons.

There's already one promising toolkit that abstracts away some of the work in building a peer-to-peer infrastructure in .NET: Intel's freely downloadable Peer-to-Peer Accelerator Kit. The final part of this book examines the Intel toolkit, considers its advantages, and shows how it extends the .NET Framework. At the same time, you'll look at the Groove platform, which provides the infrastructure for peer-to-peer collaborative applications as well as an easier way to control Microsoft's own Windows Messenger network.

> **NOTE** *In short, Microsoft has identified peer-to-peer as a promising new area where they must provide cutting-edge development tools. .NET moves toward this vision, but there are likely many more revolutions ahead.*

Code Samples

It's a good idea to use the online site to download the most recent, up-to-date code samples. In addition, many of the samples presented in this book are quite lengthy, and the full code is not listed in these pages. To test them on your own system, you'll need to download the complete projects. To download the source code, go to http://www.prosetech.com. You can also download the source code from the Downloads section of the Apress website (http://www.apress.com).

All the code in this book is supported by versions 1.0 and 1.1 of the .NET Framework. For best results, compile the code on your system before executing it. Projects are provided in Visual Studio .NET 2002 format, which means that you must "upgrade" the project before using it in Visual Studio .NET 2003. This upgrading process is easy and automatic. No code changes are required.

Variable Naming

It seems that variable naming is about to become another religious issue for which there is no clear standard, even though developers take heated, uncompromising attitudes about it. Hungarian notation, the preferred standard for C++ and VB (in a slightly modified form), is showing its age. In the world of .NET, where memory management is handled automatically, it seems a little backward to refer to a variable by its data type, especially when that data type may change without any serious consequences and when the majority of variables store references to full-fledged objects.

To complicate matters, Microsoft recommends that objects use simple names for properties and methods, such as COM components and controls. This system makes a good deal of sense, as data-type considerations are becoming more and more transparent. Visual Studio .NET now takes care of some of the work of spotting the invalid use of data types, and its built-in IntelliSense automatically displays information about the data types used by a method.

In this book, data-type prefixes are not used for variables. The only significant exception is with control variables, for which it's still a useful trick to distinguish between types of controls (such as txtUserName and lstUserCountry) and some data objects. Of course, when you create your programs you're free to follow whatever variable naming convention you prefer, provided you make the effort to adopt complete consistency across all your projects (and ideally across all the projects in your organization).

> **NOTE** *This book uses an underscore to denote private variables that are linked to a property procedure. For example, if a class provides a property called Name, the data for that property will be stored in a private variable called _Name. Underscores are not used for any other variable names.*

Feedback

You can send complaints, adulation, and everything in between directly to p2p@prosetech.com. I can't solve your .NET problems or critique your own code, but I'll know what I did right and wrong (and what I may have done in an utterly confusing way) with this book from your feedback. You can also send comments about the website support.

Chapter Overview

It's easiest to read the book from start to finish because later chapters discuss alternate approaches to some of the earlier applications. However, if you're already familiar with peer-to-peer concepts, you may find it easier to skip to the chapters that interest you.

The book follows this four-part structure.

Part One: Introducing Peer-to-Peer

The first part of this book explores peer-to-peer fundamentals. Chapter 1 takes a high-level look at the peer-to-peer world. It presents the key characteristics of peer-to-peer applications, a brief history of peer-to-peer development, and the place of peer-to-peer designs in the enterprise world.

Chapter 2 tackles peer-to-peer architecture and dissects several different peer-to-peer models. In this chapter, you'll learn about the basic challenges and design decisions that face any peer-to-peer project as well as the .NET technologies that are available to meet them. By the end of the chapter, you'll be able to decide when you should (and shouldn't) use peer-to-peer designs in your own solutions.

Part Two: Peer-to-Peer with a Coordination Server

This part introduces "brokered" peer-to-peer designs, in which a central server plays an important role in helping peers communicate. This design can be easily implemented with .NET's high-level Remoting Framework, which you'll encounter in Chapter 3 in detail. Next, Chapter 4 and Chapter 5 show how Remoting can be used to build an instant-messaging application that routes messages over a network, tracks multiple clients, and uses multiple threads and locking to handle simultaneous requests seamlessly.

Finally, Chapter 6 takes a different approach by developing a model for distributed computing in which multiple clients can work together to solve a single CPU-intensive problem. You'll learn how to create a dedicated client to work with a fixed problem type, or how you can use .NET reflection and dynamic assembly loading to create task-independent peers. You'll also see the code-access security measures you'll need to make to ensure that the second approach won't become an express highway for spreading malicious worms across the Internet.

Part Three: Peer-to-Peer with a Discovery Server

Some of the most common and powerful peer-to-peer designs combine a decentralized application with a centralized repository of peer information. The second part of this book explores this model of peer-to-peer design. Chapter 7 introduces the lower level of .NET networking support that you'll need to create direct connections between peers. Chapter 8 shows you how to build a discovery server as an ASP.NET web service, and Chapter 9 brings it all together with a complete sample application for sharing files between peers.

Chapter 10 revisits the discovery service and considers how you can adapt your design for a system that uses .NET Remoting for peer-to-peer interaction. In the process, you'll develop a discovery service that you can use with the Talk .NET instant-messaging code sample presented in Chapter 4 and Chapter 5.

Part Four: Advanced Peer-to-Peer

The last part of this book tackles a few advanced topics in peer-to-peer application programming. Chapter 11 considers security and how you can use .NET's native support for cryptography to protect sensitive data and verify peer identity. Chapter 12 explores third-party toolkits for collaborative peer-to-peer applications with Windows Messenger and Groove. Finally, Chapter 13 introduces Intel's freely downloadable Peer-to-Peer Accelerator Kit, which extends .NET Remoting with valuable networking and peer connectivity features.

Part One

Introducing
Peer-to-Peer

CHAPTER 1

The Evolution
of Peer-to-Peer

PEER-TO-PEER IS an almost magical term that's often used, rarely explained, and frequently misunderstood. In the popular media, peer-to-peer is often described as a copyright-violating technology that underlies song-swapping and file-sharing systems such as Napster and Gnutella. In the world of high-tech business, peer-to-peer networking is a revolution that promises to harness the combined computing power of ordinary personal computers and revolutionize the way we communicate. And to Internet pioneers, peer-to-peer is as much a philosophy as it is a model of development, one that contains the keys needed to defeat censorship and create global communities. All of these descriptions contain part of the answer, but none will help you build your own peer-to-peer systems, or explain why you should.

In this chapter, you'll learn what distinguishes peer-to-peer applications from traditional enterprise systems, how peer-to-peer technology evolved in the early Internet, and what advantages and disadvantages the peer-to-peer model offers. You'll also preview the .NET technologies you'll need to build peer-to-peer software, and the challenges you'll face along the way. By the end of the chapter, you'll be able to decide when you should (and shouldn't) use peer-to-peer designs in your own solutions.

A Brief History of Programming

The easiest way to understand peer-to-peer applications is by comparing them to other models of programming architecture. To understand peer-to-peer programming, you need to realize that it's part revolution, part *evolution*. On the one hand, peer-to-peer programming is the latest in a long line of schisms that have shaken up the programming world. Like them, it promises to change the face of software development forever. On the other hand, peer-to-peer programming borrows heavily from the past. It's likely that peer-to-peer concepts may end up enhancing existing systems, rather than replacing them.

The Birth of Client-Server

In a traditional business environment, software is centralized around a server. In the not-so-distant past, this role was played by a mainframe. The mainframe performed all the work, processing information, accessing data stores, and so on. The clients were marginalized and computationally unimportant: "dumb terminals." They were nothing more than an interface to the mainframe.

As Windows development gained in popularity, servers replaced the mainframe, and dumb terminals were upgraded to low-cost Windows stations that assumed a more important role. This was the start of the era of *client-server* development. In client-server development, the server hosts shared resources such as the program files and back-end databases, but the application actually executed on the client (see Figure 1-1).

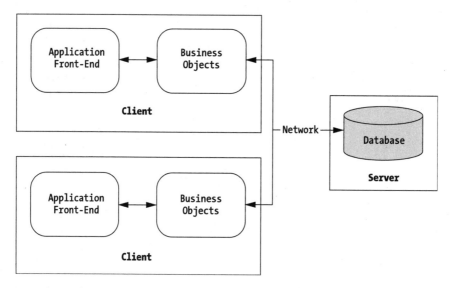

Figure 1-1. Client-server computing

This approach is far from ideal because the clients can't work together. They often need to compete for limited server resources (such as database connections), and that competition creates frequent bottlenecks. These limitations appear most often in large-scale environments and specialized systems in which client communication becomes important. In mid-scale systems, client-server development has proved enormously successful because it allows costly mainframes to be replaced by more affordable servers. In fact, though many programming books talk about the end of client-server development, this model represents the most successful programming paradigm ever applied to the business world, and it's still alive and well in countless corporations.

Distributed Computing

The more popular the Windows PC became in the business world and the more it became involved in ambitious enterprise systems, the more the limitations of client-server programming began to show. A new model was required to deal with the massive transactional systems that were being created in the business world. This new model was *distributed computing*. Distributed computing tackles the core problem of client-server programming—its lack of scalability—with a component-based model that can spread the execution of an application over multiple machines.

In a distributed system, the client doesn't need to directly process the business and data-access logic or connect directly to the database. Instead, the client interacts with a set of components running on a server computer, which in turn communicates with a data store or another set of components (see Figure 1-2). Thus, unlike a client-server system, a significant part of the business code executes on the server computer.

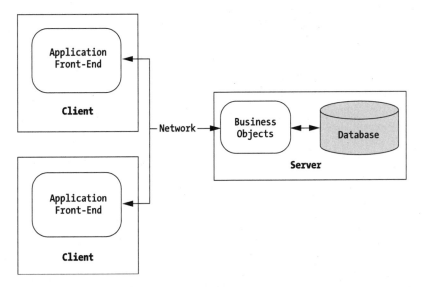

Figure 1-2. Distributed computing

By dividing an application into multiple layers, it becomes possible for several computers to contribute in the processing of a single request. This distribution of logic typically slows down individual client requests (because of the additional overhead required for network communication), but it improves the overall throughput for the entire system. Thus, distributed systems are much more scalable than client-server systems and can handle larger client loads.

Here are some of the key innovations associated with distributed computing:

- If more computing power is needed, you can simply move components to additional servers instead of providing a costly server upgrade.

- If good stateless programming practices are followed, you can replace individual servers with a clustered group of servers, thereby improving scalability.

- The server-side components have the ability to use limited resources much more effectively by pooling database connections and multiplexing a large number of requests to a finite number of objects. This guarantees that the system won't collapse under its own weight. Instead, it will simply refuse clients when it reaches its absolute processing limit.

- Distributed computing is associated with a number of good architecture practices, which make it easier to debug, reuse, and extend pieces of an application.[1]

Distributed programming is the only way to approach a large-scale enterprise-programming project. However, the classic distributed design shown in Figure 1-2 isn't suited for all scenarios. It shares some of the same problems as client-server models: namely, the overwhelming dependence on a central server or cluster of server-like computers. These high-powered machines are the core of the application—the 1 percent of the system where 99 percent of the work is performed. The resources of the clients are mostly ignored.

Peer-to-Peer Appears

The dependency on a central set of servers isn't necessarily a problem. In fact, in some environments it's unavoidable. The reliability, availability, and manageability of a distributed system such as the one shown in Figure 1-2 are hard to beat. In all honesty, you aren't likely to use peer-to-peer technology to build a transaction-processing backbone for an e-commerce website. However, there are other situations that a server-based system can't deal with nearly as well. You'll see some of these examples at the end of this section.

Peer-to-peer technology aims to free applications of their dependence on a central server or group of servers, and it gives them the ability to create global

---

1. Distributed computing is sometimes described as multitier or n-tier programming, but this is not strictly correct. Distributed computing is a physical model that splits execution over multiple computers. Multitier programming is a logical model that divides an application into distinct layers. Think of it this way: A program with a multitier design has the *option* of graduating into a distributed application. However, multitier design and component-based programming can still be used in a traditional client-server application.

communities, harness wasted CPU cycles, share isolated resources, and operate independently from central authorities. In peer-to-peer design, computers communicate directly with each other. Instead of a sharp distinction between servers that provide resources and clients that consume them, every computer becomes an equal peer that can exhibit clientlike behavior (making a request) and serverlike behavior (filling a request). This increases the value of each computer on the network. No longer is it restricted to being a passive client consumer—a peer-to-peer node can participate in shared work or provide resources to other peers.

Peer-to-peer is most often defined as a technology that takes advantage of resources "at the edges of the network" because it bypasses the central server for direct interaction. As you can see in Figure 1-3, this approach actually *complicates* the overall system.

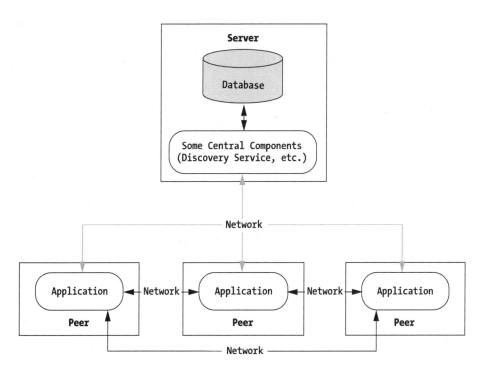

Figure 1-3. Peer-to-peer computing

Peer-to-peer programming is regarded by some as a new generation of programming design, and by others as a subset of distributed computing. In a sense, distributed architecture overlaps with peer-to-peer architecture because many of the technologies used to create distributed enterprise applications can be used to create peer-to-peer systems as well. However, peer-to-peer applications represent a dramatic shift toward a decentralized design philosophy that is quite different from what most programmers expect in an enterprise application.

Here are some of the hallmarks that distinguish a peer-to-peer application:

- The processing is performed on the peers, not farmed out to another computer (such as a high-powered server).

- The peers interact by establishing direct connections, rather than passing messages through a central authority.

- The system can deal with inconsistent connectivity (for example, peers who disappear and reappear on the network).

- The system uses a proprietary peer naming and discovery system that operates outside the Internet's Domain Name Service (DNS) registry.

Evaluating the Peer-to-Peer Model

The inevitable question is this: Can a peer-to-peer application perform better than a client-server application? Unfortunately, this question is not easily answered. It not only depends on the type of application, but on the type of peer-to-peer design, the number of users, and the overall traffic patterns. The most honest answer is probably this: There are some development niches in which peer-to-peer applications will perform better and require fewer resources. However, a peer-to-peer application can easily introduce new headaches and scalability challenges, which can't be dismissed easily. In order to create a successful peer-to-peer application, you must understand both the advantages and drawbacks of a peer-to-peer design.

Benefits and Challenges

Peer-to-peer applications hold a great deal of promise. Some of the unique properties of a peer-to-peer system are as follows:

- A large network of peers will almost always have more computing resources at hand than a powerful central server.

- A completely decentralized peer-to-peer application should have improved reliability because the server won't be a single point of failure for the system.

- A peer-to-peer application should also have improved performance because there is no central server to act as a bottleneck.

Enterprise programmers have met some of these challenges by introducing server farms and clustering technologies. However, these solutions are expensive, and minor server-side problems can still derail an entire enterprise application.

On the other hand, the advantages of peer-to-peer applications are qualified by a few significant drawbacks:

- As a peer-to-peer design becomes more decentralized, the code becomes more complex and the required network bandwidth to manage the peer discovery process increases. This might not be a problem if the bandwidth is spread out equitably over the network, but it often *does* become a problem in an intranet where the network must also be used for a critical client-server business application.

- Although peer-to-peer systems don't rely on a central server, they do rely on the cooperation of multiple peers. This cooperating can be damaged by the variable connectivity of the Internet, where peers might abruptly disappear, even in the middle of serving a request. Similarly, in fully decentralized peer-to-peer systems, low-bandwidth clients can become "mini-bottlenecks" for their part of the network.

- Peer-to-peer programming introduces significant challenges with network addressing due to the way the Internet works with dynamic IP addresses, proxy servers, network address translation (NAT), and firewalls.

It's also difficult to predict how a decentralized peer-to-peer solution will scale as the user community grows. Like all complex systems, a peer-to-peer network can display a dramatically different behavior at a certain "critical mass" of peers. Gnutella, a peer-to-peer protocol used for popular file-sharing applications, is in some respects an enormous in-progress experiment. As the network has grown wildly beyond what was originally expected, connectivity has suffered—frequently. At times, entire islands of peers have broken off from the main pool, able to communicate within their community, but unable to access other parts of the Gnutella network.

Ingenious techniques such as smart caching and optimized routing have been developed to meet the challenges of large peer-to-peer networks. However, it's still hard to predict how these solutions will play out on a large scale over a loosely connected network that might include hundreds of thousands of peers. These emergent behaviors are impossible to plan for. The only way to solve them is with an iterative process of development that involves frequent testing and updates. Ultimately, a peer-to-peer system may become more robust and perform better than a classic enterprise application, but it will take ongoing development work.

Peer-to-Peer and Security

Security is a concern with any type of application, and peer-to-peer systems are no exception. The key difference is that with server-based programming, the server is in complete control. If the server adopts rigorous privacy standards and security safeguards, your information is safe, and you're in a "benevolent dictator" situation. However, if the server falls short of its commitment in any way, you'll have no protection.

In a decentralized peer-to-peer application, peers lack the protection of the server. On the one hand, they're also free from monitoring and have control of their private information. It's difficult to track an individual peer's actions, which remain publicly exposed, but lost in a sea of information. Nevertheless, malicious peers can connect directly to other peers to steal information or cause other types of problems.

Doing away with a central authority is both liberating and dangerous. For example, a malicious user can easily place a virus in a file-swapping peer-to-peer application disguised as another popular type of application and infect countless users, without being subject to any type of punishment or even being removed from the system. In addition, the decentralized nature of peer discovery makes it difficult for an organization to enforce any kind of access control (short of blocking Internet access on certain ports). For these reasons, peer-to-peer application programmers need to consider security from the initial design stage. Some peer-to-peer applications handle security issues by allowing users to assign different levels of trust to certain peers. Other peer-to-peer systems rely on encryption to mask communication and certificates to validate peer identities. These topics are explored in Chapter 11, with cryptography, and Chapter 6, with code access security.

The Peer-to-Peer Niche

Peer-to-peer applications may not displace enterprise development, but they do tackle some increasingly difficult enterprise problems. Some of the scenarios for which a peer-to-peer design is well suited are presented in the next few sections.

Systems with Which Clients Need to Interact

The server-based model emphasizes one-way communication from the client to the server. That means that the client must initiate every interaction. This poses difficulty if you want to create a collaborative application such as a real-time chat, a multiplayer game, or a groupware application. With the introduction of a little peer-to-peer code, the problem becomes much more manageable.

Systems with Which Clients Need to Share Content

In the server-based system, everything needs to be routed through the central server. This taxes the computing power and network bandwidth of a small section of the overall network. Thus, you'll need a disproportionately powerful server to handle a relatively small volume of requests. If, however, the central server is used simply to locate other peers, it can become a "jumping off" point for a true peer-to-peer interaction, which is much more efficient. This is the infamous Napster model.

In some cases, you might use the file-sharing abilities of a peer-to-peer application to support other features. For example, some virus-scanning software packages use a form of file sharing to distribute virus catalog updates. In this model, an individual computer in an enterprise will download an updated virus catalog as needed. Other peers will then retrieve the update from the nearest local user, rather than the remote servers, thereby minimizing network traffic and the load placed on the central servers. Similar forms of resource sharing can support a variety of services, and in doing so they prove that peer-to-peer applications are about more than just swapping digital music.

Systems for Which a Central Server Would Be a Liability

This is generally the case if an application operated outside the bounds of local law (or in an area that could be subjected to future prosecution). For example, Napster, despite being partly peer-to-peer, required a central server for content lookup and for resolving peer addresses, and was thus subjected to legal intervention. Gnutella, a more radically "pure" peer-to-peer application, isn't vulnerable in the same way. Similarly, consider the case of the legendary remailer *anon.penet.fi*, which was forced to close in 1996 because the anonymity of users could not be guaranteed against court orders that might have forced it to reveal account identities. Pure peer-to-peer systems, because they have no central server, are impervious to censorship and other forms of control.

Systems That Would Otherwise Be Prohibitively Expensive

You could build many peer-to-peer applications as server-based applications, but you'd require a significant hardware investment and ongoing work from a network support team to manage them. Depending on the type of application, this might not be realistic. For example, SETI@Home could not afford a super-computer to chew through astronomical data in its search for unusual signals. However, by harnessing individual chunks of CPU time on a large network of peers, the same task could be completed in a sustainable, affordable way. Another example is a virtual file system that can provide terabytes of storage by combining small portions of an individual peer hard drive. In many ways, these applications represent the ideal peer-to-peer niche.

Thus, peer-to-peer applications don't always provide new features, but sometimes provide a more economical way to perform the same tasks as other application types. They allow specialized applications to flourish where the support would otherwise not exist. This includes every type of peer-to-peer application, from those that promote collaboration and content sharing, to those that work together to complete CPU-intensive tasks.

A New Class of Application

Of course, new technologies always lead to a few new and radical applications that could not exist with earlier technologies. These applications may not grow and flourish right away—in fact, it's impossible to predict what next-generation software will be facilitated by peer-to-peer technology.

One possibility is real-time searching technology that allows peers to share any type of resources. The immense diversity of this content, and the variety of ways it can be described, make it impossible for a central server to catalogue it effectively. However, if a peer-to-peer application that uses an effective content-description query language could be designed, it could pass a specific, highly sophisticated request out to a wide audience of peers, who would then respond according to the highly specific information they have on hand. The way we share information on networks would be revolutionized overnight.

Another example of a new sort of application that might become possible with peer-to-peer is real-time collaboration software. Currently, collaborative applications allow for relatively simple tasks, such as exchanging text messages or sketching ideas on a primitive whiteboard. In the future, we could see peer-to-peer software tailored for a specific industry or activity. There could be a collaborative application that allows groups of users to work together on complex projects such as creating an architectural model, reviewing experimental data, or teaching a virtual lesson.[2]

---

2. Microsoft's Windows Messenger includes a feature called Application Sharing, which allows users to collaborate in any ordinary application. However, a collaboration "killer app" would doubtlessly include some more insightful, specialized interfaces that would coordinate multiple users.

The Evolution of the Internet

So far we've considered peer-to-peer as it relates to the dominant architecture in enterprise applications. There's another way to look at the evolution of peer-to-peer technology: in relation to the development of the early Internet.

The Early Internet

The Internet was first envisioned in the late 1960s as a global peer-to-peer system in which all computers could participate as equals. It was assumed that computers in the early Internet would always be on and always be connected. Thus, they were assigned permanent IP addresses that were recorded in a global registry called the Domain Name Service (DNS).

> **NOTE** *An IP address is a 32-bit number that uniquely identifies a computer on a network or the Internet. An IP address is typically written as four numbers from 0-255 separated by periods (as in 168.212.226.204). IP addresses can be tied to website names (such as* http://www.amazon.com*) using the DNS registry, but they don't need to be. In any case, the IP address is the key to finding and communicating with another computer on a conventional network.*

Unlike today's Internet, the early Internet was much more open. Any computer could send a packet to another. Usenet allowed message-board postings to be propagated across the Internet in a manner not unlike the way today's peer-to-peer applications route their own proprietary messages. Client-server applications such as FTP and Telnet existed, but any computer could morph into a server and host the application. On the whole, the usage patterns of the early Internet were peer-to-peer.

The Client-Server Internet

Two trends conspired to shift the Internet into a predominantly client-server system. The first was the invention of Mosaic, the first web browser. It was at this point that a larger community of casual users began to take interest in the content that was available on the World Wide Web, and another model began to spread.

To access the Internet, a PC user needed to use a temporary dial-up connection via an Internet service provider (ISP). These PC users became second-class citizens of the Internet, interacting as clients to download information from established web servers. Because these users weren't permanently connected to the Internet, it made less sense to assign them an entry in the DNS. And because there weren't enough IP addresses available to handle the sudden onslaught of new users, ISPs began assigning IP addresses dynamically so that each user had a different IP address for every session.[3] The DNS system was never designed for this sort of environment. The creators of the Internet assumed that changing an IP address would be a rare occurrence, and as a result, it could take days for a modification to make its way through the DNS system.

The end result was that the PC user became an invisible client on the Internet, able to receive data but not able to contribute any. With the commercialization of the Internet, this one-way pattern became the norm, and the Internet became the computer-based counterpart of newspaper and television media. Early visions of the Internet as the great equalizer of communication faded.

At the same time, the cooperative model of the Internet began to break down. Network administrators reacted to the threat of malicious users by using firewalls and network address translation (NAT). Both of these changes furthered the transformation to a client-server Internet. Computers could no longer contact each other as peers. Instead, communication could only succeed if the client inside the firewall (or behind the NAT) initiated it. Even the network infrastructure of the Internet became more and more optimized for client-server communication. Internet providers built up their networks with asymmetric bandwidth with which download times are always faster than upload times.

Interestingly, much of the underlying technology that supports the Internet is still based on peer-to-peer concepts. For example, the DNS registry is not a central repository stored at a single location but a system for sharing information among peer DNS servers. Similarly, a network of mail-server peers routes e-mail. On a hardware level, the physical routers that route network traffic follow some peer-to-peer patterns: They communicate together and cooperate to optimize a path for data transmission. However, the infrastructure that's developed on top of this substrate is primarily client-server. In order for peer-to-peer to succeed, applications will need to reintroduce some of the ideas pioneered by the early Internet.

The Return of Peer-to-Peer

Recently, there's been a resurgence of peer-to-peer activity on the Internet—this time in the form of a few revolutionary applications such as Napster, SETI@Home,

---

3. The IPv6 protocol promises to solve this problem and prevent the Internet from running out of IP addresses. IPv6 uses 128-bit IP addresses with values represented as hexadecimal numbers separated by colons (as in 0528:a165:ff00:50bf:7708:0dc9:4d76). IPv6 will support an incredible one trillion machines, and one billion networks. However, it's uncertain when IPv6 will be widely implemented.

ICQ, and Gnutella. Not all of these are pure peer-to-peer applications. In fact, all but Gnutella rely on a central server for some tasks. Nevertheless, they all include a framework that allows significant peer interaction.

Part of the reason behind this latest change is the increasing value of the ordinary PC. When they first appeared on the Internet, PCs were primitive enough that it seemed appropriate to treat them as dumb terminals that did little more than download and display HTML pages. Today, PCs offer much more CPU power and contain more disk space (and thereby host more potentially valuable content). PCs have also swelled to be the largest single part of the Internet. What they can't offer in quality, they can offer through sheer numbers.

> **NOTE** *Even a conservative estimate of 100 million PCs on the Internet, each with only a 100 MHz chip and a 100 MB hard drive, arrives at a staggering total of 10 billion MHz of processing power and 10,000 TBs of storage. The real total is almost certainly much larger.*

There is one disheartening fact about all of the examples of current peer-to-peer applications. Without exception, each one has developed a proprietary system for peer discovery and communication. Some of these systems are complementary, and a few are based on more-or-less open standards. However, the next wave of peer-to-peer development will probably appear when broader standards emerge and technology companies such as Microsoft and Sun develop high-level tools that specifically address (and solve) the severe networking demands of peer-to-peer programming.

Instant Messaging

The first wave of peer-to-peer applications included instant-messaging software, which allows users to carry out real-time conversations. The key insight behind applications such as ICQ is that users would require a new kind of registry to allow them to find each other on the Internet. Or to put it another way: Communicating over the Internet is easy; locating a friend is not, because of the unreliable nature of dynamic IP addresses. ICQ solved this problem by introducing a dynamic registry that associates each user with a unique number. Later instant-messaging systems bind a user to an e-mail address or, in the case of Windows Messenger, a .NET passport. With a dynamic registry, the user's connection information (the IP address) can be changed instantly.

However, most messaging applications are not strictly peer-to-peer because they use a central server to route messages. This allows the server to store messages for offline users and route messages through a firewall. Some messaging systems provide the option of establishing direct client-to-client connections when possible and only using the server as a fallback (ICQ), while others use direct client-to-client communication when large amounts of information must be transferred (such as sending a file in Windows Messenger). There are advantages and drawbacks to both approaches, and you'll explore them in the second part of this book when you develop an instant-messaging example.

Jabber and Groove

Instant-messaging applications require their own proprietary infrastructure. However, there are at least two tools that are evolving to supply some of this infrastructure for you. One is Jabber, an open-source instant-messaging platform that began as a switching system between incompatible instant-messaging protocols. Today, you can use Jabber as an XML routing system that allows peer communication. See http://www.jabber.org and http://www.jabbercentral.com for more information.

Groove is a more ambitious platform for collaborative applications that was developed by Ray Ozzie, the creator of Lotus Notes. Groove is not an open-source project, but it's of interest to Microsoft developers because it's COM-based and includes .NET tools, which make it easy to build collaborative applications that include automatic support for routing and encryption. Essentially, Groove provides a peer-to-peer infrastructure that you can use in your own peer-to-peer applications. You will find out more about Groove in Chapter 12.

SETI@Home

SETI@Home is an innovative project that exploits the idle time on the average personal computer. SETI@Home masquerades as an ordinary screen saver. When it runs, it processes a chunk of astronomical radio data downloaded from the SETI@Home site and scans for unusual patterns. When it's finished, it uploads the results and requests another block.

The idea of using multiple ordinary computers to do the work of one supercomputer is far from new. In the early days of the Internet, distributed-computing projects were used to test encryption codes. Math hobbyists and researchers sometimes did similar independent work to generate potential prime numbers or test a theory, although the efforts were never as well integrated. SETI@Home was the first to create an effective vehicle for distributing the code (a screen saver) and combine it with a problem that could easily be factored into smaller parts. Several other companies have tried, without success, to create similar projects in the commercial arena.

In some ways, SETI@Home deviates from a true peer-to-peer system because it relies on a central server that ultimately controls the entire system. However, in another respect SETI@Home represents the ideal of peer-to-peer design:

Every computer participates in performing the heavy lifting. In Chapter 6, you'll learn how to design a peer-to-peer .NET application for distributed computing. Best of all, unlike SETI@Home, you'll learn how to make this program generic enough to handle a dynamically defined task.

For more information about SETI@Home, see http://setiathome.berkeley.edu.

Napster and Gnutella

Napster and Gnutella are examples of peer-to-peer applications designed for content sharing—specifically, for sharing MP3 music files.

Napster's genius was to combine peer-to-peer technology with a centralized peer directory. This created a hybrid system that performed and scaled extremely well. The central server never became a bottleneck because it was used for comparatively low-bandwidth activities while the actual file transfers were performed between peers on the edges of the network. Napster also exploited a niche that was particularly well suited for peer-to-peer applications: popular music. Any large group of users with music collections is certain to have a significant redundancy in catalogued songs. This redundancy allowed the overall system to work reliably, even though it was composed of thousands of unreliable clients. In other words, the chance that a given song could be found was quite high, though the chance that a given user was online was low.

Gnutella is a decentralized, pure peer-to-peer model that almost disappeared before being discovered by open-source developers. Unlike Napster, Gnutella doesn't use a central server, but relies on a message-based system in which peers forward communication to small groups. However, though all peers are given equal opportunity by the Gnutella software, they aren't all equal. When a computer is discovered with a higher bandwidth, it morphs into a super-node and is given a higher share of responsibility.

The Gnutella design has several well-known limitations. It does not provide any security to disguise user actions, or any anonymity for peers, or any way to verify the content of files. It also lacks the optimized routing and caching that allow more sophisticated peer-to-peer applications to dynamically correct load imbalances as they occur.

In Part Three, you'll use .NET's networking support to create a hybrid file-sharing application like Napster's.

Freenet

Freenet is a peer-to-peer model for a virtual pooled hard drive—with one significant difference. Freenet's goal is to ensure free and uncensored communication over the Internet. Every Freenet peer surrenders a small portion of space on their hard drive, on which encrypted data is stored. The actual content stored on a given peer changes regularly so that the most requested content is replicated while the least requested content gradually disappears. Because of its design, Freenet is quite efficient for transferring large amounts of information. It also allows any user to freely publish information to the Internet, without requiring a website. However, there is no way for a Freenet peer to determine what's being stored on the local drive. Overall, Freenet is a niche use of peer-to-peer technology, but it's an example of an elegant, completely decentralized model. For more information about Freenet, see `http://freenetproject.org`.

JXTA Search

One peer-to-peer application type that hasn't yet materialized is distributed searching. Currently, web search engines such as AltaVista and Google use spiders that continuously crawl through an unlimited series of websites, following links and cataloguing everything they find. When you perform a search with Google, you're searching the most recent results from the spider's search. Unfortunately, this doesn't necessarily reflect the content on the Web at that moment. Some of the results you retrieve may be months old, and may point to nonexisting links while omitting much more important current data. And the data stored on internal networks but not published on a website will always be beyond the reach of the search.

One idea is to supplement the current generation of searching technology with real-time searches over a peer network. Unfortunately, before a peer-searching technology can work, it needs a large network of like-minded peers with valuable content, and a content-description language that can be used to advertise resources and create queries. One early attempt to standardize such a system was Infrasearch. The technology behind Infrasearch was recently purchased by Sun and incorporated into their new JXTA platform. It's not yet ready for prime time, but it promises to change the way we find information on the Internet.

For information about JXTA, go to `http://search.jxta.org`.

.NET Terrarium

.NET Terrarium is a learning game for the Microsoft .NET platform. It allows developers to create virtual "creature" classes and insert them into a virtual ecosystem hosted by a group of peers. Like Napster and SETI@Home, .NET Terrarium is a hybrid peer-to-peer application that makes use of a central discovery server. Currently, the source code for .NET Terrarium is not available, although it's expected that some pieces will gradually appear, accompanied by helpful commentary from Microsoft's architects. You can download Terrarium at `http://www.gotdotnet.com/terrarium`.

The "Death" of Peer-to-Peer

Peer-to-peer applications are still in their infancy, and already some reports are predicting their demise. Most of these claims center around the inability of most peer-to-peer venture projects to make money, particularly such high-profile failures as Napster. However, peer-to-peer is not just a business model. It's also a framework that deals with current problems with distributed computer systems—problems that can't be resolved in any other way.

There are two schools of thought on the future of peer-to-peer. Some believe that pure peer-to-peer applications are the ultimate future of computing, and that the current trend of combining peer-to-peer concepts with more traditional client-server components is transitional. Others believe that peer-to-peer technology will be *integrated* into the current generation of applications, thereby adding new capabilities.

One interesting example is the .NET learning game Terrarium, which was initially envisioned as a straight peer-to-peer application. When the resulting network traffic became difficult to manage, the team switched to a hybrid system with sever-based peer discovery. The final solution incorporates .NET web services (primarily a client-server technology) with peer-to-peer networking. Lance Olson, Terrarium's lead program manager, describes it this way:

> *I think that the peer-to-peer hype was sold as a new application model and an entirely new world around which we would build applications. And I think that the truth of the matter is that it's much more evolutionary. . . . Peer-to-peer is certainly not dead. However, the hype and the notion of peer-to-peer as just a stand-alone concept is probably . . . more of an evolutionary step than something that is just an entirely new model. And so the peer-to-peer world as I see it in the future is more one of applications that are more fault tolerant or are more interactive and have a better ability to contact other resources that are available on the network. So they're just like the applications today, only better in those senses.*[4]

Recently, more and more developers have been speaking out in favor of hybrid peer-to-peer designs. Quite simply, enterprise companies are unwilling to give up their servers. They need to be able to access a central component they can control, support, back up, and protect. Enterprise companies are much more interested in systems that centralize some core services but still allow for client interactions using peer-to-peer protocols.

---

4. From Episode 21, " 'Terrarium' and Peer-to-Peer," of "The .NET Show" (see http://msdn.microsoft.com/theshow/).

> **NOTE** *This book focuses on the hybridization of peer-to-peer concepts. In other words, you'll learn how to create solutions that incorporate peer-to-peer design, but the book may make use of server components that aren't necessarily pure peer-to-peer systems. Pure peer-to-peer implementations require a significant amount of messy network coding, and .NET does not yet provide high-level ways to deal with these problems. (Other platforms, such as JXTA, are also evolving to tackle these problems.) Peer-to-peer—like .NET—is a compromise. It's your challenge to integrate it the best way you can for your development.*

Peer-to-Peer Technologies in .NET

The .NET class library provides multiple technologies for communicating between computers. Some of these are layered on top of one another. You choose a high-level or low-level technology based on how much control you need and how much simplicity you would like.

Some of these technologies include

- The low-level networking classes in the System.Net.Sockets namespace, which wrap the Windows Sockets (Winsock) interface and allow you to create and access TCP channels directly. These classes are the heart of most peer-to-peer applications.

- The networking classes in the System.Net namespace, which allow you to use a request or response access pattern with a URI over (HTTP).

- The higher-level Remoting infrastructure, which allows you to interact with (or create) objects in other application domains using pluggable channels including TCP and HTTP and formats including binary encoding or SOAP. These classes can also be used in a peer-to-peer application, with some adaptation.

- The higher-level web services infrastructure, which provides fixed services as static class methods. This model is not suited for peer-to-peer communication, but is useful when creating a discovery service.

In addition, there are several .NET technologies that you'll need to use and understand as part of any peer-to-peer application that isn't trivially simple. This includes threading, serialization, code access security, and encryption. You'll get a taste of all of these in this book.

Finally, it's worth mentioning a few third-party tools that you'll see in Part Four of this book.

- Windows Messenger is Microsoft's instant-messaging product. There is some published information available on the Windows Messenger protocol, and even a .NET library that allows you to harness it in your own software. See Chapter 12 for more information.

- Groove is a platform for collaborative applications that manages the synchronization of a shared space. It's not free, but it's powerful, and Chapter 12 shows how it can help your applications.

- Intel provides a free .NET Peer-to-Peer Accelerator Kit, which extends .NET's Remoting infrastructure with support for security, discovery, and limited firewall traversal. It's still an early product, but it promises to eliminate some of the connectivity headaches with peer-to-peer on the Web. You'll consider Intel's toolkit in Chapter 13.

The Last Word

Peer-to-peer applications represent a fundamental shift from most other types of enterprise development and a return to some of the concepts that shaped the early Internet. They provide the key to collaboration and distributed computing, but require a new programming model that offers additional complexity and isn't yet built into development platforms such as .NET. You'll explore some of the new considerations required for peer-to-peer programming and take a closer look at different peer-to-peer models in the next chapter.

Perhaps the most interesting thing about a peer-to-peer system is that the work it performs is often more than the sum of its parts. Peers in a peer-to-peer application are a bit like ants in a colony. Each individual peer contributes relatively little at any one moment, but the sum of the work performed by all peers is surprisingly powerful.

CHAPTER 2

Peer-to-Peer Architecture

BEFORE YOU DIVE INTO a full-fledged peer-to-peer application, you need to understand some of the design issues that affect every peer-to-peer project. These are questions about peer identity, discovery, communication, and interaction. In this chapter, you'll investigate these issues and dissect different types of peer-to-peer architecture.

You'll notice that this is a fairly short chapter. There's a reason for that. Although peer-to-peer architecture is important, it's often more helpful to see live examples than volumes of theory. This chapter is only meant to introduce the basics that you need to understand the peer-to-peer examples developed throughout the book.

Peer-to-Peer Characteristics

One characteristic you *won't* find in the peer-to-peer world is consistency. The more you learn about different peer-to-peer applications, the more you'll see the same problems solved in different ways. This is typical of any relatively new programming model in which different ideas and techniques will compete in the field. In the future, peer-to-peer applications will probably settle on more common approaches. But even today, most of these techniques incorporate a few core ingredients, which are discussed in the following sections.

Peer Identity

In a peer-to-peer system, a peer's identity is separated into two pieces: a unique identifier, and a set of information specifying how to contact the peer. This separation is important—it allows users in a chat application to communicate based on user names, not IP addresses, and it allows peers to be tracked for a long period of time, even as their connection information changes.

The connectivity information that you need depends on the way you are connecting with the peer, although it typically includes information such as a port number and IP address. (We'll examine this information in detail in

Chapter 7, which explains core networking concepts.) The peer ID is a little trickier. How can you guarantee that each peer's identifier is unique on a large network that changes frequently?

There are actually two answers. One approach is to create a central component that stores a master list of user information. This is the model that chat applications such as Windows Messenger use. In this case, the central database needs to store authentication information as well, in order to ensure that peers are who they claim to be. It's an effective compromise, but a departure from pure peer-to-peer programming.

A more flexible approach is to let the application create a peer identifier dynamically. The best choice is to use a globally unique identifier (GUID). GUIDs are 128-bit integers that are represented in hexadecimal notation (for example, 382c74c3-721d-4f34-80e5-57657b6cbc27). The range of GUID values is such that a dynamically generated GUID is statistically unique—in other words, the chance of two randomly generated GUIDs having the same value is so astonishingly small that it can be ignored entirely.

In .NET, you can create GUIDs using the System.Guid structure. A peer can be associated with a new GUID every time it joins the network, or a GUID value can be generated once and stored on the peer's local hard drive if you need a more permanent identity. Best of all, GUIDs aren't limited to identifying peers. They can also track tasks in a distributed-computing application (such as the one in Chapter 6) or files in a file-sharing application (as shown in Chapter 9). GUIDs can also be used to uniquely identify messages as they are routed around a decentralized peer-to-peer network, thereby ensuring that duplicate copies of the same message are ignored.

Regardless of the approach you take, creating a peer-to-peer application involves creating a *virtual namespace* that maps peers to some type of peer identifier. Before you begin to code, you need to determine the type of peer identifier and the required peer connection information.

Peer Discovery

Another challenge in peer-to-peer programming is determining how peers find each other on a network. Because the community of peers always changes, joining the network is not as straightforward as connecting to a well-known server to launch a client-server application.

The most common method of peer discovery in .NET applications is to use a central discovery server, which will provide a list of peers that are currently online. In order for this approach to work, peers must contact the discovery server regularly and update their connectivity information. If no communication is received from a peer within a set amount of time, the peer is considered to be no longer active, and the peer record is removed from the server.

When a peer wants to communicate with another peer, it first contacts the discovery server to learn about other active peers. It might ask for a list of nearby peers, or supply a peer identifier and request the corresponding connectivity information it needs to connect to the peer. The peer-to-peer examples presented in the second and third part of this book all use some form of centralized server.

The discovery-server approach is the easiest way to quickly implement a reliable peer-to-peer network, but it isn't suitable for all scenarios. In some cases, there is no fixed server or group of servers that can play the discovery role. In this case, peers need to use another form of discovery. Some options include

- Sending a network broadcast message to find any nearby peers. This technique is limited because broadcast messages cannot cross routers from one network to another.

- Sending a multicast broadcast message to find nearby peers. This technique can cross networks, but it only works if the network supports multicasting.

- Reading a list of super-peers from some location (typically a text file or a web page), and trying to contact them directly. This requires a fixed location to post the peer information.

The last approach is not perfect, but it's the one most commonly used in decentralized peer-to-peer applications such as Gnutella. You'll learn about broadcasting in Chapter 9.

The Server-Mode/Client-Mode Model

Peer to peer applications often play two roles, and act both as a client and server. For example, in a file-sharing application every interaction is really a client-server interaction in which a client requests a file and a server provides it. The difference with peer-to-peer applications is every peer can play both roles, usually with the help of threading code that performs each task simultaneously. This is known as the server-mode/client-mode (SM/CM) model, as shown in Figure 2-1.

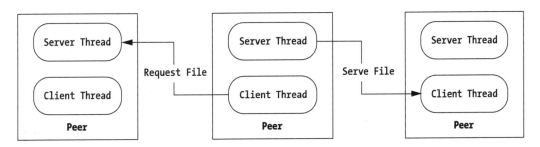

Figure 2-1. The server-mode/client-mode model

The dual roles in a file-sharing application are fairly obvious, but there are some types of applications that require more server work. For example, in a distributed-computing application, a work manager typically divides a task into multiple task segments, assigns it to a group of workers, and assembles their responses into a final solution. In some respects, this kind of application doesn't appear to be a true peer-to-peer application at all, because it centralizes functionality in a dedicated server module. However, you can make this application into more of a peer-to-peer solution by applying the SM/CM model. For example, you might create a peer that has the ability to request work and perform work for other requesters, as you will in our example in Chapter 6.

Remember, in a single interaction, the parts of a peer-to-peer system are not equivalent. One peer will take the role of a server, while the other acts as a client. However, over a longer time frame, each peer has the capability to play different roles.

Network Addressing Challenges

Firewalls and network address translation (NAT) devices are the bane of all peer-to-peer applications and can make it all but impossible for peers to interact.

Firewalls act as gatekeepers separating the public Internet and an internal network (or individual computer). Firewalls typically work as a kind of one-way gate, allowing outgoing traffic, but preventing arbitrary outside computers from sending information to a computer inside the Internet. In some cases, firewalls can be configured to allow or deny connections on specific ports, thereby authorizing some channels for peer-to-peer communication, although it's becoming increasingly common for firewalls to lock down almost *everything*. Further complicating life is NAT, which hides a client's IP address so it's not publicly accessible. The NAT is intelligent enough to be able to route a response from a server to the original client, but other peers can't communicate with the hidden computer. Thus, a peer could work in client-mode, but not server-mode, which would cripple the functionality of the system.

The peer-to-peer working group (http://peer-to-peerwg.org) identifies some of the most common approaches for interacting over a firewall or NAT. Two basic techniques include

- Reversing the connection. If PeerA can't contact PeerB due to a firewall, have PeerA contact PeerC, which will then notify PeerB. PeerB can then initiate the connection to PeerA. This won't work if both PeerA and PeerB are behind firewalls.

- Using a relay peer. If PeerA and PeerB need to communicate but are separated by a firewall, have them route all communication through some PeerC that is visible to both. JXTA and Gnutella use variations of this approach.

Coding this sort of low-level networking logic is a chore at best. If you need to create peer-to-peer applications over a wide network that can tunnel through firewalls, your best choice may be a third-party tool such as the ones we'll explore in Part Four of this book. Or, you may want to incorporate some centralized components. For example, a typical chat application such as Windows Messenger avoids firewall problems because all clients connect directly to the server, rather than to each other. However, some features (for example, file transfer) use direct connections and are consequently not supported by all peers. You may want to take this approach in your own applications to guarantee basic functionality, while giving peers the option of using direct connections for some features whenever possible.

> **TIP** *You can often tell whether the current computer is behind a NAT by examining its IP address. RFC 1918 spells out common NAT addresses: 10.0.0.0–10.255.255.255, 172.16.0.0–172.31.255.255, 192.168.0.0–192.168.255.255. If your IP address falls within one of these ranges, you'll be able to create outgoing connections, but won't be able to accept incoming ones.*

Peer-to-Peer Topology

Peer-to-peer applications don't necessarily abolish the central server completely. In fact, there are a variety of peer-to-peer designs. Some are considered "pure" peer-to-peer, and don't include any central components, while others are hybrid designs.

Peer-to-Peer with a Discovery Server

One of the most common peer-to-peer compromises involves a discovery server, which is a repository that lists all the connected peers. Often, a discovery server maps user names to peer connectivity information such as an IP address. When users start the application, they're logged in and added to the registry. After this point, they must periodically contact the discovery server to confirm that they're logged in and that their connection information hasn't changed.

There is more than one way for peers to use the information in a discovery server. In a simple application, peers may simply download a list of nearby users and contact them directly with future requests. However, it's also possible that the peer will need to communicate with a specific user (for example, in the case of a chat application). In this scenario, the discovery server can be structured to allow peer lookups by name, e-mail address, or some other fixed unique identifier. The peer interaction works like this:

1. The peer contacts the discovery server with a request to find the contact information for a specific user (for example, `someone@somewhere.com`).

2. The discovery server returns the user's IP address and port information.

3. The peer contacts the desired user directly.

This approach is also known as *brokered* or *mediated* peer-to-peer because the discovery server plays a central role in facilitating user interaction.

> **NOTE** *This approach is much easier to scale than a pure peer-to-peer model. Although pure peer-to-peer models can be made efficient and scalable, the "plumbing" code is significantly more difficult. If you can rely on a discovery server in your applications, it will greatly simplify most solutions.*

Peer-to-Peer with a Coordination Server

Some peer-to-peer applications benefit from a little more help on the server side. These applications combine peer-to-peer interaction with a central component that not only contains peer lookup information, but also includes some application-specific logic.

One example is Napster, which uses a central discovery and lookup server. In this system, peers register their available resources at periodic intervals. If a user needs to find a specific resource, the user queries the lookup server, which will then return a list of peers that have the desired resource. This helps to reduce network traffic and ensures that the peers don't waste time communicating if they have nothing to offer each other. The file-transfer itself is still peer-to-peer. This blend of peer-to-peer and traditional application design can greatly improve performance. By using a centralized server intelligently for a few critical tasks, network traffic can be reduced dramatically.

One question that arises with this sort of design is exactly how much responsibility the central server should assume. For example, you might create a messaging application in which communication is routed through the centralized server so that it can be analyzed or even logged. Similarly, you might design a content-sharing application that caches files on the server. These designs will add simplicity, but they can also lead to massive server bottlenecks for large peer-to-peer systems. As you'll discover in this book, a key part of the art of peer-to-peer programming with .NET is choosing the right blend between pure peer-to-peer design and more traditional enterprise programming.

Pure Peer-to-Peer

A pure peer-to-peer application has no central server of any kind. A typical user only communicates with a small group of nearby peers. In this scenario, even basic message routing and caching becomes a challenge. Typically, every message is automatically given several pieces of information, including the following:

- A unique GUID

- A field that records the "number of hops"—in other words, how many peers have already forwarded this copy of the message

- A setting that determines the maximum number of hops the message will be allowed to live for

- The sender's identifier (a GUID), and optionally, its connectivity information

To make a request, a peer creates a new message and sends it to its local group of peers. When a peer receives a message, it performs the following steps:

1. The peer checks that the message hasn't been recently received (probably by comparing it with a collection that caches the last 50 messages). If it has been received, the message is discarded.

2. The peer increments the number-of-hops field.

3. The peer checks the number of hops against the maximum number of hops allowed. If the number of hops exceeds the allowed lifetime, the message is discarded. This helps to prevent the same message from being continuously rerouted to the same peers over the network.

4. The peer forwards the message along to all the peers it knows about in a decentralized system such as Gnutella. The peers themselves will decide if they can satisfy the request. In a decentralized system such as Overnet, the peer now examines the message to determine the requested resource and compares that with a collection of information compiled by other peers. This information will probably be a hashtable that maps resource names to peers. When it finds a peer that can fulfill the request, it forwards the message to that peer only.

5. All the peers that have received the message start the same process at step 1.

This branching-out process is shown in Figure 2-2.

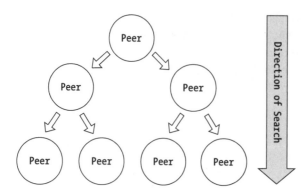

Figure 2-2. A pure peer-to-peer search

When a peer is found that can satisfy the request, it sends back a response. Typically, this response is sent back over the network in the same patch it took to arrive, thereby increasing the likelihood that it will be able to traverse the network. Alternatively, the peer could attempt to open a direct connection to the requesting peer to notify it that it has the requested resource.

Using this technique, a computer can indirectly contact a large network in a short time. There is no central server, and hence no single point of failure, and no possibility for out-of-date information. However, there are other drawbacks. The network traffic is likely to be high and the coding is complicated because each peer needs to maintain two things: a cache of peer-discovery data (which maps peer identifiers to peer connectivity information) and a cache of recently processed messages (which prevents a message from being rerouted to peers that have already processed it). It's also possible for some peer groups to become disconnected from the rest of the network, leading to multiple peer pockets instead of one large global network. This is most common when the number of peers is small.

One problem with pure peer-to-peer applications is the initial connection to the peer network. To find other peers, the application can use network-broadcasting techniques (such as IP multicast), but these can exert a significant overhead and won't work in all network environments. These approaches are most useful in an intranet in which the infrastructure required for multicast is known to exist.

Another approach is for the peer to use a list of well-known nodes to become connected at startup. This list might be retrieved from a configuration file (which can be updated every time the application is used successfully), or a fixed location on a network. An example of a pure peer-to-peer application that uses this approach is Gnutella.

The Last Word

The challenges that face peer-to-peer applications are far from trivial. Some challenges, such as the connectivity hurdles set in place by firewalls, proxy servers, and NAT, are quite difficult to overcome (and won't be fully resolved in this book). That said, hybrid designs, such as those pioneered by Napster and instant-messaging applications, have met with wild popularity, and are much easier to implement in .NET. In this book, you'll focus on these hybrid designs and consider the design decisions (and the trade-offs) you'll face when building such a system. This book also looks forward to the future of peer-to-peer and introduces some of the tools and add-ons that may eventually evolve into a richer peer-to-peer programming framework.

In the next chapter, you'll be introduced to Remoting, which will provide the framework for a peer-to-peer messaging application.

Part Two

Peer-to-Peer with a Coordination Server

CHAPTER 3

Remoting
Essentials

IN A PEER-TO-PEER APPLICATION, clients communicate over a network (or the network of networks, the Internet). You can select the protocol used for communication and the encoding used for messages. Most other models for distributed applications aren't nearly as flexible.

One approach for peer-to-peer communication in the .NET world is Remoting, a high-level abstraction that wraps networking code. Remoting is an attractive choice for communication in a peer-to-peer system because it's flexible, reliable, and easy to configure. With Remoting, the common language runtime (CLR) takes care of basic infrastructure chores such as releasing unneeded objects, creating and closing connections, and managing simultaneous requests with a pool of threads. Remoting also has some limitations—namely, because of the way it's designed, it works better for brokered communication with a coordination server than for decentralized peer-to-peer applications.

In this chapter, you'll learn all the Remoting basics that you need to create a peer-to-peer application such as the Messenger program presented in the next two chapters. You'll learn how objects communicate out-of-process, how to serialize data that must be sent across the network, and how to handle concurrent access. You'll also learn the ins and outs of some trickier aspects of Remoting, such as bidirectional communication, callbacks and events, and object lifetime. You'll also see why Remoting code is used differently in a peer-to-peer application than in a typical .NET enterprise system.

But before we begin, it helps to take a broad look at what Remoting is, how it fits into the grand scheme of distributed application technologies, and what its advantages and shortcomings are.

Inter-Process Communication

Every .NET program consists of one or more threads inside an *application domain*. Application domains are isolated logical processes that can't communicate directly. To bridge the gap between more than one application domain, you can use .NET Remoting.

Remoting is often described as the way that programs communicate with each other in .NET. This description is accurate, but it ignores the fact that there are literally dozens of different ways for applications to communicate on any platform. Some of the options for inter-process communication include

- Serializing information to a data store that both applications can access (such as a database or a file)

- Sending a custom message to a Microsoft Message Queuing queue

- Calling an ASP.NET web service with a SOAP message

- Creating a connection by directly using .NET's networking support, which provides classes that wrap Transmission Control Protocol (TCP) and User Datagram Protocol (UDP) channels, or raw sockets

- Using an operating system service such as named pipes or COM/DCOM (or see Microsoft Knowledge Base Article Q95900 for some other legacy choices)

All of these approaches have dramatically different characteristics, and different niches in the programming world. For example, the first choice (serializing information to a data store) is never workable if you need to provide instantaneous communication. In order to receive new messages regularly, multiple applications would need to poll the data source continuously, thereby creating an unbearable burden on your system. I've seen examples of chat applications that rely on this sort of continuous polling and, as a result, cannot scale beyond a small set of users without crippling the server.

On the other hand, the second option (using a message queue) is extremely scalable because it uses a disconnected message-based architecture. Every machine has its own queue that it monitors for received messages. To send a message, you simply need to know the queue name of the recipient. However, this approach is rarely used for peer-to-peer applications because it ties each client to a specific machine (the one on which the queue exists). It also requires a Windows PC with Microsoft Message Queuing installed and properly configured. Finally, message queuing only allows one-way "fire-and-forget" communication. To respond to a message, a new message must be created and sent to the original sender's queue. This means that a complex interaction (such as querying a computer for a list of files and initiating a download) could require several back-and-forth messages, thereby increasing the complexity and possibility for error. As a result, it's much more likely to find message queuing at work in the enterprise world (for example, as the backbone of an internal order processing system).

The third option, web services, excels at no-nonsense cross-platform communication. Unfortunately, it's too feature-limited for a peer-to-peer application. The problem is that web services are essentially a client-server technology. To use a web service, a client contacts the web server, makes a request, and waits for a response. There's no way for the server to contact the client at a later time, and there's no way for multiple clients to interact (unless they too are configured as web servers running ASP.NET and providing their own web services). Web services are the ticket when you wish to provide server-side functionality to all kinds of clients. They aren't any help if you want to build a system of equal peers that work together.

The final two options suggest some more useful ways to create a peer-to-peer application. Direct networking in .NET is an important technique, and you'll look into it in the third part of this book. However, direct networking can be complicated, and it will dramatically inflate the amount of code you need to write. To simplify your life, you can make use of one of the higher-level abstractions provided by Microsoft. In the past, this was the quirky technology of COM/DCOM. Today, DCOM is replaced by a newer and more flexible standard: .NET Remoting.

Introducing Remoting

Remoting is a generic method of inter-process and remote communication in .NET. It allows applications in different processes and different computers to communicate seamlessly. Like DCOM, Remoting is designed to let you use the objects in another application in the same way that you use local objects. The heavy lifting takes place behind the scenes and requires little programmer intervention.

The real strength of Remoting, however, is the fact that it abstracts the way you use remote objects from the way you communicate with them. When you use Remoting, you have the choice of different activation types, transport protocols, serialization formats, and object-lifetime policies. You can change these options with a few lines of code or a configuration file, but the code for *using* the remote object remains unchanged, and your application stays blissfully unaware of how the communication takes place.

Remoting Advantages

Remoting is a boon for any sort of distributed application developer. Some of its advantages include the following:

- Remoting can be used with different protocols and even in cross-platform projects. Because Remoting supports the ability to send SOAP-formatted messages, you can bring a Java client into the mix, although it won't be quite as easy as it is with web services.

- Remoting handles state management and object lifetime, ensuring that objects time out when the client isn't using them (thereby preventing potential memory leaks).

- Remoting is extensible. You can create building blocks for other transport channels or formats that will plug in to the Remoting infrastructure.

- Remoting is scalable. Remote requests are handled by a pool of listener threads provided by the CLR. If too many concurrent requests are sent to the same object, the excess requests will be politely queued and may time out without damaging the performance of the overall system.

- When used in conjunction with Internet Information Server (IIS), Remoting allows you to use Secure Sockets Layer (SSL) security to encrypt messages.

Even though Remoting hides some infrastructure details, it's inherently trickier than programming a local application. You'll need to perform extra work to make events, custom structures, and object creation work the way you expect with remote objects. You'll also need to accept some significant trade-offs.

Remoting supports several types of objects, including client-activated, SingleCall, and Singleton objects. For reasons you'll discover shortly, a peer-to-peer application requires Singleton objects. Singleton objects are, generally speaking, the most complex types of objects because they need to deal with the reality that multiple clients may use them at once. (In other words, a single computer in your peer-to-peer system may be simultaneously contacted by several peers, each of which will call methods on the same object.) In order to handle this possibility, you'll need to introduce threading code at some point, as explained in Chapter 5.

Remoting Drawbacks

Programming with Remoting means that you're programming at a higher level than with raw sockets and channels. Although this means you're insulated from a number of costly errors, it can also restrict some of the things that you can do. Here are a few examples:

- Remoting imposes some rules about how objects are exposed. For example, you can't tie objects in the same application domain to separate channels.

- Remoting is inextricably tied up with objects. Clients interact with a remotable object by calling any of its public methods. Typically, this means you need to create a dedicated Remoting "front end" for any application that requires remote communication.

- Remoting is not designed for on-the-fly configuration. Although it's possible to create an application that dynamically unregisters Remoting channels and creates new ones, you would need to do more work to implement it. Usually, Remoting applications are designed with the assumption that it's acceptable to restart the hosting application if the configuration information changes.

- Remoting sends objects in all-or-nothing chunks. If you need to stream large files across the network, this may not be the best approach. It's for this reason that we'll use a different approach in the third part of this book to build a file-sharing application.

- You have no control of the thread pool used to handle Remoting requests. That means you can't fine-tune details such as the number of maximum requests.

For the most part, Remoting is a perfect compromise between flexibility and safety. For example, the fact that you can't configure how the CLR allocates its thread pool is usually a benefit. The CLR handles requests very efficiently, and by performing its work automatically, it ensures that you won't unwittingly choose an ill-suited setting that would harm the scalability of your system. (It's for a similar reason that you can't configure how frequently the garbage collector runs or how much memory is initially allocated to an application.)

The next two chapters will discuss some of these issues in more detail as they develop a messaging application using Remoting. The remainder of this chapter introduces the basics of the Remoting infrastructure.

> **NOTE** *In this chapter, you'll look at Remoting in terms of objects, and consider how these objects interact across application domain boundaries. We won't consider how remotable objects are used for communication in a peer-to-peer application yet—those design decisions will be considered in the next chapter.*

Remoting Architecture

For the purposes of Remoting, you can divide all .NET classes into three types:

- Remotable classes. Any class that derives directly or indirectly from MarshalByRefObject automatically gains the ability to be exposed remotely and invoked by .NET peers in other application domains.

- Serializable classes. Any class that is marked with the <Serializable> attribute can be copied across application boundaries. Serializable types must be used for the parameters or return values of methods in a remotable class.

- Ordinary classes. These classes can't be used to send information across application boundaries, and they can't be invoked remotely. This type of class can still be used in a remotable application, even though it doesn't play a part in Remoting communication.

Figure 3-1 shows both remotable and serializable types in action. Incidentally, it's possible for a class to be both serializable and remotable, but it's not recommended. (In this case, you could interact with a remote instance of the object or send a copy of it across the network.)

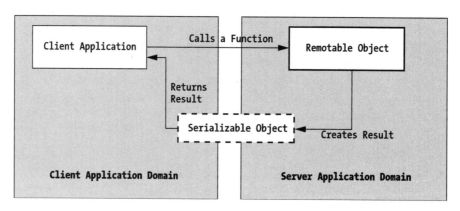

Figure 3-1. Remotable and serializable types

Figure 3-1 shows a good conceptual model of what takes place with Remoting, but it omits the work that takes place behind the scenes. For example, serializable types are not moved, but rather copied by converting them into a stream of bytes. Similarly, remotable types aren't accessed directly, but through a proxy mechanism provided by the CLR (see Figure 3-2). This is similar to the way that many high-level distributed technologies work, including web services and COM/DCOM.

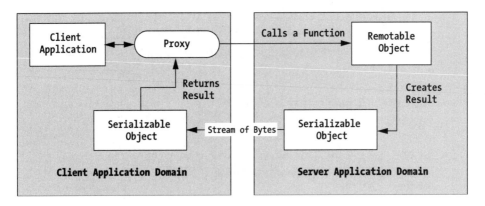

Figure 3-2. The Remoting proxy mechanism

With proxy communication, you interact with a remote object by using a local proxy that provides all the same methods. You call a method on the proxy class in exactly the same way that you would call a method on a local class in your application. Behind the scenes, the proxy class opens the required networking channel (with the help of the CLR), calls the corresponding method of the remote object, waits for the response, deserializes any returned information, and then returns it to your code. This entire process is transparent to your .NET code. The proxy object behaves just like the original object would if it were instantiated locally.

In the next two examples, we'll consider serializable and remotable types in more detail, and show you how to make your own.

Serializable Types

A serializable type is one that .NET can convert to a stream of bytes and reconstruct later, potentially in another application domain. Serializable classes are a basic feature of .NET programming and are used to persist objects to any type of stream, including a file. (In this case, you use the methods of the BinaryFormatter in the System.Runtime.Serialization.Formatters.Binary namespace or the SoapFormatter in the System.Runtime.Serialization.Formatters.Soap namespace to perform manual serialization.) Serialized classes are also used with Remoting to copy objects from one application domain to another.

All basic .NET types are automatically serializable. That means that you can send integers, floating point numbers, bytes, strings, and date structures to other .NET clients without worry. Some other serializable types include the following:

- Arrays and collection classes (such as the ArrayList). However, the content or the array or collection must also be serializable. In other words, an array of serializable objects can be serialized, but an array of non-serializable objects cannot.

- The ADO.NET data containers, such as the DataTable, DataRow, and DataSet.

- All .NET exceptions. This allows you to fire an exception in a remotable object that an object in another application domain can catch.

- All EventArgs classes. This allows you to fire an event from a remotable object and catch it in another application domain.

Many, but not all .NET types are serializable. To determine if a given type is serializable, look it up in the class library reference and check if the type definition is preceded with the <Serializable> attribute.

You can also make your own serializable classes. Here's an example:

```
<Serializable> _
Public Class Message

    Public Text As String
    Public Sender As String

End Class
```

A serializable class must follow several rules:

- You must indicate to .NET that the class can be serialized by adding the <Serializable> attribute just before the class declaration.

- Every member variable and property must also be serializable. The previous example works because the Message class encapsulates two strings, and strings are serializable.

- If you derive from a parent class, this class must also be serializable.

- Both the client and recipient must understand the object. If you try to transmit an unrecognized object, the recipient will simply end up with a stream of uninterpretable bytes. Similar problems can occur if you change the version of the object on one end.

Remember, when you send a serializable object you're in fact copying it. Thus, if you send a Message object to another peer, there will be two copies of the message: one in the application domain of the sender (which will probably be released because it's no longer important) and one in the application domain of the recipient.

When a class is serialized, every object it references is also serialized. This can lead to transmitting more information than you realize. For example, consider this revised version of the Message class that stores a reference to a previous message:

```
<Serializable> _
Public Class Message

    Public Text As String
    Public Sender As String
    Public PreviousMessage As Message

End Class
```

When serializing this object, the Message referred to by the PreviousMessage member variable is also serialized and transmitted. If this message refers to a third message, it will also be serialized, and so on. This is a dangerous situation for data integrity because it can lead to duplicate copies of the same object in the remote application domain.

Finally, if there's any information you don't want to serialize, add the <NonSerialized> attribute just before it. The variable will be reinitialized to an empty value when the object is copied, as follows:

```
<Serializable> _
Public Class Message

    Public Text As String
    Public Sender As String
    <NonSerialized> Public PreviousMessage As Message

End Class
```

This technique is useful if you need to omit information for security reasons (for example, a password), or leave out a reference that may not be valid in another application domain (for example, file handles).

> **TIP** *You may be familiar with web-service serialization. However, the serialization mechanism used in Remoting has little in common with the one used in web services, even if you're using SOAP-formatted messages. This difference is necessary because web services place a greater emphasis on cross-platform compatibility and restrict many types that would have no meaning to non-.NET clients. As a result, there are serializable classes that you use with Remoting that can't be sent to a web service.*

Remotable Types

A remotable type is one that can be accessed from another application domain. Following is an example of a simple remotable object. It's identical to any other .NET class, except for the fact that it derives from the System.MarshalByRefObject class.

```
Public Class RemoteObject
    Inherits MarshalByRefObject

    Public Sub ReceiveMessage(ByVal message As Message)
        Console.WriteLine("Received message: " & message.Text)
    End Sub

End Class
```

Every public property, method, and member variable in a remotable class is automatically accessible to any other application. In the previous example, this means that any .NET application can call RemoteObject.ReceiveMessage(), as long as it knows the URL where it can find the object. All the ByVal parameters used by ReceiveMessage() must be serializable. ByRef parameters, on the other hand, must be remotable. (In this case, the ByRef parameter would pass a proxy reference to the original object in the sender's application domain.)

In this example, RemoteObject represents the complete, viable code for a remote object that writes a message to a console window. With the aid of configuration files, we'll develop this into a working example.

> **TIP** *Like any public method, the ReceiveMessage() method could also be called by another class in the same application. However, to prevent confusion, it's best to only include methods that are designed exclusively for remote communication in a MarshalByRefObject.*

Remoting Hosts

MarshalByRefObject instances have the ability to be invoked remotely. However, simply creating a MarshalByRefObject doesn't make it available to other applications. Instead, you need a server application (also called a component host) that listens for requests, and provides the remotable objects as needed. The component host also determines the URL the client must use to locate or create the remote object, and configures how the remote object is activated and how long it should live. This information is generally set in the component host's configuration file. Any executable .NET application can function as a component host, including a Windows application, console application, or Windows service.

A component host requires very little code because the Remoting infrastructure handles most of the work. For example, if you place your configuration information into a single file, you can configure and initialize your component host with a single line of code, as follows:

```
RemotingConfiguration.Configure(ConfigFileName)
```

In this case, ConfigFileName is a string that identifies a configuration file that defines the application name, the protocol used to send messages, and the remote objects that should be made available. We'll consider these settings in the next section.

Once you have called the RemotingConfiguration.Configure() method, the CLR will maintain a pool of threads to listen for incoming requests, as long as the component host application is running. If it receives a request that requires the creation of a new remotable object, this object will be created in the component host's application domain. However, these tasks take place on separate threads. The component host can remain blissfully unaware of them and continue with other tasks, or—more commonly—remain idle (see Figure 3-3).

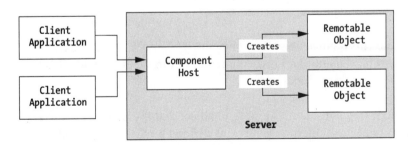

Figure 3-3. The component host in an enterprise system

This model is all well and good for a distributed enterprise application, but it's less useful in a peer-to-peer scenario. In an enterprise application, a component host exposes useful server-side functionality to a client. Typically, each client will create a separate object, work with it, and then release it. By using Remoting, the object is allowed to execute on the server, where it can reap a number of benefits including database connection pooling and the use of higher-powered server hardware.

In a peer-to-peer application, however, the component host and the remote component are tied together as one application that supports remote communication. This means that every peer in a peer-to-peer application consists of a remotable interface that's exposed to the world and a component host that contains the rest of the application. Figure 3-4 diagrams this approach.

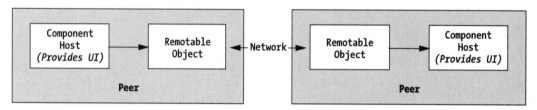

Figure 3-4. The component host in a peer-to-peer system

These two models are dramatically different. Enterprise systems use a stateless approach. Communication is usually initiated by the client and all functionality is held at the server (much like the client-server model). Peer-to-peer applications use a stateful model in which independent peers converse through Remoting front-ends.

This difference between enterprise development and peer-to-peer applications becomes evident when you need to choose an *activation type* for a remote object. Remotable types can be configured with one of three activation types, depending on the configuration file settings:

- SingleCall. This defines a stateless object that is automatically created at the start of every method invocation and destroyed at the end. This is similar to how web services work.

- Client-activated. This defines a stateful object that is created by the client and lives until its set lifetime expires, as defined by client usage and configuration settings. Client-activated objects are the most similar to local .NET objects.

- Singleton. This defines a stateful object that is accessible to the remote client, but has a lifetime controlled by the server.

Generally, SingleCall objects are perfect for enterprise applications that simply want to expose server resources. They can't be used in a peer-to-peer application as the basis for bidirectional communication between long-running applications. In a peer-to-peer application, you need to use the Singleton type, which associates an endpoint with a single object instance. No matter how many clients connect, there's only ever one remote object created. Or, to put it another way, a Singleton object points to a place where a specific object exists. SingleCall and client-activated addresses point to a place where a client can create its own instance of a remotable object. In this book, we'll focus on the Singleton activation type.

There is one other twist to developing with Remoting. In order for another application to call a method on a remote object, it needs to know some basic information about the object. This information takes the form of .NET metadata. Without it, the CLR can't verify your remote network calls (checking, for example, that you have supplied the correct number of parameters and the correct data types). Thus, in order to successfully use Remoting to communicate, you need to distribute the assembly for the remote object to the client and add a reference to it.

There are some ways of minimizing this inconvenience, either by pre-generating a proxy class or by using interfaces. We'll use the latter method in the next chapter when we develop a real Remoting example.

> **NOTE** *It may seem counterintuitive that you need to distribute the assembly for remote objects to all clients. This is one of the quirks of using an object-based model for remote communication (such as Remoting or web services). This problem won't appear when we use a lower-level networking approach in the third part of this book.*

Configuration Files

The configuration files use an XML format to define the channels and ports that should be used for communication, the type of formatting for messages, and the objects that should be exposed. In addition, they can specify additional information such as a lifetime policy for remotable objects. Here's the basic framework for a configuration file with Remoting:

```
<configuration>
    <system.runtime.remoting>
        <application>
```

```
        <service>
            <!-- Information about the supported (remotable) objects. -->
        </service>

        <channels>
            <!-- Information about the channels used for communication. -->
        </channels>

        <!-- Optional information about the lifetime policy (tag below). -->
        <lifetime />

        </application>
    </system.runtime.remoting>
</configuration>
```

You can create this configuration file outside of Visual Studio .NET, provided you place it in the *bin* directory where the compiled application will be executed. A simpler approach is to add your configuration file to the Visual Studio .NET project. Simply right-click on the project in the Solution Explorer and select Add → New Item. Then, choose Application Configuration File under the Utility node (see Figure 3-5).

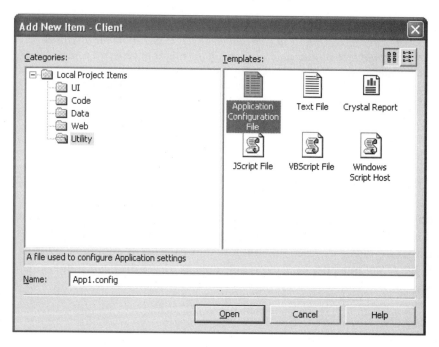

Figure 3-5. Adding a configuration file to a project

The application configuration file is automatically given the name *app.config*. When Visual Studio .NET compiles your project, it will copy the *app.config* file to the appropriate directory and give it the full name (the name of the application executable, plus the *.config* extension). To see this automatically generated configuration file for yourself, select Project ➤ Show All Files from the menu. Once you compile your project, you'll see the appropriate file appear in the *bin* directory (see Figure 3-6).

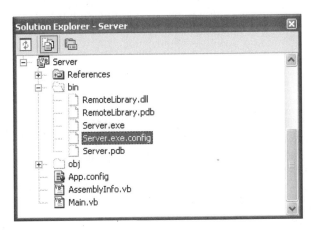

Figure 3-6. An automatically generated configuration file

Configuration files are required for every application that needs to communicate using Remoting. This includes a component host and any client that wants to interact with a remote object. The next section shows specific configuration file examples.

A Basic Remoting Example

To make all this clear, we'll consider a stripped-down Remoting example. To start, we'll create two console applications: a client and a server. The client will send a message to the server, which will display it in a console window.

> **TIP** *There's a reason we're beginning with a simple console example rather than a Windows Form application. The Console object is guaranteed to be thread-safe, meaning that there's no possibility for error if multiple clients call the same remote object at once. With a Windows Form, life isn't always as easy.*

We'll also need to create a class library project that contains the remote object. That way, you can easily add a reference to the remote object from the client. Without this extra step, the client would lack the metadata that tells the CLR how it should verify method invocations, and communication wouldn't be possible.

If you coded the remote object directly in the server application, you would face the same problem in a different way. Because the server application is an executable assembly, you can't add a reference to it in your client. It's possible to circumvent this restriction using interfaces, as you'll see in the next chapter. Without them you *must* separate the remotable parts of an application into a separate assembly.

The Remote Object

You can begin by creating the remote object for the server. If you're using Visual Studio .NET, you'll begin by creating a new class library (DLL) project. This example reuses the RemoteObject class presented earlier, but replaces the custom Message object with a simple string for simplicity's sake.

```
Public Class RemoteObject
    Inherits MarshalByRefObject

    Public Sub ReceiveMessage(ByVal message As String)
        Console.WriteLine("Received message: " & message)
    End Sub

End Class
```

Because this object will be created in the server's application domain, it can use the Console object to display a message. A similar interaction would be possible if the server were a Windows Form application, but you would need a little extra threading code to prevent glitches when interacting with user-interface controls. The Console object, however, is always guaranteed to be thread-safe.

The Server

The server (or component host) is the main console application. If you're using Visual Studio .NET, you'll begin by creating a new console application. This application registers the Remoting settings defined in the *Server.exe.config* file, displays a message, and waits for the user to press Enter, at which point it will end.

```
Imports System.Runtime.Remoting

Public Module ServerApplication

    Public Sub Main()

        Console.WriteLine("Configuring remotable objects....")
        RemotingConfiguration.Configure("Server.exe.config")

        Console.WriteLine("Waiting for a request.")
        Console.WriteLine("Press any key to exit the application.")

        ' The CLR will monitor for requests as long as this application
        ' is running. When the user presses Enter, it will end.
        Console.ReadLine()

    End Sub

End Module
```

> **TIP** *The name* Server.exe.config *is used because the application executable file is* Server.exe. *According to .NET conventions, settings for an executable application should always be stored in a configuration file that has the same name as the executable, and adds the* .config *extension. In some cases, .NET will read and apply these settings automatically, although this is not the case for Remoting settings (and so it's technically possible to use any file name you like).*

The Server Configuration File

The server configuration file defines the object it will expose and the channel it will open for client requests. Remember, if you're using Visual Studio .NET, you should always give the application configuration file the name *app.config*. When Visual Studio .NET compiles your project, it will copy the *app.config* file to the appropriate directory, and give it the correct name.

Here's a sample configuration file for a component host:

```
1   <configuration>
2      <system.runtime.remoting>
3         <application name="Server">
4            <service>
5               <wellknown mode="Singleton"
6                           type="RemoteLibrary.RemoteObject, RemoteLibrary"
7                           objectUri="RemoteObject" />
8            </service>
9            <channels>
10              <channel ref="tcp server" port="8000" />
11           </channels>
12        </application>
13     </system.runtime.remoting>
14  </configuration>
```

It contains several important pieces of information:

- The application is assigned the name "Server" (line 3).

- The Singleton mode is used (line 5), ensuring that only a single instance of the object will be created on the server.

- The remotable object has the fully qualified class name of RemoteLibrary.RemoteObject (first part of line 6). The remotable object can be found in the DLL assembly RemoteLibrary.dll (second part of line 6). Both of these pieces of information must match exactly. Note that the assembly name does not include the extension *.dll*. This is simply a matter of convention.

- The remoteable object is given the URI "RemoteObject" (line 7). Together with the computer name and port number, this specifies the URL the client needs to use to access the object.

- A TCP/IP server channel is defined on port 8000 (line 10). This channel can receive messages and respond to them. By default, this channel will use binary encoding for all messages, although you'll see how to tweak this later on.

In this case, the port number isn't terribly important. The next chapter discusses port numbers in more detail.

NOTE *Ports are generally divided into three groups: well-known ports (0–1023), registered ports (1024–49151), and dynamic ports (49152–65535). Historically, well-known ports have been used for server-based applications such as web servers (80), FTP (20), and POP3 mail transfer (110). In your application, you would probably do best to use a registered or dynamic port that's not frequently used. These are less likely to cause a conflict (although more likely to be blocked by a firewall). For example, 6346 is most commonly used by Gnutella. For a list of frequently registered ports, refer to the* C:\{WinDir}\System32\Drivers\Etc\Services *file, or the* http://www.iana.org/assignments/port-numbers *site.*

The Client

The client is also created as a console application. It performs a continuous loop asking the user for an input string, and only exits if the user enters the keyword "exit." Every time a message is entered, the client sends this object to the remote application domain simply by calling the remote object's ReceiveMessage() method.

```
Imports System.Runtime.Remoting

Public Module ClientApplication

    Public Sub Main()

        Console.WriteLine("Configuring remote objects....")
        RemotingConfiguration.Configure("Client.exe.config")

        Do
            Console.WriteLine()
            Console.WriteLine("Enter the message you would like to send.")
            Console.WriteLine("Or type 'exit' to exit the application.")
            Console.Write(">")
            Dim Message As String = Console.ReadLine()
            If Message.ToUpper() = "EXIT" Then Exit Do

            ' Create the remote object.
            Dim TestObject As New RemoteLibrary.RemoteObject()

            ' Send the message to the remote object.
            TestObject.ReceiveMessage(Message)
```

```
                    Console.WriteLine()
                    Console.WriteLine("Message sent.")
              Loop

         End Sub

    End Module
```

In order for the client to be able to use the RemoteObject class, you must add a reference to the class library assembly that contains this type.

When the client creates the TestObject, it's actually creating a proxy class that mimics the remote object. When the client calls TestObject.ReceiveMessage(), the TestObject proxy class makes a call over the network and transmits the information needed to the real remote object instance.

This proxy layer has a couple of other side effects. For example, when the client creates the proxy class, it doesn't create the server-side object. If the remote object doesn't yet exist, it will be created the first time the ReceiveMessage() method is called. Similarly, the .NET Framework will not destroy the object if it goes out of scope or if the proxy reference is set to Nothing. Instead, the remote object behaves according to a specific *lifetime lease*. In this case, because the lifetime lease has not been explicitly configured, the default settings will prevail. That means that the object will have an initial lifetime of about five minutes, after which it will be destroyed if it experiences two minutes of inactivity. Thus, if the client sends multiple messages within a two-minute time period, it will reuse the same remote object instance, even though the proxy class is re-created with each iteration of the loop. We'll look at more advanced leasing options later in this chapter.

The Client Configuration File

The client configuration file loosely resembles the server configuration. It defines what channel to use to send communication, what URL to contact, and what object to communicate with.

```
1   <configuration>
2      <system.runtime.remoting>
3         <application name="Client">
4            <client>
5               <wellknown url="tcp://localhost:8000/RemoteObject"
6                          type="RemoteLibrary.RemoteObject, RemoteLibrary"/>
```

```
7              </client>
8              <channels>
9                  <channel ref="tcp client"/>
10             </channels>
11          </application>
12      </system.runtime.remoting>
13  </configuration>
```

The file contains several pieces of information:

- The application is assigned the name "Client" (line 3). This designation has no particular significance because the client will not be contacted by URL.

- The URL for the remote object is specified (line 5). This URL consists of the computer name, port, and object URI. (In this example, the machine name is identified only as "localhost," which is a loopback alias that always points to the current computer.) The full object URL takes the following form:

```
<client url="[Protocol]://[MachineName]:[Port]/[ObjectURI]">
```

- The remotable object has the fully qualified class name of RemoteLibrary.RemoteObject (first part of line 6). The remotable object can be found in the DLL assembly RemoteLibrary.dll (second part of line 6). Both of these pieces of information must match exactly. Note that the assembly name does not include the extension *.dll*. This is simply a matter of convention.

- A TCP/IP client channel is defined without a port number (line 9). This means that .NET will dynamically choose the most suitable port to open the connection on the client. This port does not need to be hard-coded, because no other application is trying to contact this client by URL.

The Application in Action

All the parts of this application are provided with the online samples for this chapter, in the *OneWayRemoting* directory. To test this solution, you can configure Visual Studio .NET to launch both the client and the server at the same time (just make sure the server is initialized before you enter any messages in the client). To do so, simply set Visual Studio .NET to launch multiple projects, as shown in Figure 3-7.

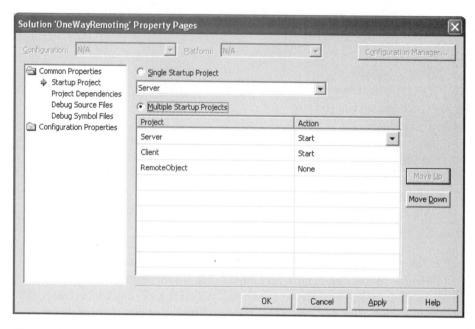

Figure 3-7. Launching multiple projects for debugging

Next, type a message into the client (Figure 3-8). After a brief delay, while the server-side object is created, the message will appear in the server's console window (Figure 3-9).

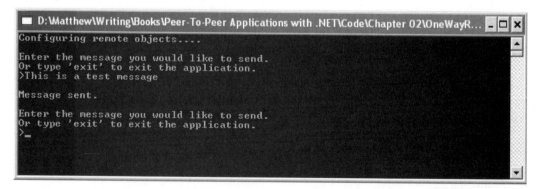

Figure 3-8. Entering a message in the client

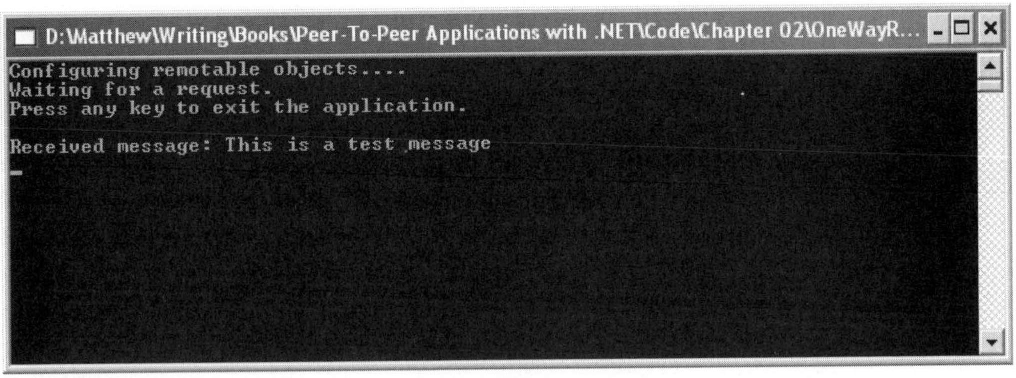

Figure 3-9. Receiving the message with the remote object

To confirm that the application is working as expected, you can perform a simple test. Modify the client by omitting the RemotingConfiguration.Configure() method call. Now, when you create the RemoteObject, a local object will be instantiated in the client's application domain. When you call the ReceiveMessage() method, the message will be processed in the client's application domain and will be output in the client's console window.

Clearly, this is a trivial example of Remoting at work. But it gives you an important overview of the following key fundamentals:

- Remoting is based on objects. While an experienced network programmer will refer to "sending a message" across the network (the terminology often used in this book), in Remoting you send this message by invoking a method on a remote object.

- Remote objects are not necessarily tied to the server that hosts them. In fact, if you do want to allow communication between the remote object and the hosting "container" (as you probably will in a peer-to-peer application), you'll need to use synchronization code because these parts of the application execute on different threads.

- Remoting uses configuration files to register available objects and define the channel that will be used. That makes it easy to change settings without recompiling. These settings are passed to the Remoting infrastructure provided by the CLR, which automatically creates channels, opens ports, and provides requested objects as needed without requiring any additional code.

Remote Object Lifetime

One of the problems with the previous generation of distributed object technology (for example, COM/DCOM) is the fact that it lacked a reliable way to handle object lifetime. In DCOM, the solution was to use keep-alive pinging messages, which increased network traffic unnecessarily and allowed greedy clients to keep objects alive indefinitely, wasting server memory. Remoting introduces a new lease-based system for handling object lifetimes that allows them to be automatically destroyed after a fixed amount of time (or a fixed period of idleness). You can set lifetime properties in several ways:

- The application domain can configure default settings for all the objects it creates by using the <lifetime> configuration section in its configuration file.

- The client using the object can manually retrieve the remote object's lease from the GetLifetimeService() method (which all MarshalByRefObject instances inherit). The client can then modify the lease settings.

- The object itself can override its InitializeLifetimeService() method (which all MarshalByRefObject instances inherit) and add code to ignore lease settings and configure its own lease properties.

- You can implement a custom lease sponsor that monitors an object and determines if its lifetime should be extended when it expires.

The lifetime leasing system plays a minor role in peer-to-peer programming, in which you typically want an object's network interface to remain as long as the application domain exists. For that reason, you'll usually want to configure an infinite lease time. The easiest way is to simply override the InitializeLifetimeService() to return a null reference:

```
' Ensures that this object will not be prematurely released.
Public Overrides Function InitializeLifetimeService() As Object
        Return Nothing
End Function
```

This works because it specifies a null reference in the place of the lease object. Alternatively, you could retrieve the ILease object and modify it to apply new settings, as shown here:

```
Public Overrides Function InitializeLifetimeService() As Object
    Dim Lease As ILease = MyBase.InitializeLifetimeService()
```

```
' Lease can only be configured if it's in an initial state.
If Lease.CurrentState = LeaseState.Initial Then
    Lease.InitialLeaseTime = TimeSpan.FromMinutes(10)
    Lease.RenewOnCallTime = TimeSpan.FromMinutes(5)
End If

Return Lease

End Function
```

This will set a lease-lifetime policy in which the object lives at least ten minutes, and is removed after not being used for a five-minute period. As discussed previously, this technique would rarely be used in a peer-to-peer application.

A Bidirectional Remoting Example

In the One-Way Remoting example, the client always contacts the server. The server can respond to the client through the method return value, but once the method call is finished, the client closes the connection and the server can no longer contact the client. This is not appropriate for a peer-to-peer system, which requires bidirectional communication.

In order to support bidirectional communication, the client must meet three criteria:

- It must provide a remotable type (a class that derives from MarshalByRefObject) that the server can call.

- It must open a bidirectional Remoting channel, which it will use to listen for calls initiated from the server.

- There must be some way to transfer the received information from the remotable client type to the main client application. This can be accomplished in a loosely coupled way by using a local event.

Once these criteria are met, there are several choices for the actual method of communication:

- The server can fire an event, which will be delivered by Remoting to the client's remotable object.

- The client can create a delegate that points to one of the methods in its remotable object, and then submit this delegate to the server. The server can then trigger the method by invoking the delegate.

- The client can create a reference to its local remotable object and pass this reference to the server. The server can then call a method on the local object directly. Alternatively, you could pass the reference as an interface implemented by the remotable object. In either case, the server must know enough about the remotable client object or its interface to be able to call one of its methods.

The first option—using events—requires the least amount of work. Multiple clients can attach event handlers to the same event, and the server doesn't need to worry about who is being contacted when it fires the event. The only consideration is making sure that the EventArgs object is serializable, so that it can leap across application domain boundaries. However, the event-based approach is less practical because it doesn't allow the flexibility for the server to call a specific client. It can also lead to problems if clients disconnect from the network without unregistering their event handlers properly.

The delegate or interface approaches are more flexible. In both cases, the server is in charge of tracking clients (typically by using some sort of collection object), and removing them from the collection when they can no longer be contacted. The instant-messaging example in the next chapter uses an interface-based approach.

The following example uses a similar, yet slightly different approach: a delegate that both the server and client recognize. This project can be found in the *TwoWayRemoting* directory with the samples for this chapter. This example uses a Windows client. The server (component host) is unchanged.

The Remote Objects

The first step is to modify the server-side remotable object so that it will attempt to contact the client after a short delay through a callback. It works like this:

1. The client calls a method in the remote object.

2. The method sets up a timer and returns.

3. When the timer ticks, a new message is sent to the client. This requires opening a new connection because the original connection has been closed. This time, the server is acting as a client because it's opening the connection.

Here's the code for our simple example:

```vbnet
Public Delegate Sub ConfirmationCallback(ByVal message As String)

Public Class RemoteObject
    Inherits MarshalByRefObject

    Private WithEvents tmrCallback As New System.Timers.Timer()
    Private Callback As ConfirmationCallback
    Private Message As String

    Public Sub ReceiveMessage(ByVal message As String, _
      ByVal callback As ConfirmationCallback)
        Me.Callback = callback
        Me.Message = "Received message: " & message
        tmrCallback.Interval = 5000
        tmrCallback.Start()
    End Sub

    Private Sub tmrCallback_Elapsed(ByVal sender As System.Object, _
      ByVal e As System.Timers.ElapsedEventArgs) _
      Handles tmrCallback.Elapsed
        tmrCallback.Stop()
        Callback.Invoke(Message)
    End Sub

End Class
```

> **NOTE** *This simple design isn't suitable for a system that experiences multiple calls in close succession because the ConfirmationCallback and Message values will be overwritten with each new call. Don't worry too much about this limitation now—the next two chapters will explore these limitations in detail and resolve them.*

The RemoteLibrary project also contains the remotable portion of the client, which is a dedicated listener object. This object is created in the client's application domain for the sole purpose of receiving the callback. It raises a local event so the client application can become notified of the callback. This is a common pattern in peer-to-peer systems with Remoting, and you'll see it again in the next chapter.

```vb
Public Class Listener
    Inherits MarshalByRefObject

    Public Event CallbackReceived(ByVal sender As Object, _
      ByVal e As MessageEventArgs)

    Public Sub ConfirmationCallback(ByVal message As String)
        RaiseEvent CallbackReceived(Me, New MessageEventArgs(message))
    End Sub

    ' Ensures that this object will not be prematurely released.
    Public Overrides Function InitializeLifetimeService() As Object
        Return Nothing
    End Function

End Class

Public Class MessageEventArgs
    Inherits EventArgs

    Public Message As String

    Public Sub New(ByVal message As String)
        Me.Message = message
    End Sub

End Class
```

The Configuration Files

The configuration files require only a single change from the previous example. In the simple One-Way Remoting example, the client declared a client-only channel (TCP client), while the server declared a server-only channel (TCP server). To remedy this design, you must configure a bidirectional channel that can create new outgoing connections *and* receive incoming connections.

The changed line looks like this in the server:

```
<channel ref="tcp" port="8000" />
```

The client configuration file requires a similar change. It doesn't define a port number because the .NET Framework will dynamically choose the first available dynamic port.

```
<channel ref="tcp"/>
```

The Client

The client is modeled after the One-Way Remoting example. It allows any
message to be dispatched to the client. The message is then returned through
a callback and handled in a local event, which displays the message box shown
in Figure 3-10.

Figure 3-10. Receiving a callback at the client

The client code is encapsulated in a single form, as follows:

```
Imports System.Runtime.Remoting

Public Class Client
    Inherits System.Windows.Forms.Form

    ' Create the local remotable object that can receive the callback.
    Private ListenerObject As New RemoteLibrary.Listener()

    ' Create the remote object.
    Private TestObject As New RemoteLibrary.RemoteObject()

    Private Sub Form1_Load(ByVal sender As System.Object, _
      ByVal e As System.EventArgs) Handles MyBase.Load

        RemotingConfiguration.Configure("Client.exe.config")

    End Sub

    Private Sub cmdSend_Click(ByVal sender As System.Object, _
      ByVal e As System.EventArgs) Handles cmdSend.Click

        ' Create the delegate that points to the client object.
        Dim Callback As New RemoteLibrary.ConfirmationCallback( _
          AddressOf ListenerObject.ConfirmationCallback)
```

```
        ' Connect the event handler to the local listener class.
        AddHandler ListenerObject.CallbackReceived, _
          AddressOf ListenerObject_CallbackReceived

        ' Send the message to the remote object.
        TestObject.ReceiveMessage(txtMessage.Text, Callback)

    End Sub

    Private Sub ListenerObject_CallbackReceived(ByVal sender As Object, _
      ByVal e As RemoteLibrary.MessageEventArgs)

        MessageBox.Show(e.Message)

    End Sub

End Class
```

> **NOTE** *You might assume that server callbacks and events work using the channel established by the client. However, due to the way that Remoting works, this isn't possible. Instead, the server opens a new channel to deliver its message, which has significant implications if the client is behind a firewall or network address translation (NAT) device. Ingo Rammer has created a proof-of-concept bidirectional TCP channel that solves this issue and allows the server to use the client-created channel (it's available at* http://www.dotnetremoting.cc/projects/modules/BidirectionalTcpChannel.asp). *Unfortunately, this sample isn't yet ready for a production environment. Your best bet may be to wait for future .NET platform releases, since Microsoft Remoting architects are actively considering this issue.*

Configuring Remoting

Remoting uses a multilayered architecture that allows developers to "snap-in" custom modules for different types of formatting, different communication channels, or additional services (such as logging or encryption). In many cases, this layered design means that you can switch the entire communication protocol of an application simply by modifying a single setting in the XML configuration file. This is a unique advantage of Remoting, and none of the lower-level approaches considered later in this book can provide anything like it.

The Remoting model shown in Figure 2-2 simplifies a few details and collapses the Remoting infrastructure down to a single layer. In reality, a Remoting call is routed through several channel sinks in a set order, each of which performs an important task. By default, the first channel sink is the formatter, which encodes the message in SOAP or binary representation. The final channel sink is always the transport channel, which routes the message using the appropriate transport protocol. This model is diagrammed in Figure 3-11.

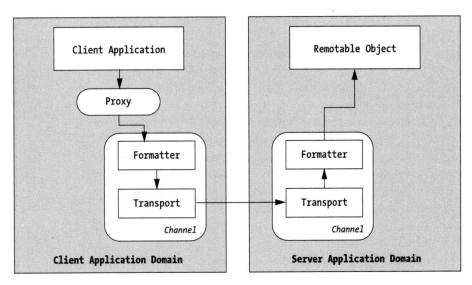

Figure 3-11. The many layers of Remoting

Formatters and Channels

The examples so far have used TCP communication and binary encoding. This is generally the most performance-optimal form of communication, although it can run into trouble in an Internet scenario, particularly when a firewall is involved. Firewalls are often configured to reject incoming TCP connections.

To switch to a more Internet-friendly HTTP channel, simply replace this line in the configuration file:

```
<channel ref="tcp"/>
```

with this one:

```
<channel ref="http"/>
```

You'll need to perform this change for both the client and server. An error will occur if the two parts of the system try to communicate using different formatters or protocols.

As with the TCP channel, there are three versions of the HTTP channel that you can use: http client, http server, and bidirectional http. These are all aliases to specific channel classes that are defined in your computer's *machine.config* file:

```
<channels>
    <channel id="http"
        type="System.Runtime.Remoting.Channels.Http.HttpChannel,
            System.Runtime.Remoting, Version=1.0.3300.0,
            Culture=neutral, PublicKeyToken=b77a5c561934e089"/>
    <channel id="http client"
        type="System.Runtime.Remoting.Channels.Http.HttpClientChannel,
            System.Runtime.Remoting, Version=1.0.3300.0,
            Culture=neutral, PublicKeyToken=b77a5c561934e089"/>
    <channel id="http server"
        type="System.Runtime.Remoting.Channels.Http.HttpServerChannel,
            System.Runtime.Remoting, Version=1.0.3300.0,
            Culture=neutral, PublicKeyToken=b77a5c561934e089"/>
    <channel id="tcp"
        type="System.Runtime.Remoting.Channels.Tcp.TcpChannel,
            System.Runtime.Remoting, Version=1.0.3300.0,
            Culture=neutral, PublicKeyToken=b77a5c561934e089"/>
    <channel id="tcp client"
        type="System.Runtime.Remoting.Channels.Tcp.TcpClientChannel,
            System.Runtime.Remoting, Version=1.0.3300.0,
            Culture=neutral, PublicKeyToken=b77a5c561934e089"/>
    <channel id="tcp server"
        type="System.Runtime.Remoting.Channels.Tcp.TcpServerChannel,
            System.Runtime.Remoting, Version=1.0.3300.0,
            Culture=neutral, PublicKeyToken=b77a5c561934e089"/>
</channels>
```

You'll also need to change the URL used to request the object over the HTTP channel, by replacing the "tcp" prefix with "http," as shown here:

```
<wellknown url="http://localhost:8000/RemoteObject"
            type="RemoteLibrary.RemoteObject, RemoteLibrary"/>
```

The port number can be used in the same manner. Any available port can be used for TCP or HTTP communication.

By default, the TCP channel uses binary encoding. The HTTP channel, on the other hand, always defaults to SOAP (XML-based text) communication. These defaults can be changed. For example, you could use binary communication over an HTTP channel to allow .NET programs to communicate efficiently over the Internet and through a firewall. This would reduce the size of the message because binary encoding is much more compact than XML encoding, but it wouldn't sacrifice any of the connectivity. Similarly, you could use SOAP over a TCP channel. This is an unlikely choice, but might have some uses if you were creating a Remoting client using a non-.NET language such as Java.

In order to specify a formatter other than the default, you must add a <serverProviders> tag inside the <channel> tag, and a <formatter> tag inside the <serverProviders> tag. You then set the ref attribute of the <formatter> tag to "soap" or "binary." You must repeat this on both the client and server configuration file.

Here's a sample configuration file that combines HTTP transport with .NET's proprietary binary encoding:

```
<configuration>
    <system.runtime.remoting>
      <application name="Server">
        <service>
          <wellknown mode="Singleton"
                     type="RemoteLibrary.RemoteObject, RemoteLibrary"
                     objectUri="RemoteObject" />
        </service>

        <channels>
          <channel ref="http server" port="8080" >
            <serverProviders>
              <formatter ref="binary" >
            </serverProviders>
          </channel>
        </channels>

      </application>
</system.runtime.remoting>
```

Dynamic Registration

The last topic this chapter considers is dynamic registration with Remoting. In the examples presented so far, all the Remoting settings have been centralized in a configuration file. The server defines the channel type and registers an available object in one step, using the RemotingConfiguration.Configure() method.

However, it's also possible to perform these tasks exclusively through .NET code. The disadvantage of this approach is that it intermingles configuration details with the application code, and it may force you to recompile your code when you change the distribution of your system. However, dynamic registration also has a number of advantages:

- It allows you to read and apply configuration information from another source, such as a database or a web service.

- It allows you to change the objects that are available or the channels that are used during the lifetime of your application.

- It allows you to make a conditional decision about what channels to use and which objects to expose.

- It allows you to use interface-based programming, as shown in the next chapter.

Dynamic registration is easy. All you need to do is create at least one instance of one of the HTTP or TCP channel classes, register it using the shared ChannelServices.RegisterChannel() method, and register an object type that you want to make available using the shared RemotingConfiguration. RegisterWellKnownServiceType() method. This method also allows you to specify the activation type of the object.

```
RemotingConfiguration.ApplicationName = "Server"

' Define the channel.
Dim Channel As New TcpServerChannel(8000)

' Register the channel.
ChannelServices.RegisterChannel(Channel)

' Register the remote object type.
RemotingConfiguration.RegisterWellKnownServiceType( _
    GetType(RemoteLibrary.RemoteObject), _
    "RemoteLibrary.RemoteObject", _
    WellKnownObjectMode.Singleton)
```

The process on the client is much the same. The only difference is that you use the RegisterWellKnownServiceType() method, instead of the RegisterWellKnownClientType() method.

```
RemotingConfiguration.RegisterWellKnownClientType( _
    GetType(RemoteLibrary.RemoteObject), _
    "tcp://localhost:8000/RemoteObject ")
```

NOTE *The channel classes are located in three namespaces: System.Runtime.Remoting.Channels, System.Runtime.Remoting.Channels.Tcp, and System.Runtime.Remoting.Channels.Http. Depending on the type of channel class you need to create, you'll have to import some of these namespaces.*

The Last Word

In this chapter you've been presented with a condensed (but thorough) primer on Remoting. While Remoting is extremely flexible, most of its assumptions are tailored to stateless enterprise applications that are squarely focused on a small group of powerful server computers. To use Remoting in a peer-to-peer application is an entirely different matter. It will force you to master threading, understand SingleCall activation, and use a central coordinator component. The rewards are a flexible, extensible system that saves you from building key parts of the peer-to-peer infrastructure from scratch.

Depending on your needs, you may even want to extend and customize the Remoting infrastructure. In this case, you'll probably want to consult a dedicated book about Remoting, such as Ingo Rammer's *Advanced .NET Remoting* (Apress 2002). In the final part of this book, you'll look at one example of a component that extends Remoting with features that are ideal for the peer-to-peer domain: the Intel Peer-to-Peer Accelerator Kit.

CHAPTER 4

Building a Simple Messenger

THE LAST CHAPTER CONDUCTED a whirlwind tour of Remoting, .NET's object-based model for communication between applications and across a network. Remoting is a surprisingly flexible technology. By default, it's tailored for traditional enterprise computing, in which all the work is performed by a central group of powerful server computers. But with a little more effort, you can use Remoting as the basis for a peer-to-peer system that uses brokered communication. In this chapter, we'll explore one such example with an instant-messaging application that relies on a central coordinator. Along the way, you'll learn the advantages and drawbacks involved with using Remoting in a peer-to-peer project.

Though Remoting is fairly easy to use, there can be a fair bit of subtlety involved in using it *correctly*. In the example presented in this chapter, it's easy to ignore threading and concurrency problems, scalability considerations, and security. These details are explored in more detail in the next chapter. In this chapter, however, we'll concentrate on creating a basic, reliable framework for a messaging application based on Remoting.

Because the code is quite lengthy, it won't be presented in this chapter all at once. Instead, it's broken down and dissected in detail throughout the chapter. But before we consider a single line of code, we need to plan the overall architecture of the system, which we'll call Talk .NET.

Envisioning Talk .NET

Every Internet user is familiar with the basic model for an instant-messaging application. Users log on to some sort of central authority, retrieve a list that indicates who else is currently online, and exchange simple text messages. Some messaging platforms include additional enhancements, such as file-transfer features and group conversations that can include more than two parties.

All current-day instant-messaging applications rely on some sort of central component that stores a list of who is currently online as well as the information needed to contact them. Depending on the way the system is set up, peers may retrieve this information and contact a chosen user directly, or they may route all activity through the central coordinator. This chapter will consider both alternatives. We'll use the central coordinator approach first.

Conceptually, there are two types of applications in Talk .NET: the single server and the clients (or peers). Both applications must be divided into two parts: a remotable MarshalByRefObject that's exposed to the rest of the world and used for communication over the network, and a private portion, which manages the user interface and local user interaction. The server runs continuously at a fixed, well-known location, while the clients are free to appear and disappear on the network. Figure 4-1 diagrams these components.

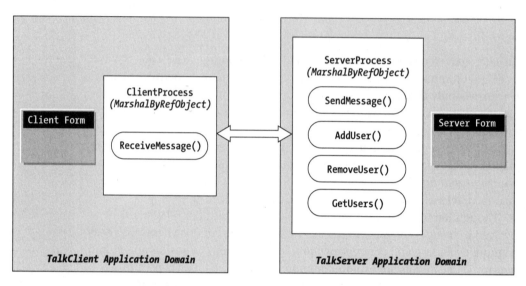

Figure 4-1. Components of the Talk .NET system

In order for the server to contact the client, the client must maintain an open bidirectional channel. When a message arrives, the server notifies the client. This notification can take place in several ways—it might use a callback or event, or the server could just call a method on the client object or interface, which is the approach taken in Talk .NET. Communication between these components uses TCP channels and binary formatting in our example, although these details are easy enough to change through the configuration files.

One of the most important aspects of the Talk .NET design is the fact that it uses interfaces to manage the communication process. Interfaces help to standardize how any two objects interact in a distributed system. Talk .NET includes two interfaces: ITalkServer, which defines the methods that a client can call on the server, and ITalkClient, which defines the methods that the server (or another client) can call on a client. Before actually writing the code for the Talk .NET components, we'll define the functionality by creating these interfaces.

> **NOTE** *You can examine the full code for Talk .NET with the online samples for this chapter. There are a total of four projects that make up this solution; each is contained in a separate directory under the* Talk *.NET directory.*

Defining the Interfaces

The first step in creating the system is to lock down the methods that will be used for communication between the server and client components. These interfaces must be created in a separate DLL assembly so that they can be used by both the TalkClient and TalkServer applications. In the sample code, this class library project is called TalkComponent. It contains the following code:

```
Public Interface ITalkServer

    ' These methods allow users to be registered and unregistered
    ' with the server.
    Sub AddUser(ByVal [alias] As String, ByVal callback As ITalkClient)
    Sub RemoveUser(ByVal [alias] As String)

    ' This returns a collection of user names that are currently logged in.
    Function GetUsers() As ICollection

    ' The client calls this to send a message to the server.
    Sub SendMessage(ByVal senderAlias As String, _
      ByVal recipientAlias As String, ByVal message As String)

End Interface

Public Interface ITalkClient

    ' The server calls this to forward a message to the appropriate client.
    Sub ReceiveMessage(ByVal message As String, ByVal senderAlias As String)

End Interface

' This delegate is primarily for convenience on some server-side code.
Public Delegate Sub ReceiveMessageCallback(ByVal message As String, _
  ByVal senderAlias As String)
```

> **TIP** *Remember to consider security when designing the interfaces. The inter-faces define the methods that will be exposed publicly to other application domains. Don't include any methods that you don't want a user at another computer to be able to trigger.*

ITalkServer defines the basic AddUser() and RemoveUser() methods for registering and unregistering users. It also provides a GetUsers() method that allows peers to retrieve a complete list of online users, and a SendMessage() method that actually routes a message from one peer to another. When SendMessage() is invoked, the server calls the ReceiveMessage() method of the ITalkClient interface to deliver the information to the appropriate peer.

Finally, the ReceiveMessageCallback delegate represents the method signature for the ITalkClient.ReceiveMessage() method. Strictly speaking, this detail isn't required. However, it makes it easier for the server to call the client asynchronously, as you'll see later.

One design decision has already been made in creating the interfaces. The information that's being transferred—the sender's user name and the message text—is represented by separate method parameters. Another approach would be to create a custom serializable Message object, which would be added to the TalkComponent project. Both approaches are perfectly reasonable.

Creating the TraceComponent

In Figure 4-1, both the client and the server are depicted as Windows applications. For the client, this design decision makes sense. For the server, however, it's less appropriate because it makes the design less flexible. For example, it might make more sense to implement the server component as a Windows service instead of a stand-alone application (as demonstrated in the next chapter).

A more loosely coupled option is possible. The server doesn't need to include any user-interface code. Instead, it can output messages to another source, such as the Windows event log. The Talk .NET server will actually output diagnostic messages using tracing code. These messages can then be dealt with in a variety of ways. They can be captured and recorded in a file, sent to an event log, shown in a console window, and so on. In the Talk .NET system, these messages will be caught by a custom trace listener, which will then display the trace messages in a Windows form. This approach is useful, flexible, and simple to code.

In .NET, any class can intercept, trace, and debug messages, provided it inherits from TraceListener in the System.Diagnostics namespace. This abstract class is the basis for DefaultTraceListener (which echoes messages to the Visual Studio .NET debugger), TextWriterTraceListener (which sends messages to a TextWriter or Stream, including a FileStream) and EventLogTraceListener (which records messages in the Windows event log).

All custom trace listeners work by overriding the Write() and WriteLine() methods. The entire process works like this:

1. The program calls a method such as Debug.Write() or Trace.Write().

2. The common language runtime (CLR) iterates through the current collection of debug listeners (Debug.Listeners) or trace listeners (Trace.Listeners).

3. Each time it finds a listener object, it calls its Write() or WriteLine() method with the message.

The solution used in this example creates a generic listener that forwards trace messages to a form, which then handles them appropriately. This arrangement is diagrammed in Figure 4-2.

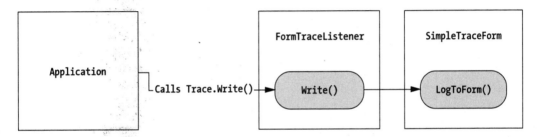

Figure 4-2. Forwarding trace messages to a form

The following is the outline for a FormTraceListener. This class is implemented in a separate class library project named TraceComponent.

```
' The form listener is a TraceListener object that
' maps trace messages to an ITraceForm instance, which
' will then display them in a window.
Public Class FormTraceListener
    Inherits TraceListener

    Public TraceForm As ITraceForm

    ' Use the default trace form.
    Public Sub New()
        MyBase.New()
        Me.TraceForm = New SimpleTraceForm()
    End Sub
```

```
' Use a custom trace form.
Public Sub New(ByVal traceForm As ITraceForm)
    MyBase.New()

    If Not TypeOf traceForm Is Form Then
        Throw New InvalidCastException( _
            "ITraceForm must be used on a Form instance.")
    End If

    Me.TraceForm = traceForm
End Sub

Public Overloads Overrides Sub Write(ByVal value As String)
    TraceForm.LogToForm(value)
End Sub

Public Overloads Overrides Sub WriteLine(ByVal message As String)
    ' WriteLine() and Write() are equivalent in this simple example.
    Me.Write(message)
End Sub

End Class
```

The FormTraceListener can send messages to any form that implements an ITraceForm interface, as shown here:

```
' Any custom form can be a "trace form" as long as it
' implements this interface.
Public Interface ITraceForm

    ' Determines how trace messages will be displayed.
    Sub LogToForm(ByVal message As String)

End Interface
```

Finally, the TraceComponent assembly also includes a sample form that can be used for debugging. It simply displays received messages in a list box and automatically scrolls to the end of the list each time a message is received.

```
Public Class SimpleTraceForm
    Inherits System.Windows.Forms.Form
    Implements ITraceForm

    ' (Designer code omitted.)
```

```
Public Sub LogToForm(ByVal message As String) Implements ITraceForm.LogToForm
    ' Add the log message.
    lstMessages.Items.Add(message)

    ' Scroll to the bottom of the list.
    lstMessages.SelectedIndex = lstMessages.Items.Count - 1
End Sub

End Class
```

This approach is useful for the Talk .NET server, but because it's implemented as a separate component, it can easily be reused in other projects.

The Coordination Server

Now that we've defined the basic building blocks for the Talk .NET system, it's time to move ahead and build the server. The TalkServer application has the task of tracking clients and routing messages from one user to another. The core of the application is implemented in the remotable ServerProcess class, which is provided to clients as a Singleton object. A separate module, called Startup, is used to start the TalkServer application. It initializes the Remoting configuration settings, creates and initializes an instance of the FormTraceListener, and displays the trace form modally. When the trace form is closed, the application ends, and the ServerProcess object is destroyed.

The startup code is shown here:

```
Imports System.Runtime.Remoting

Public Module Startup

    Public Sub Main()
        ' Create the server-side form (which displays diagnostic information).
        ' This form is implemented as a diagnostic logger.
        Dim frmLog As New TraceComponent.FormTraceListener()
        Trace.Listeners.Add(frmLog)

        ' Configure the connection and register the well-known object
        ' (ServerProcess), which will accept client requests.
        RemotingConfiguration.Configure("TalkServer.exe.config")
```

```
' From this point on, messages can be received by the ServerProcess
' object. The object will be created for the first request,
' although you could create it explicitly if desired.

' Show the trace listener form. By using ShowDialog(), we set up a
' message loop on this thread. The application will automatically end
' when the form is closed.
Dim frm As Form = frmLog.TraceForm
frm.Text = "Talk .NET Server (Trace Display)"
frm.ShowDialog()
End Sub


End Module
```

When you start the server, the ServerProcess Singleton object isn't created. Instead, it's created the first time a client invokes one of its methods. This will typically mean that the first application request will experience a slight delay, while the Singleton object is created.

The server configuration file is shown here. It includes three lines that are required if you want to run the Talk .NET applications under .NET 1.1 (the version of .NET included with Visual Studio .NET 2003). These lines enable full serialization, which allows the TalkServer to use the ITalkClient reference. If you are using .NET 1.0, these lines must remain commented out, because they will not be recognized. .NET 1.0 uses a slightly looser security model and allows full serialization support by default.

```
<configuration>
    <system.runtime.remoting>
        <application name="TalkNET">
            <service>
                <wellknown
                    mode="Singleton"
                    type="TalkServer.ServerProcess, TalkServer"
                    objectUri="TalkServer" />
            </service>
            <channels>
                <channel port="8000" ref="tcp" >
                    <!-- If you are using .NET 1.1, uncomment the lines below. -->
                    <!--
                    <serverProviders>
                        <formatter ref="binary" typeFilterLevel="Full" />
                    </serverProviders>
                    -->
```

```
            </channel>
          </channels>
        </application>
    </system.runtime.remoting>
</configuration>
```

Most of the code for the ServerProcess class is contained in the methods implemented from the ITalkServer interface. The basic outline is shown here:

```
Public Class ServerProcess
    Inherits MarshalByRefObject
    Implements ITalkServer

    ' Tracks all the user aliases, and the "network pointer" needed
    ' to communicate with them.
    Private ActiveUsers As New Hashtable()

    Public Sub AddUser(ByVal [alias] As String, ByVal client As ITalkClient) _
      Implements TalkComponent.ITalkServer.AddUser
        ' (Code omitted.)
    End Sub

    Public Sub RemoveUser(ByVal [alias] As String) _
      Implements TalkComponent.ITalkServer.RemoveUser
        ' (Code omitted.)
    End Sub

    Public Function GetUsers() As System.Collections.ICollection _
      Implements TalkComponent.ITalkServer.GetUsers
        ' (Code omitted.)
    End Function

    <System.Runtime.Remoting.Messaging.OneWay()> _
    Public Sub SendMessage(ByVal senderAlias As String, _
      ByVal recipientAlias As String, ByVal message As String) _
      Implements TalkComponent.ITalkServer.SendMessage
        ' (Code omitted.)
    End Sub

End Class
```

You'll see each method in more detail in the next few sections.

Tracking Clients

The Talk .NET server tracks clients using a Hashtable collection. The Hashtable provides several benefits compared to arrays or other types of collections:

- The Hashtable is a key/value collection (unlike some collections, which do not require keys). This allows you to associate two pieces of information: the user name and a network reference to the client.

- The Hashtable is optimized for quick key-based lookup. This is ideal, because users send messages based on the user's name. The server can speedily retrieve the client's location information.

- The Hashtable allows easy synchronization for thread-safe programming. We'll look at these features in the next chapter.

The collection stores ITalkClient references, indexed by user name. Technically, the ITalkClient reference really represents an instance of the System.Runtime.Remoting.ObjRef class. This class is a kind of network pointer— it contains all the information needed to generate a proxy object to communicate with the client, including the client channel, the object type, and the computer name. This ObjRef can be passed around the network, thus allowing any other user to locate and communicate with the client.

Following are the three collection-related methods that manage user registration. They're provided by the server.

```
Public Sub AddUser(ByVal [alias] As String, ByVal client As ITalkClient) _
   Implements TalkComponent.ITalkServer.AddUser
      Trace.Write("Added user '" & [alias] & "'")
      ActiveUsers([alias]) = client
End Sub


Public Sub RemoveUser(ByVal [alias] As String) _
   Implements TalkComponent.ITalkServer.RemoveUser
      Trace.Write("Removed user '" & [alias] & "'")
      ActiveUsers.Remove([alias])
End Sub


Public Function GetUsers() As System.Collections.ICollection _
   Implements TalkComponent.ITalkServer.GetUsers
      Return ActiveUsers.Keys
End Function
```

The AddUser() method doesn't check for duplicates. If the specified user name doesn't exist, a new entry is created. Otherwise, any entry with the same key is overwritten. The next chapter introduces some other ways to handle this behavior, but in a production application, you would probably want to authenticate users against a database with password information. This allows you to ensure that each user has a unique user name. If a user were to log in twice in a row, only the most recent connection information would be retained.

Note that only one part of the collection is returned to the client through the GetUsers() method: the user names. This prevents a malicious client from using the connection information to launch attacks against the peers on the system. Of course, this approach isn't possible in a decentralized peer-to-peer situation (wherein peers need to interact directly), but in this case, it's a realistic level of protection to add.

Sending Messages

The process of sending a message requires slightly more work. The server performs most of the heavy lifting in the SendMessage() method, which looks up the appropriate client and invokes its ReceiveMessage() method to deliver the message. If the recipient cannot be found (probably because the client has recently disconnected from the network), an error message is sent to the message sender by invoking *its* ReceiveMessage() method. If neither client can be found, the problem is harmlessly ignored.

```
Public Sub SendMessage(ByVal senderAlias As String, _
   ByVal recipientAlias As String, ByVal message As String) _
   Implements TalkComponent.ITalkServer.SendMessage

    ' Deliver the message.
    Dim Recipient As ITalkClient
    If ActiveUsers.ContainsKey(recipientAlias) Then
        Trace.Write("Recipient '" & recipientAlias & "' found")
        Recipient = CType(ActiveUsers(recipientAlias), ITalkClient)
    Else
        ' User wasn't found. Try to find the sender.
        If ActiveUsers.ContainsKey(senderAlias) Then
            Trace.Write("Recipient '" & recipientAlias & "' not found")
            Recipient = CType(ActiveUsers(senderAlias), ITalkClient)
            message = "'" & message & "' could not be delivered."
            senderAlias = "Talk .NET"
```

```
        Else
            Trace.Write("Recipient '" & recipientAlias & "' and sender '" & _
                        senderAlias & "' not found")
            ' Both sender and recipient weren't found.
            ' Ignore this message.
        End If
    End If

    Trace.Write("Delivering message to '" & recipientAlias & "' from '" & _
                senderAlias & "'")
    If Not Recipient Is Nothing Then
        Dim callback As New ReceiveMessageCallback( _
          AddressOf Recipient.ReceiveMessage)
        callback.BeginInvoke(message, senderAlias, Nothing, Nothing)
    End If

End Sub
```

You'll see that the server doesn't directly call the ClientProcess.ReceiveMessage()
method because this would stall the thread and prevent it from continuing other
tasks. Instead, it makes the call on a new thread by using the BeginInvoke()
method provided by all delegates. It's possible to use a server-side callback to
determine when this call completes, but in this case, it's not necessary.

This completes the basic framework for the TalkServer application. The next
step is to build a client that can work with the server to send instant messages
around the network.

The TalkClient

The client portion of Talk .NET is called TalkClient. It's designed as a Windows
application (much like Microsoft's Windows Messenger). It has exactly two
responsibilities: to allow the user to send a message to any other online user and
to display a log of sent and received messages.

When the TalkClient application first loads, it executes a startup procedure,
which presents a login form and requests the name of the user that it should register. If one isn't provided, the application terminates. Otherwise, it continues by
taking two steps:

- It creates an instance of the ClientProcess class and supplies the user name. The ClientProcess class mediates all communication between the remote server and the client user interface.

- It creates and shows the main chat form, named Talk, around which most of the application revolves.

The startup code is shown here:

```
Public Class Startup

    Public Shared Sub Main()
        ' Create the login window (which retrieves the user identifier).
        Dim frmLogin As New Login()

        ' Only continue if the user successfully exits by clicking OK
        ' (not the Cancel or Exit button).
        If frmLogin.ShowDialog() = DialogResult.OK Then
            ' Create the new remotable client object.
            Dim Client As New ClientProcess(frmLogin.UserName)

            ' Create the client form.
            Dim frm As New Talk()
            frm.TalkClient = Client

            ' Show the form.
            frm.ShowDialog()
        End If
    End Sub

End Class
```

On startup, the ClientProcess object registers the user with the coordination server. Because ClientProcess is a remotable type, it will remain accessible to the server for callbacks throughout the lifetime of the application. These callbacks will, in turn, be raised to the user interface through local events. We'll dive into this code shortly.

The login form (shown in Figure 4-3) is quite straightforward. It exposes a public UserName property, which allows the Startup routine to retrieve the user name without violating encapsulation. This property could also be used to pre-fill the txtUser textbox by retrieving the previously used name, which could be stored in a configuration file or the Windows registry on the current computer.

```vbnet
Public Class Login
    Inherits System.Windows.Forms.Form

  ' (Designer code omitted.)

  Private Sub cmdExit_Click(ByVal sender As System.Object, _
    ByVal e As System.EventArgs) Handles cmdExit.Click
      Me.Close()
  End Sub

  Public Property UserName()
      Get
          Return txtUser.Text
      End Get
      Set(ByVal Value)
          txtUser.Text = UserName
      End Set
  End Property

End Class
```

Figure 4-3. The login form

The Remotable ClientProcess Class

The ClientProcess class does double duty. It allows the TalkClient to interact
with the TalkServer to register and unregister the user or send a message
destined for another user. The ClientProcess also receives callbacks from the
TalkServer and forwards these to the TalkClient through an event. In the Talk .NET
system, the only time the TalkServer will call the ClientProcess is to deliver

a message sent from another user. At this point, the ClientProcess will forward the message along to the user interface by raising an event. Because the server needs to be able to call ClientProcess.ReceiveMessage() across the network, the ClientProcess class must inherit from MarshalByRefObject. ClientProcess also implements ITalkClient.

Here's the basic outline for the ClientProcess class. Note that the user name is stored as a member variable named _Alias, and exposed through the public property Alias. Because alias is a reserved keyword in VB .NET, you will have to put this word in square brackets in the code.

```
Imports System.Runtime.Remoting
Imports TalkComponent

Public Class ClientProcess
    Inherits MarshalByRefObject
    Implements ITalkClient

    ' This event occurs when a message is received.
    ' It's used to transfer the message from the remotable
    ' ClientProcess object to the Talk form.
    Event MessageReceived(ByVal sender As Object, _
      ByVal e As MessageReceivedEventArgs)

    ' The reference to the server object.
    ' (Technically, this really holds a proxy class.)
    Private Server As ITalkServer

    ' The user ID for this instance.
    Private _Alias As String
    Public Property [Alias]() As String
        Get
            Return _Alias
        End Get
        Set(ByVal Value As String)
            _Alias = Value
        End Set
    End Property

    Public Sub New(ByVal [alias] As String)
        _Alias = [alias]
    End Sub
```

```
' This override ensures that if the object is idle for an extended
' period, waiting for messages, it won't lose its lease and
' be garbage collected.
Public Overrides Function InitializeLifetimeService() As Object
    Return Nothing
End Function

Public Sub Login()
    ' (Code omitted.)
End Sub

Public Sub LogOut()
    ' (Code omitted.)
End Sub

Public Sub SendMessage(ByVal recipientAlias As String, _
  ByVal message As String)
    ' (Code omitted.)
End Sub

Private Sub ReceiveMessage(ByVal message As String, _
  ByVal senderAlias As String) Implements ITalkClient.ReceiveMessage
    ' (Code omitted.)
End Sub

Public Function GetUsers() As ICollection
    ' (Code omitted.)
End Function

End Class
```

The InitializeLifetimeService() method must be overridden to preserve the life of all ClientProcess objects. Even though the startup routine holds a reference to a ClientProcess object, the ClientProcess object will still disappear from the network after its lifetime lease expires, unless you explicitly configure an infinite lifetime. Alternatively, you can use configuration file settings instead of overriding the InitializeLifetimeService() method, as described in the previous chapter.

One other interesting detail is found in the ReceiveMessage() method. This method is accessible remotely to the server because it implements ITalkClient.ReceiveMessage. However, this method is also marked with the Private keyword, which means that other classes in the TalkClient application won't accidentally attempt to use it.

The Login() method configures the client channel, creates a proxy to the server object, and then calls the ServerProcess.AddUser() method to register the client. The Logout() method simply unregisters the user, but it doesn't tear down the Remoting channels—that will be performed automatically when the application exits. Finally, the GetUsers() method retrieves the user names of all the users currently registered with the coordination server.

```
Public Sub Login()

    ' Configure the client channel for sending messages and receiving
    ' the server callback.
    RemotingConfiguration.Configure("TalkClient.exe.config")

    ' You could accomplish the same thing in code by uncommenting
    ' the following two lines:
    ' Dim Channel As New System.Runtime.Remoting.Channels.Tcp.TcpChannel(0) and
    ' ChannelServices.RegisterChannel(Channel).

    ' Create the proxy that references the server object.
    Server = CType(Activator.GetObject(GetType(ITalkServer), _
                    "tcp://localhost:8000/TalkNET/TalkServer"), ITalkServer)

    ' Register the current user with the server.
    ' If the server isn't  running, or the URL or class information is
    ' incorrect, an error will most likely occur here.
    Server.AddUser(_Alias, Me)

End Sub

Public Sub LogOut()
    Server.RemoveUser(_Alias)
End Sub

Public Function GetUsers() As ICollection
    Return Server.GetUsers()
End Function
```

Following is the client configuration, which only specified channel information. The client port isn't specified and will be chosen dynamically from the available ports at runtime. As with the server configuration file, you must enable full serialization if you are running the Talk .NET system with .NET 1.1. Otherwise, the TalkClient will not be allowed to transmit the ITalkClient reference over the network to the server.

```
<configuration>
   <system.runtime.remoting>
      <application>
         <channels>
            <channel port="0" ref="tcp" >
               <!-- If you are using .NET 1.1, uncomment the lines below. -->
               <!--
               <serverProviders>
                   <formatter ref="binary" typeFilterLevel="Full" />
               </serverProviders>
               -->
            </channel>
         </channels>
      </application>
   </system.runtime.remoting>
</configuration>
```

You'll notice that the Login() method mingles some dynamic Remoting code (used to create the TalkServer instance) along with a configuration file (used to create the client channel). Unfortunately, it isn't possible to rely exclusively on a configuration file when you use interface-based programming with Remoting. The problem is that the client doesn't have any information about the server, only an interface it supports. The client thus cannot register the appropriate object type and create it directly because there's no way to instantiate an interface. The previous solution, which uses the Activator.GetObject() method, forces you to include several distribution details in your code. This means that if the object is moved to another computer or exposed through another port, you'll need to recompile the code.

You can resolve this problem in several ways. One option is simply to add a custom configuration setting with the full object URI. This will be an application setting, not a Remoting setting, so it will need to be entered in the <appSettings> section of the client configuration file, as shown here:

```
<configuration>

   <appSettings>
      <add key="TalkServerURL"
           value="tcp://localhost:8000/TalkNET/TalkServer" />
   </appSettings>
```

```
<system.runtime.remoting>
  <application>
    <channels>
      <channel port="0" ref="tcp" >
        <!-- If you are using .NET 1.1, uncomment the lines below. -->
        <!--
        <serverProviders>
            <formatter ref="binary" typeFilterLevel="Full" />
        </serverProviders>
        -->
      </channel>
    </channels>
  </application>
</system.runtime.remoting>
```

```
</configuration>
```

You can then retrieve this setting using the ConfigurationSettings.AppSettings collection:

```
Server = CType(Activator.GetObject(GetType(ITalkServer), _
                ConfigurationSettings.AppSettings("TalkServer")), ITalkServer)
```

Note that in this example, we use the loopback alias localhost, indicating that the server is running on the same computer. You should replace this value with the name of the computer (if it's on your local network), the domain name, or the IP address where the server component is running.

The last ingredient is the ClientProcess methods for sending and receiving messages. The following code shows the SendMessage() and ReceiveMessage() methods. The SendMessage() simply executes the call on the server and the ReceiveMessage() raises a local event for the client, which will be handled by the Talk form.

```
Public Sub SendMessage(ByVal recipientAlias As String, ByVal message As String)
    Server.SendMessage(_Alias, recipientAlias, message)
End Sub

Private Sub ReceiveMessage(ByVal message As String, _
  ByVal senderAlias As String) Implements ITalkClient.ReceiveMessage
    RaiseEvent MessageReceived(Me, New MessageReceivedEventArgs(message, _
                                senderAlias))
End Sub
```

The MessageReceived event makes use of the following custom EventArgs class, which adds the message-specific information:

```
Public Class MessageReceivedEventArgs
    Inherits EventArgs

    Public Message As String
    Public SenderAlias As String

    Public Sub New(ByVal message As String, ByVal senderAlias As String)
        Me.Message = message
        Me.SenderAlias = senderAlias
    End Sub

End Class
```

The Talk Form

The Talk form is the front-end that the user interacts with. It has four key tasks:

- Log the user in when the form loads and log the user out when the form closes.

- Periodically refresh the list of active users by calling ClientProcess.GetUsers(). This is performed using a timer.

- Invoke ClientProcess.SendMessage() when the user sends a message.

- Handle the MessageReceived event and display the corresponding information on the form.

The form is shown in Figure 4-4. Messages are recorded in a RichTextBox, which allows the application of formatting, if desired. The list of clients is maintained in a ListBox.

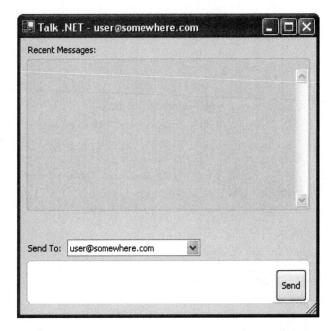

Figure 4-4. The Talk form

The full form code is shown here:

```
Public Class Talk
    Inherits System.Windows.Forms.Form

    ' (Designer code omitted.)

    ' The remotable intermediary for all client-to-server communication.
    Public WithEvents TalkClient As ClientProcess

    Private Sub Talk_Load(ByVal sender As System.Object, _
      ByVal e As System.EventArgs) Handles MyBase.Load

        Me.Text &= " - " & TalkClient.Alias

        ' Attempt to register with the server.
        TalkClient.Login()

        ' Ordinarily, a user list is periodically fetched from the
        ' server. In this case, the code enables the timer and calls it
        ' once (immediately) to initially populate the list box.
        tmrRefreshUsers_Tick(Me, EventArgs.Empty)
```

```
        tmrRefreshUsers.Enabled = True
        lstUsers.SelectedIndex = 0


End Sub


Private Sub TalkClient_MessageReceived(ByVal sender As Object, _
    ByVal e As MessageReceivedEventArgs) Handles TalkClient.MessageReceived

        txtReceived.Text &= "Message From: " & e.SenderAlias
        txtReceived.Text &= " delivered at " & DateTime.Now.ToShortTimeString()
        txtReceived.Text &= Environment.NewLine & e.Message
        txtReceived.Text &= Environment.NewLine & Environment.NewLine

End Sub


Private Sub cmdSend_Click(ByVal sender As System.Object, _
    ByVal e As System.EventArgs) Handles cmdSend.Click

        ' Display a record of the message you're sending.
        txtReceived.Text &= "Sent Message To: " & lstUsers.Text
        txtReceived.Text &= Environment.NewLine & txtMessage.Text
        txtReceived.Text &= Environment.NewLine & Environment.NewLine

        ' Send the message through the ClientProcess object.
        Try
            TalkClient.SendMessage(lstUsers.Text, txtMessage.Text)
            txtMessage.Text = ""
        Catch Err As Exception
            MessageBox.Show(Err.Message, "Send Failed", _
                            MessageBoxButtons.OK, MessageBoxIcon.Exclamation)
        End Try

End Sub


' Checks every 30 seconds.
Private Sub tmrRefreshUsers_Tick(ByVal sender As System.Object, _
    ByVal e As System.EventArgs) Handles tmrRefreshUsers.Tick

        ' Prepare list of logged-in users.
        ' The code must copy the ICollection entries into
        ' an ordinary array before they can be added.
        Dim UserArray() As String
        Dim UserCollection As ICollection = TalkClient.GetUsers
        ReDim UserArray(UserCollection.Count - 1)
        UserCollection.CopyTo(UserArray, 0)
```

```
' Replace the list entries. At the same time,
' the code will track the previous selection and try
' to restore it, so the update won't be noticeable.
Dim CurrentSelection As String = lstUsers.Text
lstUsers.Items.Clear()
lstUsers.Items.AddRange(UserArray)
lstUsers.Text = CurrentSelection

End Sub


Private Sub Talk_Closed(ByVal sender As Object, _
   ByVal e As System.EventArgs) Handles MyBase.Closed
     TalkClient.LogOut()
   End Sub


End Class
```

The timer fires and refreshes the list of user names seamlessly every 30 seconds. In a large system, you would lower this value to ease the burden on the coordinator. For a very large system with low user turnover, it might be more efficient to have the server broadcast user-added and user-removed messages. To support this infrastructure, you would add methods such as ITalkClient.NotifyUserAdded() and ITalkClient.NotifyUserRemoved(). Or you might just use a method such as ITalkClient.NotifyListChanged(), which tells the client that it must contact the server at some point to update its information.

The ideal approach isn't always easy to identify. The goal is to minimize the network chatter as much as possible. In a system with 100 users who query the server every 60 seconds, approximately 100 request messages and 100 response messages will be sent every minute. If the same system adopts user-added and user-removed broadcasting instead, and approximately 5 users join or leave the system in a minute, the server will likely need to send 5 messages to each of 100 users, for a much larger total of 500 messages per minute. The messages themselves would be smaller (because they would not contain the full user list), but the network overhead would probably be great enough that this option would work less efficiently.

In a large system, you might use "buddy lists" so that clients only receive a user list with a subset of the total number of users. In this case, the server broadcast approach would be more efficient because a network exchange would only be required for those users who are on the same list as the entering or departing peer. This reduces the total number of calls dramatically. Overall, this is probably the most sustainable option if you want to continue to develop the Talk .NET application to serve a larger audience.

Because the client chooses a channel dynamically, it's possible to run several instances of the TalkClient on the same computer. After starting the new instances, the user list of the original clients will quickly be refreshed to represent the full user list. You can then send messages back and forth, as shown in Figure 4-5. Clients can also send messages to themselves.

Figure 4-5. Multiple client interaction

In each case, the coordination server brokers the communication. The trace output for a sample interaction on the server computer is shown in Figure 4-6.

Figure 4-6. The server trace display

Enhancing Talk .NET

Talk .NET presents a straightforward way to reinvent the popular instant-messaging application in .NET code. However, as it currently stands, it's best suited for small groups of users and heavily reliant on a central coordination server. In fact, in many respects it's hard to call this a true peer-to-peer application at all.

Fortunately, Talk .NET is just a foundation that you can build on. This section considers possible enhancements, stumbling blocks, and a minor redesign that allows true peer-to-peer communication.

Cleaning Up After Clients

Currently, the system assumes that all clients will log out politely when they've finished using the system. Due to network problems, program error, or some other uncontrollable factor, this may not be the case. Remember, one of the defining characteristics of any peer-to-peer system is that it must take into account the varying, fragile connectivity of users on the Internet. For this reason, Talk .NET needs to adopt a more defensive approach.

Currently, the SendMessage() method raises an unhandled exception if it can't contact the specified user. This exception will propagate back to the user-interface code, where it will be handled and will result in a user error message. The problem with this approach is that the user remains in the server's collection and continues to "appear" online. If another user attempts to send a message to this user, valuable server seconds will be wasted attempting to contact the offline user, thereby raising the exception. This problem will persist until the missing user logs back in to the system.

To account for this problem, users should be removed from the collection if they cannot be contacted. Here's the important portion of the SendMessage() code, revised accordingly:

```
If Not Recipient Is Nothing Then

    Dim callback As New ReceiveMessageCallback( _
      AddressOf Recipient.ReceiveMessage)

    Try
        callback.BeginInvoke(message, senderAlias, Nothing, Nothing)
    Catch Err As Exception
        ' Client could not be contacted.
        Trace.Write("Message delivery failed")
        ActiveUsers.Remove(recipientAlias)
    End Try

End If
```

You may also want to send a message explaining the problem to the user. However, you also need to protect yourself in case the user who sent the message can't be contacted or found. To prevent the code from becoming too fragmented, you can rewrite it using recursion, as shown here:

```
Public Sub SendMessage(ByVal senderAlias As String, _
  ByVal recipientAlias As String, ByVal message As String) _
  Implements TalkComponent.ITalkServer.SendMessage

    Dim Recipient As ITalkClient
    If ActiveUsers.ContainsKey(recipientAlias) Then
        Trace.Write("Recipient '" & recipientAlias & "' found")
        Recipient = CType(ActiveUsers(recipientAlias), ITalkClient)

        If Not Recipient Is Nothing Then

            Trace.Write("Delivering message to '" & recipientAlias & "' from _
                        '" & senderAlias & "'")
            Dim callback As New ReceiveMessageCallback( _
              AddressOf Recipient.ReceiveMessage)

            ' Deliver the message.
            Try
                callback.BeginInvoke(message, senderAlias, Nothing, Nothing)

            Catch Err As Exception
                ' Client could not be contacted.
                ActiveUsers.Remove(recipientAlias)

                If senderAlias <> "Talk .NET"
                    ' Try to send a warning message.
                    message = "'" & message & "' could not be delivered."
                    SendMessage("Talk .NET", senderAlias, message)

            End Try
        End If

    Else
        ' User was not found. Try to find the sender.
        Trace.Write("Recipient '" & recipientAlias & "' not found")
```

```
    If senderAlias <> "Talk .NET"
        ' Try to send a warning message.
        message = "'" & message & "' could not be delivered."
        SendMessage("Talk .NET", senderAlias, message)
    End If

  End If

End Sub
```

Of course, in order for this approach to work, you'll need to ensure that no other user can take the user name "Talk .NET." You could add this restriction in your logon or authentication code.

Toward Decentralization

Talk .NET will always requires some sort of centralized server component in order to store information about logged-on users and their locations. However, it's not necessary to route all communication through the server. In fact, Remoting allows clients to communicate directly—with a few quirks.

Remoting is designed as an object-based networking technology. In order for clients to communicate directly, they need to have a reference to each other's remotable ClientProcess object. As you've already learned, you can create this reference through a configuration file or .NET Remoting code, if you know the appropriate URL. This is how the client contacts the coordination server in the Talk .NET system—by knowing the computer and port where it's located. But there's also another approach: by passing an object reference. The server calls the client back by using one of its stored ITalkClient references.

The ITalkClient reference isn't limited to exchanges between the server and client. In fact, this reference can be passed to any computer on the network. Because ITalkClient references a remotable object (in this case, ClientProcess), whenever the reference travels to another application domain, it actually takes the form of an ObjRef: a network pointer that encapsulates all the information needed to describe the object and its location on the network. With this information, any .NET application can dynamically construct a proxy and communicate with the client it references. You can use the ObjRef as the basis for decentralized communication.

To see this in action, modify the ITalkServer interface to expose an additional method that returns an ITalkClient reference for a specific user:

```
Public Interface ITalkServer

    ' (Other code omitted.)
    Function GetUser(ByVal [alias] As String) As ITalkClient

End Interface
```

Now, implement the GetUser() method in the ServerProcess class:

```
Public Function GetUser(ByVal [alias] As String) As TalkComponent.ITalkClient _
    Implements TalkComponent.ITalkServer.GetUser

    Return ActiveUsers([alias])

End Function
```

Now the ClientProcess class can call GetUser() to retrieve the ITalkUser reference of the peer it wants to communicate with; it can then call the ITalkClient.ReceiveMessage() method directly:

```
Public Sub SendMessage(ByVal recipientAlias As String, ByVal message As String)

    Dim Peer As ITalkClient = Server.GetUser(recipientAlias)
    Peer.ReceiveMessage(message, Me.Alias)

End Sub
```

With this change in place, the system will work exactly the same. However, the coordination server is now simply being used as a repository of connection information. Once the lookup is performed, it's no longer required.

> **NOTE**   *You can find this version of the application in the* Talk .NET *Decentralized directory with the online samples for this chapter.*

Which approach is best? There's little doubt that the second choice is more authentically peer-to-peer. But the best choice for your system depends on your needs. Some of the benefits of the server-focused approach include the following:

- The server can track system activity, which could be useful, depending on your reporting needs. If you run the second version of this application, you'll see that the server trace log reflects when users are added or removed, but it doesn't contain any information when messages are sent.

- The connectivity is likely to be better. Typically, if a client can contact the server, the server will be able to call the client. However, two arbitrary clients may not be able to interact, depending on firewalls and other aspects of network topology.

- The server can offer some special features that wouldn't be possible in a decentralized system, such as multiuser broadcasts that involve thousands of users.

On the other hand, the benefits of the decentralized approach include the following:

- The server has no ability to monitor conversations. This translates into better security (assuming peers don't fully trust the behavior of the server).

- The possibility for a server bottleneck decreases. This is because the server isn't called on to deal with messages, but rather, only to provide client lookup, thereby reducing its burden and moving network traffic out to the edges of the network.

Most peer-to-peer supporters would prefer the decentralized approach. However, the current generation of instant-messaging applications avoid it for connectivity reasons. Instead, they use systems that more closely resemble the client-server model.

In some cases you might want to adopt a blended approach that makes use of both of these techniques. One option is to allow the client to specify the behavior through a configuration setting. Another option would be to use peer-to-peer communication only when large amounts of data need to be transmitted. This is the approach used in the next section to provide a file transfer service for Talk .NET.

In any case, if you adopt the decentralized approach, you can further reduce the burden on the central coordinator by performing the client lookup once, and then reusing the connection information for all subsequent messages. For example, you could cache the retrieved client reference in a local ActiveUsers collection, and update it from the server if an error is encountered while sending a message. Or, you might modify the system so that the GetUsers() method returns the entire collection, complete with user names and ITalkClient network pointers. The central coordinator would then simply need to support continuous requests to three methods: AddUser(), RemoveUser(), and GetUsers(). This type of design works well if you use "buddy lists" to determine who a user can communicate with. That way, users will only retrieve information about a small subset of the total number of users when they call GetUsers().

Adding a File Transfer Feature

Using the decentralized approach, it's easy to implement a file transfer feature that's similar to the one provided by Microsoft's Windows Messenger. This feature wouldn't be practical with the centralized approach because it encourages the server to become a bottleneck. Although transferring files isn't a complex task, it can take time, and the CLR only provides a limited number of threads to handle server requests. If all the threads are tied up with sending data across the network (or waiting as data is transferred over a low-bandwidth connection), subsequent requests will have to wait—and could even time out.

The file transfer operation can be broken down into four steps:

1. Peer A offers a file to Peer B.

2. Peer B accepts the file offer and initiates the transfer.

3. Peer A sends the file to Peer B.

4. Peer B saves the file locally in a predetermined directory.

These steps require several separate method calls. Typically, in step 2, the user will be presented with some sort of dialog box asking whether the file should be transferred. It's impractical to leave the connection open while this message is being displayed because there's no guarantee the user will reply promptly, and the connection could time out while waiting. Instead, the peer-to-peer model requires a looser, disconnected architecture that completely separates the file offer and file transfer.

The first step needed to implement the file transfer is to redefine the ITalkClient interface. It's at this point that most of the coding and design decisions are made.

```
Public Interface ITalkClient

    ' (Other code omitted.)
```

```
Sub ReceiveFileOffer(ByVal filename As String, _
   ByVal fileIdentifier As Guid, ByVal senderAlias As String)
Function TransferFile(ByVal fileIdentifier As Guid, _
   ByVal senderAlias As String) As Byte()
```

```
End Interface
```

You'll notice that both methods use a globally unique identifier (GUID) to identify the file. There are several reasons for this approach, all of which revolve around security. If the TransferFile() method accepted a full file name, it would be possible for the client to initiate a transfer even if the file had not been offered, thereby compromising data security. To circumvent this problem, all files are identified uniquely. The identifier used is a GUID, which guarantees that a client won't be able to guess the identifier for a file offered to another user. Also, because GUIDs are guaranteed to be unique, a peer can offer multiple files to different users without confusion. More elaborate security approaches are possible, but this approach is a quick and easy way to prevent users from getting ahold of the wrong files.

The file itself is transferred as a large byte array. While this will be sufficient in most cases, if you want to control how the data is streamed over the network, you'll need to use a lower-level networking class, such as the ones described in the second part of this book.

Once the ITalkClient interface is updated, you can begin to revise the ClientProcess class. The first step is to define a Hashtable collection that can track all the outstanding file offers since the application was started:

```
Private OfferedFiles As New Hashtable()
```

To offer a file, the TalkClient calls the public SendFileOffer() method. This method looks up the client reference, generates a new GUID to identify the file, stores the information, and sends the offer.

```
Public Function SendFileOffer(ByVal recipientAlias As String, _
   ByVal sourcePath As String)

   ' Retrieve the reference to the other user.
   Dim peer As ITalkClient = Server.GetUser(recipientAlias)

   ' Create a GUID to identify the file, and add it to the collection.
   Dim fileIdentifier As Guid = Guid.NewGuid()
   OfferedFiles(fileIdentifier) = sourcePath
```

```
' Offer the file.
peer.ReceiveFileOffer(Path.GetFileName(sourcePath), fileIdentifier, Me.Alias)

End Function
```

Notice that only the file name is transmitted, not the full file path. The full file path is stored for future reference in the Hashtable collection, but it's snipped out of the offer using the Path class from the System.IO namespace. This extra step is designed to prevent the recipient from knowing where the offered file is stored on the offering peer.

> **TIP** *Currently, the TalkClient doesn't go to any extra work to "expire" an offered file and remove its information from the collection if it isn't transferred within a set period of time. This task could be accomplished using a separate thread that would periodically examine the collection. However, because the in-memory size of the OfferedFiles collection will always remain relatively small, this isn't a concern, even after making a few hundred unclaimed file offers.*

The file offer is received by the destination peer with the ReceiveFileOffer() method. When this method is triggered, the ClientProcess class raises a local event to alert the user:

```
Event FileOfferReceived(ByVal sender As Object, _
   ByVal e As FileOfferReceivedEventArgs)

Private Sub ReceiveFileOffer(ByVal filename As String, _
   ByVal fileIdentifier As System.Guid, ByVal senderAlias As String) _
   Implements TalkComponent.ITalkClient.ReceiveFileOffer

      RaiseEvent FileOfferReceived(Me, _
        New FileOfferReceivedEventArgs(filename, fileIdentifier, senderAlias))

End Sub
```

The FileOfferReceivedEventArgs class simply provides the file name, file identifier, and sender's name:

```
Public Class FileOfferReceivedEventArgs
     Inherits EventArgs
```

```
    Public Filename As String
    Public FileIdentifier As Guid
    Public SenderAlias As String

    Public Sub New(ByVal filename As String, ByVal fileIdentifier As Guid, _
      ByVal senderAlias As String)
        Me.Filename = filename
        Me.FileIdentifier = fileIdentifier
        Me.SenderAlias = senderAlias
    End Sub

End Class
```

The event is handled in the form code, which will then ask the user whether the transfer should be accepted. If it is, the next step is to call the ClientProcess.AcceptFile() method, which initiates the transfer.

```
Public Sub AcceptFile(ByVal recipientAlias As String, _
  ByVal fileIdentifier As Guid, ByVal destinationPath As String)

    ' Retrieve the reference to the other user.
    Dim peer As ITalkClient = Server.GetUser(recipientAlias)

    ' Create an array to store the data.
    Dim FileData As Byte()

    ' Request the file.
    FileData = peer.TransferFile(fileIdentifier, Me.Alias)
    Dim fs As FileStream

    ' Create the local copy of the file in the desired location.
    ' Warning: This method doesn't bother to check if it's overwriting
    ' a file with the same name.
    fs = File.Create(destinationPath)
    fs.Write(FileData, 0, FileData.Length)

    ' Clean up.
    fs.Close()

End Sub
```

There are several interesting details in this code:

- It doesn't specify the destination file path and file name. This information is supplied to the AcceptFile() method through the destinationPath parameter. This allows the form code to stay in control, perhaps using a default directory or prompting the user for a destination path.

- It includes no exception-handling code. The assumption is that the form code will handle any errors that occur and inform the user accordingly.

- It doesn't worry about overwriting any file that may already exist at the specified directory with the same name. Once again, this is for the form code to check. It will prompt the user before starting the file transfer.

The peer offering the file sends it over the network in its TransferFile() method, which is in many ways a mirror image of AcceptFile().

```
Private Function TransferFile(ByVal fileIdentifier As System.Guid, _
   ByVal senderAlias As String) As Byte() _
   Implements TalkComponent.ITalkClient.TransferFile

    ' Ensure that the GUID corresponds to a valid file offer.
    If Not OfferedFiles.Contains(fileIdentifier) Then
        Throw New ApplicationException( _
           "This file is no longer available from the client.")
    End If

    ' Look up the file path from the OfferedFiles collection and open it.
    Dim fs As FileStream
    fs = File.Open(OfferedFiles(fileIdentifier), FileMode.Open)

    ' Fill the FileData byte array with the data from the file.
    Dim FileData As Byte()
    ReDim FileData(fs.Length)
    fs.Read(FileData, 0, FileData.Length)

    ' Remove the offered file from the collection.
    OfferedFiles.Remove(fileIdentifier)

    ' Clean up.
    fs.Close()
```

```
' Transmit the file data.
Return FileData

End Function
```

The only detail we haven't explored is the layer of user-interface code in the Talk form. The first step is to add an "Offer File" button that allows the user to choose a file to send. The file is chosen using the OpenFileDialog class.

```
Private Sub cmdOffer_Click(ByVal sender As System.Object, _
    ByVal e As System.EventArgs) Handles cmdOffer.Click

    ' Prompt the user for a file to offer.
    Dim dlgOpen As New OpenFileDialog()
    dlgOpen.Title = "Choose a File to Transmit"

    If dlgOpen.ShowDialog() = DialogResult.OK Then
        Try
            ' Send the offer.
            TalkClient.SendFileOffer(lstUsers.Text, dlgOpen.FileName)
        Catch Err As Exception
            MessageBox.Show(Err.Message, "Send Failed", _
                            MessageBoxButtons.OK, MessageBoxIcon.Exclamation)
        End Try
    End If

End Sub
```

The Talk form code also handles the FileOfferReceived event, prompts the user, and initiates the transfer if accepted (see Figure 4-7).

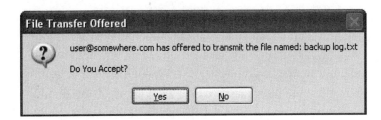

Figure 4-7. Offering a file transfer

```
Private Sub TalkClient_FileOfferReceived(ByVal sender As Object, _
  ByVal e As TalkClient.FileOfferReceivedEventArgs) _
  Handles TalkClient.FileOfferReceived

    ' Create the user message describing the file offer.
    Dim Message As String
    Message = e.SenderAlias & " has offered to transmit the file named: "
    Message &= e.Filename & Environment.NewLine
    Message &= Environment.NewLine & "Do You Accept?"

    ' Prompt the user.
    Dim Result As DialogResult = MessageBox.Show(Message, _
      "File Transfer Offered", MessageBoxButtons.YesNo, MessageBoxIcon.Question)

    If Result = DialogResult.Yes Then

        Try
            ' The code defaults to the TEMP directory, although a more
            ' likely option would be to read information from a registry or
            ' configuration file setting.
            Dim DestinationPath As String = "C:\TEMP\" & e.Filename

            ' Receive the file.
            TalkClient.AcceptFile(e.SenderAlias, e.FileIdentifier, _
                                  DestinationPath)

            ' Assuming no error occurred, display information about it
            ' in the chat window.
            txtReceived.Text &= "File From: " & e.SenderAlias
            txtReceived.Text &= " transferred at "
            txtReceived.Text &= DateTime.Now.ToShortTimeString()
            txtReceived.Text &= Environment.NewLine & DestinationPath
            txtReceived.Text &= Environment.NewLine & Environment.NewLine

        Catch Err As Exception
            MessageBox.Show(Err.Message, "Transfer Failed", _
                            MessageBoxButtons.OK, MessageBoxIcon.Exclamation)

        End Try

    End If

End Sub
```

Figure 4-8. A completed file transfer

> **NOTE** *Adding a file transfer feature such as this one is a notorious security risk. Because the communication is direct, there's no way to authenticate the recipient. (A central server, on the other hand, could verify that users are who they claim to be.) That means that a file could be offered to the wrong user or a malicious user who is impersonating another user. To reduce the risk, the server component could require user ID and password information before returning any information from the GetUsers() collection. We'll deal with security more closely in Chapter 11.*

Scalability Challenges with the Simple Implementation

In its current form, the Talk .NET application is hard pressed to scale in order to serve a large audience. The key problem is the server component, which could become a critical bottleneck as the traffic increases. To reduce this problem, you can switch to the decentralized approach described earlier, although this is only a partial solution. It won't deal with the possible problems that can occur if the number of users grows so large that storing them in an in-memory hashtable is no longer effective.

Databases and a Stateless Server

To combat this problem, you would need to store the list of logged-on users and their connection information in an external data store such as a database. This would reduce the performance for individual calls (because they would require database lookups), but it would increase the overall scalability of the system (because the memory overhead would be lessened).

This approach also allows you to create a completely stateless coordination server. In this case, you could replace your coordination server by a web farm of computers, each of which would access the same database. Each client request could be routed to the computer with the least traffic, guaranteeing performance. Much of the threading code presented in the next chapter would not be needed anymore, because all of the information would be shared in a common database that would provide its own concurrency control. In order to create the cluster farm and expose it under a single IP, you would need to use hardware clustering or a software load-balancing solution such as Microsoft's Application Center. All in all, this is a fairly good idea of how a system such as Microsoft's Windows Messenger works. It's also similar to the approach followed in the third part of this book, where you'll learn how to create a discovery server using a web service.

OneWay Methods

There is also a minor messaging enhancement you can implement using the OneWay attribute from the System.Runtime.Remoting.Messaging namespace. When you apply this attribute to a method, you indicate that, when this method is called remotely, the caller will disconnect immediately without waiting for the call to complete. This means that the method cannot return a result or modify a ByVal parameter. It also means that any exception thrown in the method will not be detected by the caller. The advantage of this approach is that it eliminates waiting. In the Talk .NET system, the coordination server automatically calls a client if a message cannot be delivered. Thus, there's no reason for the client to wait while the message is actually being delivered.

There are currently two methods that could benefit from the OneWay attribute: ClientProcess.ReceiveMessage() and ServerProcess.SendMessage(). Here's an example:

```
<System.Runtime.Remoting.Messaging.OneWay()> _
Private Sub ReceiveMessage(ByVal message As String, _
   ByVal senderAlias As String) Implements ITalkClient.ReceiveMessage
      ' (Code omitted.)
End Sub
```

Note that there's one reason you might *not* want to apply the OneWay attribute to ServerProcess.SendMessage(). If you do, you won't be able to detect an error that might result if the user has disconnected without logging off correctly. Without catching this error, it's impossible to detect the problem, notify the sender, and remove the user from the client collection. This error-handling approach is implemented in the next chapter.

Optional Features

Finally, there are a number of optional features that you can add to Talk .NET. These include variable user status, user authentication with a password, and buddy lists. The last of these is probably the most useful, because it allows you to limit the user list information. With buddy lists, users only see the names of the users that they want to contact. However, buddy lists must be stored on the server permanently, and so can't be held in memory. Instead, this information would probably need to be stored in a server-side database.

Another option would be to store a list on the local computer, which would then be submitted with the login request. This would help keep the system decentralized, but it would also allow the information to be easily lost, and make it difficult for users to obtain location transparency and use the same buddy list from multiple computers. As you'll see, users aren't always prepared to accept the limitations of decentralized peer-to-peer applications.

Firewalls, Ports, and Other Issues

Remoting does not provide any way to overcome some of the difficulties that are inherent with networking on the Internet. For example, firewalls, depending on their settings, can prevent communication between the clients and the coordination server. On a local network, this won't pose a problem. On the Internet, you can lessen the possibility of problems by following several steps:

- Use the centralized design in which all communication is routed through the coordination server.

- Make sure the coordination server is not behind a firewall (in a company network, you would place the coordination server in the demilitarized zone, or DMZ). This helps connectivity because often communication will succeed when the client is behind a firewall, but not when both the client and server are behind firewalls.

- Change the configuration files so that HTTP channels are used instead. They're typically more reliable over the Internet and low-bandwidth connections. You should still use binary formatting, however, unless you're trying to interoperate with non-.NET clients.

It often seems that developers and network administrators are locked in an endless battle, with developers trying to extend the scope of their applications while network administrators try to protect the integrity of their network. This battle has escalated to such a high point that developers tout new features such as .NET web services because they use HTTP and can communicate through a firewall. All this ignores the fact that, typically, the firewall is there to *prevent* exactly this type of communication. Thwarting this protection just means that firewall vendors will need to go to greater lengths building intelligence into their firewall products. They'll need to perform more intensive network analysis that might reject SOAP messages or deny web-service communication based on other recognizable factors. These changes, in turn, raise the cost of the required servers and impose additional overhead.

In short, it's best to deal with firewall problems by configuring the firewall. If your application needs to use a special port, convince the network administrators to open it. Similarly, using port 80 for a peer-to-peer application is sure to win the contempt of system administrators everywhere. If you can't ensure that your clients can use another port, you may need to resort to this sleight-of-hand, but it's best to avoid the escalating war of Internet connectivity altogether.

> **NOTE** *Ports are generally divided into three groups: well-known ports (0–1023), registered ports (1024–49151), and dynamic ports (49152–65535). Historically, well-known ports have been used for server-based applications such as web servers (80), FTP (20), and POP3 mail transfer (110). In your application, you would probably do best to use a registered or dynamic port that isn't frequently used. These are less likely to cause a conflict (although more likely to be blocked by a firewall). For example, 6346 is most commonly used by Gnutella. For a list of frequently registered ports, refer to the* C:\{WinDir}\System32\Drivers\Etc\Services *file or the* http://www.iana.org/assignments/port-numbers *site.*

Remoting and Network Address Translation

.NET Remoting, like many types of distributed communication, is challenged by firewalls, proxy servers, and network address translation (NAT). Many programmers (and programming authors) assume that using an HTTP channel will solve these problems. It may—if the intervening firewall restricts packets solely based on whether they contain binary information. However, this won't solve a much more significant problem: Most firewalls allow outgoing connections but prevent all incoming ones. Proxy servers and NAT devices work in the same way. This is a significant limitation. It means that a Talk .NET peer can contact the server (and the server can respond), but the server cannot call back to the client to deliver a message.

There's more than one way to solve this problem, but none is easy (or ideal). You could implement a polling mechanism, whereby every client periodically connects to the server and asks for any unsent messages. The drawback of this approach is that the message latency will be increased, and the load on the server will rise dramatically with the number of clients.

Another approach is to use some sort of bidirectional communication method. For example, you might want to maintain a connection and allow the server to fire its event or callback at any time using the existing connection. This also reduces the number of simultaneous clients the server can handle, and it requires a specially modified type of Remoting channel. Ingo Rammer has developed one such channel, and it's available at `http://www.dotnetremoting.cc/ projects/modules/BidirectionalTcpChannel.asp`. However, this bidirectional channel isn't yet optimized for a production environment, so enterprise developers will need to wait.

Unfortunately, neither of these two proposed solutions will work if you want to use decentralized communication in which peers contact each other directly. In this case, you'll either need to write a significant amount of painful low-level networking code (which is beyond the scope of this book), or use a third-party platform such as those discussed in Part Three.

The Last Word

In this chapter, we developed an instant-messaging application using Remoting and showed how it could be modified into a peer-to-peer system with a central lookup service. However, the current version of the Talk .NET system still suffers from some notable shortcomings, which will become particularly apparent under high user loads. If different users attempt to register, unregister, or send messages at the same time, the user collection may be updated incorrectly, and information could be lost. To guard against these problems, which are almost impossible to replicate under modest loads, you'll need to add multithreading, as described in the next chapter.

CHAPTER 5

Threading the Coordination Server

IN THE PREVIOUS CHAPTER, WE developed an instant-messaging application that relies on a central coordinator. As it stands, the central coordinator isn't equipped to handle concurrent requests, which could lead to subtle problems when registering and removing users. There are two approaches that can handle these problems.

The first option is to move the user registry into a database. This approach has a cost. Though a database will ensure scalability and eliminate the possibility of concurrency problems, it will also slow down individual client requests. Using a database makes the most sense if you intend to scale the system to an extremely large audience (with hundreds of simultaneous users). The database approach is demonstrated with the discovery service in Chapter 7.

The second option is to revise the central coordinator and add the .NET threading code needed to safely handle access to the user collection. This approach is ideal when creating a peer-to-peer system for a smaller community (for example, inside the private network of a single organization). This is the approach we'll develop in this chapter.

This chapter also introduces a few additional enhancements to the Talk.NET system. These include the following:

- Mechanisms to handle users who supply duplicate user names and users who disconnect from the system without properly logging out.

- Client-side threading code to properly handle user-interface refreshes, particularly when multiple messages are received at once.

- A modified TalkService component recast as a Windows service, so it can load automatically and run in the background without user intervention.

Threading Essentials

The common language runtime (CLR) uses a thread pool to listen for requests for remotable objects. That means that if more than one user attempts to call a method at the same time, the tasks will complete simultaneously on different threads. With a sufficiently high number of simultaneous requests, every thread in the pool will be busy, and some users will have to wait for a thread to become free before their task can be completed (or, in extreme cases, until a time-out occurs and an error is raised on the client). With thread pools, threads are kept alive indefinitely and reused as long as there's outstanding work to complete.

Generally, thread pools ensure optimum performance. For the most part, clients won't need to wait (as they probably would if the server provided only one thread). On the other hand, no matter how heavy the traffic, the CLR will never create so many threads that the server computer becomes swamped and unable to complete any of the work before a time-out occurs (which could occur if a new thread was created to serve each and every request).

Multithreaded systems always add a few new wrinkles for the application programmer to worry about. These mainly come in the form of *concurrency errors*. If these problems aren't anticipated, they can be fiendishly difficult to diagnose and resolve once the application is deployed in the field.

Concurrency errors occur when more than one thread modifies the same piece of memory. The problem is that the last update always takes precedence, even if it doesn't take into account the work performed by other threads. The canonical example of a concurrency error is a global counter that's being incremented by several threads. A concurrency error can occur if all threads attempt to increment the counter at once.

For example, consider the case in which the global counter is currently at 5 and there are two threads at work. Here's how it might unfold for the worse:

1. Thread A reads the value 5.

2. Thread B reads the value 5.

3. Thread A increments the value of the counter to 6.

4. Thread B increments the value of the counter to 6.

In this case, the last update wins and the counter stands at 6, even though it should really be set to 7 to represent both of the increment operations. This is just one example of a concurrency problem.

Threading and the Coordination Server

The ServerProcess class contains only a single piece of shared data: the collection of client information. Unfortunately, this is enough to cause trouble because the collection object is not intrinsically thread-safe. If more than one thread attempts to perform work with the collection at the same time, it's possible that the collection won't be properly updated. For example, if two users are registered at the same time, only one update might persist, leading to an unregistered user. Even worse, iterating through a collection isn't a thread-safe operation, which means that trying to register a new user and look up an existing user for a message delivery at the same time could conceivably cause a problem. These errors could be rare, but they're never worth the risk because they tend to grow increasingly more significant and frequent as an application becomes more successful and is used by a larger and larger user base.

Resolving concurrency problems is fairly easy. The Hashtable collection provides a thread-safe wrapper that you can use with a minimum of fuss, or you can take control of the situation yourself with Visual Basic's SyncLock statement. Both of these techniques ensure that only one client can access the collection at a time. However, these approaches can reduce performance. Every time you use locking, you force some code to execute synchronously, meaning that other clients attempting the same task or requiring access to the same resource could be stalled. If your locks are too coarse, held too long, and applied too often, the overall performance of your application may be unacceptable for a large number of users. This is the key compromise with multithreaded programming, and it requires an experienced developer to strike the right balance.

The next few sections show how you can add locking to the ServerProcess class, and how you can do so to minimize the performance overhead.

Synchronizing Collection Access

The easiest methods to deal with are the AddUser() and RemoveUser() methods, which manage the user registration process. There are three ways you could apply a lock, and we'll consider the trade-offs and advantages of each one.

First, you can create what's known as a *critical section* by locking the entire ServiceProcess object. It looks like this:

```
Public Sub AddUser(ByVal [alias] As String, ByVal client As ITalkClient) _
    Implements TalkComponent.ITalkServer.AddUser

    SyncLock Me
        Trace.Write("Added user '" & [alias] & "'")
        ActiveUsers([alias]) = client
    End SyncLock

End Sub
```

When a thread hits this patch of code, the SyncLock statement is used to lock the entire ServiceProcess object. That means that no other thread will be able to use ServiceProcess until the first thread completes its task. This is true even if the other thread is calling an innocent, unrelated method that wouldn't pose any threat. Clearly, this coarse lock can create frequent bottlenecks.

A more fine-tuned option is shown in the next example. In this case, only the ActiveUsers collection itself is locked. Other threads can continue working with ServiceProcess, until they hit a line of code that requires the ActiveUsers collection, at which point they'll be stalled:

```
Public Sub AddUser(ByVal [alias] As String, ByVal client As ITalkClient) _
    Implements TalkComponent.ITalkServer.AddUser

    Trace.Write("Added user '" & [alias] & "'")
    SyncLock ActiveUsers
         ActiveUsers([alias]) = client
    End SyncLock

End Sub
```

> **TIP** *SyncLock can only be used with objects, not simple value types such as integers. Because ActiveUsers is a Hashtable object, this technique works perfectly. If an unhandled error occurs inside the SyncLock block, the lock is automatically released.*

Note that the lock is only used around the single statement that interacts with the collection. The Trace.Write() method call is not included in the block. This ensures that the lock is held for the shortest possible time, and helps to wring every possible degree of concurrency out of this solution.

Finally, you can accomplish exactly the same thing by using the synchronized wrapper provided by the Hashtable collection as shown here:

```
Public Sub AddUser(ByVal [alias] As String, ByVal client As ITalkClient) _
    Implements TalkComponent.ITalkServer.AddUser

    Trace.Write("Added user '" & [alias] & "'")
    Dim SynchronizedCollection As Hashtable
    SynchronizedCollection = Hashtable.Synchronized(ActiveUsers)
    SynchronizedCollection([alias]) = client

End Sub
```

The synchronized wrapper returned by the Hashtable.Synchronized() method is identical to the original Hashtable in every respect except for the fact that it wraps all its methods with locking statements to prevent concurrency problems. Thus, the previous code sample is equivalent to manually locking the collection.

> **TIP** *In some cases, it's better to manually lock the collection yourself rather than use the synchronized wrapper. This is primarily the case if you need to perform several tasks with the collection, one after the other. In this case, it will be better to lock the object once and perform the work, rather than use the synchronized wrapper, which will obtain and release the lock with each individual method call.*

Either one of these approaches provides a good solution for the AddUser() and RemoveUser() methods, because they typically execute quite quickly and hold the lock for mere fractions of a second. However, it's still possible to coax a little more performance from your locking code by using the System.Threading.ReaderWriterLock class. This class allows you to create a lock that permits only one user to write to the collection at a time, but allows multiple users to read from it. By implementing this design, you could protect the AddUser() and RemoveUser() methods without locking out the harmless GetUsers() method.

To implement reader and writing locking, you must first create a member variable in the ServerProcess class that represents the lock:

```
Private ActiveUsersLock As New ReaderWriterLock()
```

In the GetUsers() method, you would acquire a reader lock by using the AcquireReaderLock() method. This method accepts a TimeSpan object that represents the interval of time to wait while attempting to acquire the lock before giving up. You can use –1 to specify an infinite wait, meaning the code won't time out (although the network connection eventually will, if the lock is never obtained). In this case, we specify a more reasonable maximum of one minute. If the lock is not acquired within this time period, an exception will be thrown.

```
Public Function GetUsers() As System.Collections.ICollection _
  Implements TalkComponent.ITalkServer.GetUsers

    ActiveUsersLock.AcquireReaderLock(TimeSpan.FromMinutes(1))
    Return ActiveUsers.Keys
    ActiveUsersLock.ReleaseReaderLock()

End Function
```

The AddUser() and RemoveUser() methods use the AcquireWriterLock() method, as shown in the following code snippet.

```
Public Sub AddUser(ByVal [alias] As String, ByVal client As ITalkClient) _
    Implements TalkComponent.ITalkServer.AddUser

    Trace.Write("Added user '" & [alias] & "'")
    ActiveUsersLock.AcquireWriterLock(TimeSpan.FromMinutes(1))
    ActiveUsers[alias] = client
    ActiveUsersLock.ReleaseWriterLock()

End Sub
```

Now multiple users can call the GetUsers() method and read from the collection at the same time without causing an error. However, if the AddUser() or RemoveUser() method is executed, an exclusive lock will be required, which will temporarily prevent any other read or write operation.

Remember, when using the ReaderWriterLock class, you should make sure to explicitly release the lock if an exception occurs after you acquire it.

Creating a Delivery Service

Synchronizing the collection access with AddUser() and RemoveUser() is straightforward, once you understand a few threading concepts. Doing the same with the message delivery isn't quite as easy. In an average system, the number of messages will be quite high. It's not practical to lock the user collection each time you need to search for a message recipient, because the entire system could shudder to a standstill.

Another option is to use a dedicated delivery service that runs on a separate thread, routing messages as needed. This delivery service wouldn't use the ActiveUsers collection but rather a recent copy of the collection. This reduces *thread contention*, which occurs when multiple clients try to grab the same resource, and some are left waiting. Best of all, the delivery service will operate on a different thread from the pool of threads used to handle incoming requests. This ensures that the server won't become a bottleneck, even if there's a measurable delay required in order to contact a remote client and transmit a message.

The delivery service should have the following basic skeleton:

```
Public Class DeliveryService

    ' Stores a copy of the ActiveUsers collection.
    Private RegisteredUsers As New Hashtable()
```

```
' Stores messages that haven't been delivered yet.
Private Messages As New Queue()


' Adds a message to the queue.
Public Sub RegisterMessage(ByVal message As Message)
    ' (Code omitted.)
End Sub


' Updates the user list.
Public Sub UpdateUsers(ByVal users As Hashtable)
    ' (Code omitted.)
End Sub


' Keep the thread active as long as there are messages.
' After that, suspend it.
Public Sub Deliver()
    ' (Code omitted.)
End Sub


' Look up the remote client and send the message.
Private Sub DeliverMessages()
    ' (Code omitted.)
End Sub


End Class
```

In this example, messages are stored in a Queue object. Queues are first-in-first-out (FIFO) collections. Using a queue ensures that messages are dealt with in the order that they're received, and none are delayed unreasonably.

The RegisterMessage() and UpdateUsers() methods are quite straightforward and need simple locking code to ensure that no concurrency errors will occur as messages are registered or the user list is updated:

```
Public Sub RegisterMessage(ByVal message As Message)
    SyncLock Messages
        Messages.Enqueue(message)
    End SyncLock
End Sub


Public Sub UpdateUsers(ByVal users As Hashtable)
    SyncLock (RegisteredUsers)
        RegisteredUsers = users
    End SyncLock
End Sub
```

Messages are submitted as instances of the Message class, which encapsulates all the relevant information, including the sender, recipient, and message text. Here's the class you'll need:

```
Public Class Message
    Private _SenderAlias As String
    Private _RecipientAlias As String
    Private _MessageBody As String

    Public Property SenderAlias() As String
        Get
            Return _SenderAlias
        End Get
        Set(ByVal Value As String)
            _SenderAlias = Value
        End Set
    End Property

    Public Property RecipientAlias() As String
        Get
            Return _RecipientAlias
        End Get
        Set(ByVal Value As String)
            _RecipientAlias = Value
        End Set
    End Property

    Public Property MessageBody() As String
        Get
            Return _MessageBody
        End Get
        Set(ByVal Value As String)
            _MessageBody = Value
        End Set
    End Property

    Public Sub New(ByVal sender As String, ByVal recipient As String, _
        ByVal body As String)
        Me.SenderAlias = sender
        Me.RecipientAlias = recipient
        Me.MessageBody = body
    End Sub

End Class
```

Message Delivery with the Delivery Service

The message delivery is performed in the DeliverMessages() method, while the Deliver() method keeps the thread alive, looping continuously, and calling DeliverMessages() if there are items in the Messages queue. Remember, once a thread completes, it cannot be resurrected. The only way to keep the message delivery thread alive is to use a loop in the Deliver() method and explicitly suspend the thread when there's no work to do.

```
Public Sub Deliver()

    Do
        Trace.Write("Starting message delivery")
        DeliverMessages()

        ' Processing is complete. The thread can be put on hold.
        Trace.Write("Suspending thread")
        Thread.CurrentThread.Suspend()
    Loop


End Sub
```

Another option would be to use some sort of timer to periodically scan the Messages queue and deliver messages. However, this could lead to latency when delivering messages. If your timer fires every five seconds, for example, messages may take over five seconds to be transmitted to their destination. Also, you would need to manually disable the timer while a message deliver was in process, and re-enable it afterwards. Similar logic can be accomplished more efficiently using threads.

The majority of the work takes place in the DeliverMessages() method. The Messages collection is locked only to retrieve the next message object, by calling Dequeue(). Calling this method retrieves the Message object and removes it from the queue. The RegisteredUsers collection is locked during the lookup operation.

```
Private Sub DeliverMessages()

    Do While Messages.Count > 0
        Trace.Write("Retrieving next message")

        Dim NextMessage As Message
        SyncLock Messages
            NextMessage = CType(Messages.Dequeue(), Message)
        End SyncLock
```

```vb
        Dim Recipient As ITalkClient
        Dim MessageBody As String
        Dim Sender As String

        ' Look up the recipient.
        SyncLock RegisteredUsers

            If RegisteredUsers.ContainsKey(NextMessage.RecipientAlias) Then
                Recipient = CType(RegisteredUsers(NextMessage.RecipientAlias), _
                                ITalkClient)
                MessageBody = NextMessage.MessageBody
                Sender = NextMessage.SenderAlias
            Else
                ' User wasn't found. Try to find the sender.
                If RegisteredUsers.ContainsKey(NextMessage.SenderAlias) Then
                    Recipient = CType(RegisteredUsers(NextMessage.SenderAlias), _
                                ITalkClient)
                    MessageBody = "'" & NextMessage.MessageBody & _
                                "' could not be delivered."
                    Sender = "Talk .NET"
                Else
                    ' Both sender and recipient were not found.
                    ' Ignore this message.
                End If
            End If

        End SyncLock

        ' Deliver the message.
        If Not Recipient Is Nothing Then
            Trace.Write("Performing message delivery callback")
            Dim callback As New ReceiveMessageCallback(AddressOf _
              Recipient.ReceiveMessage)
            Try
                callback.BeginInvoke(MessageBody, Sender, Nothing, Nothing)
            Catch Err As Exception
                Trace.Write("Message delivery failed")
            End Try
        End If
    Loop

End Sub
```

NOTE *Error handling is mandatory in the DeliverMessages() method. Because this method isn't directly called by the client, exceptions will not propagate to the user-interface level. Any problems will simply derail the delivery thread, halting all message delivery.*

The threading used here is quite efficient. Because the RegisteredUsers collection is only updated periodically, and because there's only ever one delivery operation running at a time on this thread, there's little likelihood of thread contention (when one thread needs to wait for another one to finish using a resource and release its lock). The same is true of the Messages collection, which is only locked briefly to retrieve or add a message.

Using the Delivery Service

To start using the new delivery service, you'll need to modify the server code. The first step is to create two additional member variables in the ServerProcess class: MessageDelivery and DeliveryThread. MessageDelivery stores a reference to an instance of the DeliveryService class, and DeliveryThread references the System.Threading.Thread object where it executes.

```
Public Class ServerProcess
    Inherits MarshalByRefObject
    Implements ITalkServer

    ' The object used for delivering messages.
    Private MessageDelivery As New DeliveryService()

    ' The thread where the message delivery takes place.
    Private DeliveryThread As New Thread(AddressOf MessageDelivery.Deliver)

    Public Sub New()
        MyBase.New()
        DeliveryThread.IsBackground = True
    End Sub

    ' (Other code omitted.)

End Class
```

When the ServerProcess is first created, the delivery thread is configured to run in the background. This means that it will automatically be aborted when the ServerProcess thread is destroyed. You could also use the ServerProcess constructor to configure the priority of the delivery thread.

ServerProcess also needs to update the DeliveryService.RegisteredUsers collection periodically. One possibility is to update this copy of the collection only when a user is *added* to the collection. At this point the server clones a new copy of the user collection, and submits it to the delivery service. This ensures that the delivery service can always locate message recipients. It also doesn't use much additional memory, because the duplicate collection actually references the same set of ITalkClient objects. It's only the memory references that are actually duplicated.

```
Public Sub AddUser(ByVal [alias] As String, ByVal client As ITalkClient) _
    Implements TalkComponent.ITalkServer.AddUser

    Trace.Write("Added user '" & [alias] & "'")
    SyncLock ActiveUsers
        ActiveUsers([alias]) = client
        MessageDelivery.UpdateUsers(ActiveUsers.Clone())
    End SyncLock


End Sub
```

There's not much point to refresh the collection when users are removed because this won't help the delivery service, and it will increase the potential for thread contention. Note that it's not necessary to lock the DeliveryService.Registered Users collection because the DeliveryService.UpdateUsers() method performs this step on its own.

The ServerProcess.SendMessage() method also needs to change. It will no longer send the message directly. Instead, it will just submit the message to the delivery service.

```
Public Sub SendMessage(ByVal senderAlias As String, _
    ByVal recipientAlias As String, ByVal message As String) _
    Implements TalkComponent.ITalkServer.SendMessage

    ' Register the message.
    Trace.Write("Queuing message to '" & recipientAlias & "_
                ' from '" & senderAlias & "'")
    Dim NewMessage As New Message(senderAlias, recipientAlias, message)
    MessageDelivery.RegisterMessage(NewMessage)

    ' Resume the thread if needed.
    If (DeliveryThread.ThreadState And ThreadState.Unstarted) = _
        ThreadState.Unstarted Then
            Trace.Write("Start delivery thread")
            DeliveryThread.Start()
```

```
ElseIf (DeliveryThread.ThreadState And ThreadState.Suspended) = _
   ThreadState.Suspended Then
     Trace.Write("Resuming delivery thread")
     DeliveryThread.Resume()

End If

End Sub
```

Once the message is queued, the status of the thread is checked. It's then started for this first time, if needed, or unsuspended. If the thread is already actively delivering messages, it will not suspend itself. Instead, it will pick up the new message as soon as it finishes delivering all the others.

Figure 5-1 and Figure 5-2 show two different views of this process. Figure 5-1 shows the interaction of the DeliveryService and the ServiceProcess objects. Figure 5-2 shows the threading picture (where the code is executed). As you can see, when ServiceProcess calls DeliveryService the code executes on the same thread. This is why synchronization code is needed: to prevent the Remoting threads from conflicting with the delivery process.

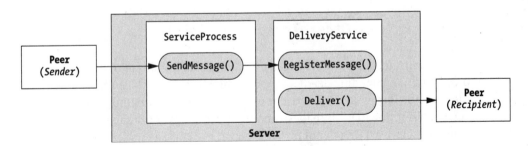

Figure 5-1. Interaction with the DeliveryService

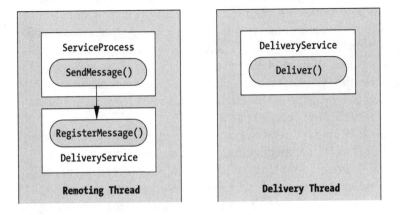

Figure 5-2. The threaded message delivery

Finally, Figure 5-3 shows the typical trace output after sending messages between clients.

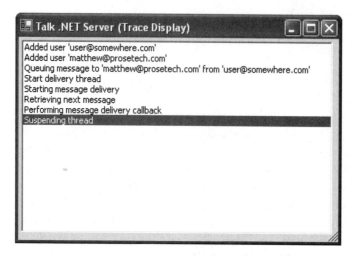

Figure 5-3. Trace output for the threaded Talk .NET

Deadlocks and Other Threading Nightmares

We've haven't discussed some of the other potential hurdles of multithreaded programming, including deadlocking and thread starvation. That's because these problems are unlikely to occur in Talk .NET. Deadlocks only appear when you're attempting to acquire locks on multiple objects at the same time or when objects are trying to obtain locks on each other. The end result is a stand-off where multiple segments of code wait for each other to surrender the lock they desire. Contrary to what some programmers may have told you, deadlocks aren't always that difficult to avoid. The best advice is to never hold more than one lock at a time, and to use fine-grained locks instead of coarse-grained critical sections. If you really must obtain multiple locks at once, always make sure that you obtain them in the same order. Finally, if you're writing some really intricate threading code, you would do well to master some of the more advanced classes in the System.Threading namespace. For example, using the Monitor class, you can write intelligent threading code that prevents deadlocks by releasing all locks if it can't complete its task.

A more realistic danger is thread starvation, the condition that occurs when you have too many threads competing for the CPU, and some threads never have the processor's attention for long enough to complete some reasonable work. This problem most often occurs when you create too many threads, so that the operating system wastes a large amount of time tracking, scheduling, and splicing from one thread to another. In the current delivery service, this isn't a problem because only one additional thread is created and this thread is reused for all message delivery operations. In the next section, however, you'll learn about an alternate design in which thread starvation is a real possibility and you'll see how the ThreadPool class can reduce the risk dramatically.

Using the ThreadPool

The delivery service design presented here will typically work very well, but it isn't the only option. Another solution is to create multiple threads to handle the message delivery. This design is possible because each message delivery is a separate operation. Using multiple threads allows the delivery of multiple messages to be performed asynchronously, potentially increasing delivery times if the system is large and networking delays are significant. But it also requires more memory, because each thread will have its own copy of the collection of registered users. In a real-world application, you would probably test both approaches with a scaled-down, automated version of the application before you begin coding the full solution.

The basic operation of the system is shown in Figure 5-4. The idea is that a thread is created every time a message needs to be delivered.

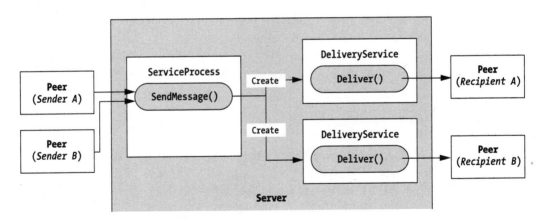

Figure 5-4. Multiple thread message delivery

If you implemented this design by using the System.Threading.Thread class, you would quickly run into a few terrible headaches. The overhead of creating and destroying threads would waste valuable server resources, and the system would perform poorly under heavy user loads because it would create far too many threads for the CPU to track and manage effectively. Instead, most of the computer's resources would be dedicated to tracking and scheduling threads, and the system would collapse under its own weight.

Luckily, there's a better approach: using a thread pool. A thread pool is a dedicated group of threads that are reused indefinitely (in much the same way the Remoting infrastructure uses threads to handle user requests). The advantages of thread pools include the following:

- Threads are only created once, so the overhead of creating and destroying threads is negligible.

- Several operations can complete at the same time. With Remoting, this means that other messages won't be stalled while the delivery service attempts to contact a disconnected client.

- Thread pools multiplex a large number of requests to a small number of threads (typically about 25). This ensures that the system never creates more threads than it can handle.

You can create a thread pool system on your own, but you'll need significant code to monitor the threads and distribute the work appropriately. Thankfully, .NET provides a simple thread pool through the System.Thread.ThreadPool class. Using the ThreadPool class is easy—the only disadvantages are threefold: you lack any way to configure how many threads it uses; you can't set relative priorities; and you can't cancel tasks after they have been submitted. By default, the ThreadPool allocates about 25 threads per CPU.

To perform a task asynchronously with the ThreadPool, simply use the static QueueUserWorkItem() method with a delegate that points to the method that should be executed.

```
ThreadPool.QueueUserWorkItem(AddressOf WorkMethod)
```

This schedules the task. When there is a free thread, the CLR will use it to execute the specified code.

To use the ThreadPool class with Talk .NET, you would first simplify the DeliveryService class:

```
Public Class DeliveryService

    Private RegisteredUsers As Hashtable
    Private NextMessage As Message

    Public Sub New (ByVal users As Hashtable, ByVal nextMessage As Message)
        RegisteredUsers = users
        NextMessage = nextMessage
    End Sub

    Public Sub DeliverMessage(state As Object)
```

```
        ' Deliver the message.
        Dim Recipient As ITalkClient
        Dim MessageBody As String
        Dim Sender As String

        ' There's no need to lock anything, because no other part of the
        ' application will communicate with this class once it is started.
        If RegisteredUsers.ContainsKey(NextMessage.RecipientAlias) Then
            Recipient = CType(RegisteredUsers(NextMessage.RecipientAlias), _
                            ITalkClient)
            MessageBody = NextMessage.MessageBody
            Sender = NextMessage.SenderAlias

        Else
            ' User wasn't found. Try to find the sender.
            If RegisteredUsers.ContainsKey(NextMessage.SenderAlias) Then
                Recipient = CType(RegisteredUsers(NextMessage.SenderAlias), _
                                ITalkClient)
                MessageBody = "'" & NextMessage.MessageBody & _
                                "' could not be delivered."
                Sender = "Talk .NET"
            Else
                ' Both sender and recipient were not found.
                ' Ignore this message.
            End If
        End If

        ' Deliver the message.
        If Not Recipient Is Nothing Then
            Trace.Write("Performing message delivery callback")
            Dim callback As New ReceiveMessageCallback(AddressOf _
              Recipient.ReceiveMessage)
            Try
              SyncLock Recipient
                callback.BeginInvoke(MessageBody, Sender, Nothing, Nothing)
              End SyncLock
            Catch Err As Exception
                Trace.Write("Message delivery failed")
            End Try
        End If

    End Sub

End Class
```

There's no longer any need to provide a form-level reference to the delivery object and thread in the ServerProcess class (although you could store this information in a collection, if needed). The ServerProcess.SendMessage() method creates a new DeliveryService object and queues it with the thread pool.

```
Public Sub SendMessage(ByVal senderAlias As String, _
   ByVal recipientAlias As String, ByVal message As String) _
   Implements TalkComponent.ITalkServer.SendMessage

    Dim NewMessage As New Message(senderAlias, recipientAlias, message)
    Dim NewDelivery As New DeliveryService(ActiveUsers.Clone(), NewMessage)

    Trace.Write("Queuing message to '" & recipientAlias & "_
                ' from '" & senderAlias & "'")
    ThreadPool.QueueUserWorkItem(NewDelivery.DeliverMessage)

End Sub
```

> **NOTE** *In this example, each thread is given a separate copy of the user collection. However, you must still lock the ITalkClient object before you attempt to send a message, to prevent a problem that could occur if more than one delivery thread tries to send a message to the same user at the same time. Remember, when you clone a collection, it still contains the same objects.*

There's only one such ThreadPool per application domain, so if you use it in more than one part of your application, all work items will be constrained to the set number of threads.

Cleaning Up Disconnected Clients

Currently, neither of these examples go the extra length to remove a client when message delivery fails. In these multithreaded examples, this step isn't as easy as it was in the nonthreaded version of Talk .NET. The problem is that it's not enough to remove the user from the DeliveryService copy of the collection—if you do, it will simply reappear the next time the collection is copied over, and it won't affect the contact list downloaded by the clients. Instead, the DeliveryService class needs to call the ServerProcess.RemoveUser() method to make sure the central collection is modified.

In order to add this functionality, you need to create a DeliveryService class that stores a reference to the ServerProcess.

```
Public Class DeliveryService

    Public Server As ServerProcess

    ' (Other code omitted)

End Class
```

You could set this reference in the DeliveryService constructor. Then, you can use this reference to call RemoveUser() as needed:

```
Try
    callback.BeginInvoke(MessageBody, Sender, Nothing, Nothing)
Catch Err As Exception
    Trace.Write("Message delivery failed")
    Server.RemoveUser(Recipient)
End Try
```

Threading and the Client

The most important place for threading code is at the coordination server, because it will regularly deal with simultaneous client requests. That's why the last few sections have dealt exhaustively with server-side threading issues. However, the peers in the system also expose an object through Remoting (called ClientProcess). That means that each client also has a pool of threads—provided by the CLR—listening for remote method calls. The ClientProcess object will be invoked on a different thread from the rest of the application, and multiple requests from different peers could be received at once.

What's worse, the code commits one of the cardinal sins of Windows programming: manipulating the user interface from a thread that doesn't own it. To deal with this reality and prevent another level of subtle, maddening bugs, you need to fortify the client and add some synchronization code.

> **TIP** *To verify that the event handlers for events such as MessageReceived and FileOfferReceived don't execute on the user-interface thread, you can perform a simple test. Display the unique numeric identifier for the current thread (Thread.CurrentThread.Hashcode), either by showing a MessageBox or writing a debug statement. You'll see that the identifier for it isn't the same in the event handler as it is in other form methods.*

Unfortunately, you can't lock user interface elements (such as controls). Instead, you need to ensure that code that interacts with the user interface executes on the user-interface thread. The base .NET Control class provides an Invoke() method designed for exactly this purpose. In order to execute a method on the user-interface thread, pass a reference to this method to the Invoke() method, using the MethodInvoker delegate.

```
MyControl.Invoke(New MethodInvoker(AddressOf MyMethod))
```

The MethodInvoker delegate can point to any method that takes no parameters. This means you need to perform a little bit more work if you want the method to have access to one or more variables. For example, in TalkClient, the method must have access to a string variable with the message text in it. The easy way to allow this is to create a dedicated class that combines the method with the required information. Here's the class used in the revised TalkClient:

```
Public Class UpdateControlText

    Private NewText As String

    ' The reference is retained as a generic control,
    ' allowing this helper class to be reused in other scenarios.
    Private ControlToUpdate As Control

    Public Sub New(ByVal newText As String, ByVal controlToUpdate As Control)
        Me.NewText = newText
        Me.ControlToUpdate = controlToUpdate
    End Sub

    ' This method must execute on the user-interface thread.
    Public Sub Update()
        Me.ControlToUpdate.Text &= NewText
    End Sub

End Class
```

As you can see, some effort has been made to ensure that this class is as generic as possible. It can be used to update the Text property of any control in a thread-safe manner. Here's how you'll put it to work when receiving a message:

```
Private Sub TalkClient_MessageReceived(ByVal sender As Object, _
    ByVal e As MessageReceivedEventArgs) Handles TalkClient.MessageReceived
```

```
' Define the text.
Dim NewText As String
NewText = "Message From: " & e.SenderAlias
NewText &= " delivered at " & DateTime.Now.ToShortTimeString()
NewText &= Environment.NewLine & e.Message
NewText &= Environment.NewLine & Environment.NewLine

' Create the object.
Dim ThreadsafeUpdate As New UpdateControlText(NewText, txtReceived)

' Invoke the update on the user-interface thread.
Me.Invoke(New MethodInvoker(AddressOf ThreadsafeUpdate.Update))

End Sub
```

Ideally, all methods that access the user interface should be performed on the user-interface thread. That means you'll need to update the code that prompts the user to accept a file transfer in response to the FileOfferReceived method. Here's one option:

```
Private Sub TalkClient_FileOfferReceived(ByVal sender As Object, _
  ByVal e As TalkClient.FileOfferReceivedEventArgs) _
  Handles TalkClient.FileOfferReceived

    ' Create the user message describing the file offer.
    Dim Message As String
    Message = e.SenderAlias & " has offered to transmit the file named: "
    Message &= e.Filename & Environment.NewLine
    Message &= Environment.NewLine & "Do You Accept?"

    'Fortunately the MessageBox.Show method is thread-safe,
    'saving some work.
    Dim Result As DialogResult = MessageBox.Show(Message, _
      "File Transfer Offered", MessageBoxButtons.YesNo, MessageBoxIcon.Question)

    If Result = DialogResult.Yes Then

        Try
            Dim DestinationPath As String = "C:\TEMP\" & e.Filename

            ' Receive the file.
            TalkClient.AcceptFile(e.SenderAlias, e.FileIdentifier, _
                            DestinationPath)
```

```
' Display information about it in the chat window.
Dim NewText As String
NewText = "File From: " & e.SenderAlias
NewText &= " transferred at " & DateTime.Now.ToShortTimeString()
NewText &= Environment.NewLine & DestinationPath
NewText &= Environment.NewLine & Environment.NewLine

Dim ThreadsafeUpdate As New UpdateControlText(NewText, txtReceived)
Me.Invoke(New MethodInvoker(AddressOf ThreadsafeUpdate.Update))

Catch err As Exception
    MessageBox.Show(err.Message, "Transfer Failed", _
                    MessageBoxButtons.OK, MessageBoxIcon.Exclamation)
End Try
End If

End Sub
```

You won't need to take any extra steps when updating the user list—this call is performed on the user-interface thread thanks to a UI-friendly timer. This is the key difference between the System.Windows.Forms.Timer class and other classes in the System.Timers namespace.

Refining Talk .NET

So far this chapter has investigated threading intricacies and rewritten all the parts of the Talk .NET system that are vulnerable to threading problems. At this point, it's worth considering a few additional enhancements that you can make to round out Talk .NET.

Client Lifetime

Currently, there are only two ways that a client is removed from the user list: if the client logs out or if an error occurs when sending that client a message. To improve the system and ensure it more accurately reflects the clients that are currently connected, you can add an expiry time to the client login information. This expiry date should be fairly generous (perhaps 15 minutes) to prevent the system from being swamped by frequent network messages. Unfortunately, there will always be a trade-off between ensuring the up-to-date accuracy of the system, and ensuring the optimal performance of the system.

In order to use an expiry policy, the ActiveUsers collection will need to store expiry dates (or last update times) and client references. You handle this by creating a new class that aggregates these two pieces of information, such as the ClientInfo class shown here:

```
Public Class ClientInfo

    Public ProxyRef As ITalkClient
    Public LastUpdated As DateTime

End Class
```

The ActiveUsers collection will then only store ClientInfo objects.

Once the expiry dates are in place, there are two ways to implement an expiry policy:

- You could give the server the responsibility for calling a "dummy" method in the client that simply returns True. If this method can be called without a networking error, the client's expiry date will be updated accordingly.

- You can give the client the responsibility of contacting the server and logging in periodically before the expiry date is reached.

Both methods are used in the current generation of peer-to-peer applications. The latter is generally preferred, because it simplifies the server-side coding. It also ensures that the server won't have to wait for a communication error to detect an improperly disconnected client. Instead, it will just inspect the expiry date. Because the server is a critical component in the system, you should reduce its work as much as possible.

In either case, the server needs to periodically examine the list of logged-in users and remove invalid entries. This could be performed on a separate thread or in response to a timer. The separate thread would probably create a copy of the collection before examining it for expired users, in order to minimize locking possibilities. It would then double-check the live collection and call the RemoveUser() method.

In Talk .NET, there's another, potentially more efficient approach. The client expiry date could be refreshed every time the client calls the GetUsers() method. This reduces network traffic because the client is already calling GetUsers() as long as it's active in order to keep its list of contacts up to date. To accommodate this design, you would need to modify the GetUsers() signature so that it accepts the client name (or, in a secure application, a security token of some kind). Here's an example:

```
Public Sub GetUsers(requestingUser As String)

    SyncLock ActiveUsers
        ' Refresh the client last update time.
        CType(ActiveUsers(requestingUser), ClientInfo).LastUpdated = DateTime.Now

        ' Return the client list.
        Return ActiveUsers.Keys
    End SyncLock

End Sub
```

> **NOTE** *We will deal with expiry dates again in more detail when we create a discovery service in the third part of this book.*

Duplicate Users

The current TalkServer makes no effort to prevent duplicate users. This is a problem because if there's more than one user that logs on with the same name, only the most recent user will be entered in the collection (and will be able to receive messages).

To overcome this problem, you simply need to modify the ServerProcess.AddUser() method so that it refuses attempts to create an already existing user.

```
Public Function AddUser(ByVal [alias] As String, ByVal client As ITalkClient) _
    As Boolean Implements TalkComponent.ITalkServer.AddUser

    SyncLock Me
        If ActiveUsers.Contains([alias])
            Return False
        Else
            ActiveUsers[alias] = client
            Return True
    End SyncLock

End Sub
```

Similarly, TalkClient should be modified so that it will refuse to continue until it receives acceptance from the server:

```
Public Shared Sub Main()
    Dim frmLogin As New Login()

    Do
        If frmLogin.ShowDialog() = DialogResult.OK Then
            ' Create the new remotable client object.
            Dim Client As New ClientProcess(frmLogin.UserName)

            If frm.TalkClient.Login() Then
                ' Create the client form.
                Dim frm As New Talk()
                frm.TalkClient = Client

                ' Show the form.
                frm.ShowDialog()
            Else
                ' Login attempt failed. The loop will try it again.
            End If
        Else
            ' User chose to exit the application.
            Exit Do
        End If
    Loop

End Sub
```

Unfortunately this approach is still a little too restrictive. What happens in the legitimate case that a user wants to log in again after the application disconnected due to network problems? The user could use a new alias or wait for the old information to expire, but this is still far from ideal. One option is to add a "dummy" method to the ClientProcess. When faced with a duplicate login request, the server could then call this dummy method and, if it receives an error, it would determine that the current client is invalid and allow the new login request.

If you implement an authentication system, this code may change. In the case of an authentication system, it's safe to assume that if a user who already exists logs in again, the old information should be replaced without asking any questions, provided the user's identity is confirmed (typically by comparing the supplied password against a database).

Using a Windows Service

Remoting and Windows services make a great match. Currently, the TalkServer component host uses a Windows Form interface. This imposes some limits—namely, it requires someone to launch the application, or at least log on to a server computer so it can be loaded automatically. Windows services, on the other hand, require no user intervention other than starting the computer. The TalkServer, if implemented as a Windows service, will run quietly in the background, logged in under a preset account, even if the computer isn't currently in use, or is still at the Windows Login screen. Administrators using the computer can interact with Windows Services through the Service Control Manager (SCM), which allows services to be started, stopped, paused, and resumed.

This book won't explore Windows services in much detail, as they're already covered in many introductory .NET books, and they aren't specific to peer-to-peer development. However, it's surprisingly easy to create a simple Windows service to host the Talk .NET peer-to-peer system, and it's worth a quick digression.

The first requirement is to understand a few basics about programming a Windows service in .NET. Here's a quick summary of the most important ones:

- Windows services use the classes in the System.ServiceProcess namespace. These include ServiceBase (from which every Windows service class must derive), and ServiceInstaller and ServiceProcessInstaller (which are used to install a service).

- Windows services cannot be tested in the Visual Studio .NET environment. Instead, you must install the service and start it using the SCM.

- When you start a Windows service, the corresponding OnStart() method is called in the service class. This method only has 30 seconds to set up the service, usually by enabling a timer or starting a new thread. The OnStart() method does not actually perform the required task.

- When the service is stopped, the OnStop() method is called. This tears down whatever resources the OnStart() method sets up.

To create a Windows service, Visual Studio .NET programmers can start by creating a Windows service project. The project will contain a single class that inherits from ServiceBase as well as the installation classes that you'll generate later.

In Talk .NET, the Windows service plays a simple role. It configures the .NET Remoting channels in the OnStart() method and unregisters them in the OnStop() method. Once these channels are in existence, the Talk .Net ServiceProcess object will be created with the first client requests, and preserved until the service is stopped.

Following is a simple service that does exactly that. The code sample includes a portion of the hidden designer code, so you can better see how it works.

```vbnet
Imports System.ServiceProcess
Imports System.Runtime.Remoting
Imports System.Runtime.Remoting.Channels

Public Class TalkNetService
    Inherits System.ServiceProcess.ServiceBase

    Public Sub New()
        MyBase.New()
        InitializeComponent()
    End Sub

    Private Sub InitializeComponent()
        ' (The code for all design-time property configuration appears here.)
        Me.ServiceName = "Talk .NET Service"
    End Sub

    <MTAThread()> _
    Shared Sub Main()
        ServiceBase.Run(New TalkNetService())
    End Sub

    ' Register the listening channels.
    Protected Overrides Sub OnStart(ByVal args() As String)
        RemotingConfiguration.Configure("SimpleServer.exe.config")
    End Sub

    ' Remove all the listening channels.
    Protected Overrides Sub OnStop()
        Dim Channel As IChannel
        For Each Channel In ChannelServices.RegisteredChannels()
            ChannelServices.UnregisterChannel(Channel)
        Next
    End Sub

End Class
```

The lifetime of a service runs something like this:

1. When the service is installed or when the computer is started, the Main() method is invoked. The Main() method creates a new instance of the service and passes it to the base ServiceBase.Run() method. This loads the service into memory and provides it to the SCM, but does actually start it.

2. The next step depends on the service configuration—it may be started automatically, or the user may have to manually start it by selecting it with a tool such as the Computer Management utility.

3. When the service is started, the SCM calls the OnStart() method of your class. However, this method doesn't actually perform the work, it just prepares it (starting a new thread, creating a timer, or something else). If OnStart() doesn't return after approximately 30 seconds, the start attempt will be aborted and the service will be terminated.

4. Afterward, the service does its actual work. This may be performed continuously on a separate thread, in response to a timer tick or another event, or (as in this example) in response to client requests through the Remoting infrastructure.

Installing the Windows Service

Windows service applications cannot be executed from inside Visual Studio .NET. To test your service, you need to create an installer. Visual Studio .NET will perform this step automatically: Just click on your service code file, switch to the design (component) view, and click the Add Installer link that appears in the Properties window (see Figure 5-5). A new *ProjectInstaller.vb* file will be added to your project, which contains all the code required to install the service.

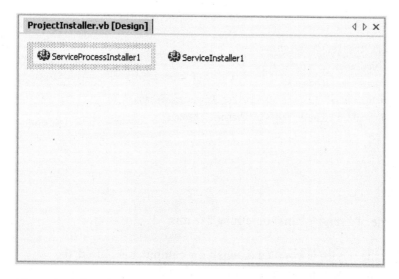

Figure 5-5. Creating a service installer in Visual Studio .NET

> **TIP** *You can configure some of the default service settings before you install the service by configuring the properties of the ServiceProcessInstaller and ServiceInstaller classes. Set the ServiceProcessInstaller.Account property to LocalService if you want the service to run under a system account, rather than the account of the currently logged-in user. Set the ServiceInstaller.StartType property to Automatic if you want the service to be configured to start automatically when the computer boots up. Both of these details can be configured manually using the Computer Management utility.*

At this point, you can either use the generated installation components in a custom setup application, or you can use the InstallUtil.exe utility included with .NET. First, build the project. Then, browse to the directory where the executable was created (typically the *bin* directory) and type in the following instruction:

```
InstallUtil TalkNetService.exe
```

The output for a successful install operation is shown in Figure 5-6.

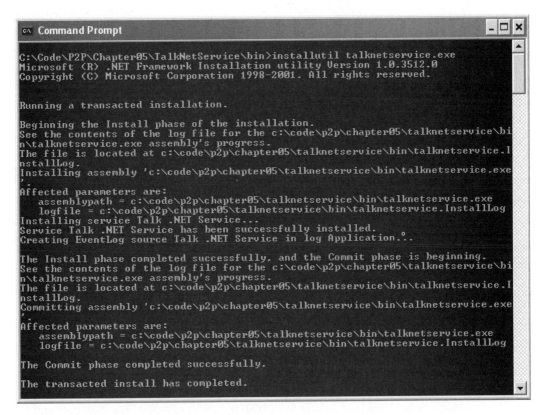

Figure 5-6. Installing a service with InstallUtil.exe

You can now find and start the service using the Computer Management administrative tool. In the Control Panel, select Computer Management from the Administrative Tools group, and right-click the Talk .NET Service (see Figure 5-7).

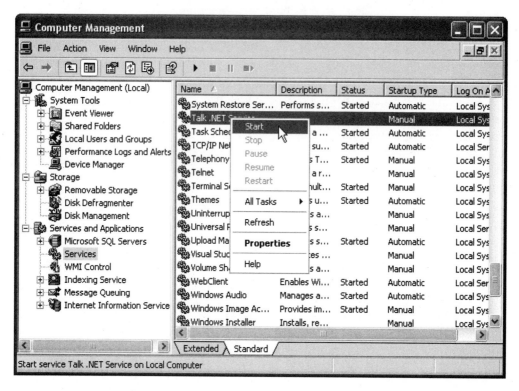

Figure 5-7. Starting the service through the SCM

To update the service, you need to recompile the executable, uninstall the existing service, and then reinstall the new service. To uninstall a service, simply use the /u parameter with InstallUtil:

```
InstallUtil TalkNetService.exe /u
```

Debugging the Windows Service

This implementation works exactly the same as before, except trace messages will no longer be captured by the TraceFormListener. Also, the only way to end the service will be through the SCM, not by closing the trace form.

What happens if you want to capture the trace messages and inspect them later? As discussed in Chapter 4, you can use another type of TraceListener and write messages to a text file or an event log. If you don't want to create a permanent record of messages, but you want to watch the messages "live," and possibly debug the service source code, you can still use the Visual Studio .NET debugger. You simply need to attach the debugger to the service manually.

Here's how it works. First you start Visual Studio .NET. Then, you open the TalkService project. This step isn't required, but it allows you to set breakpoints and single-step through the code easily. Finally, assuming the Talk .NET Service is running, select Tools ➤ Debug Processes from the Visual Studio .NET menu. The Processes window will appear, as shown in Figure 5-8.

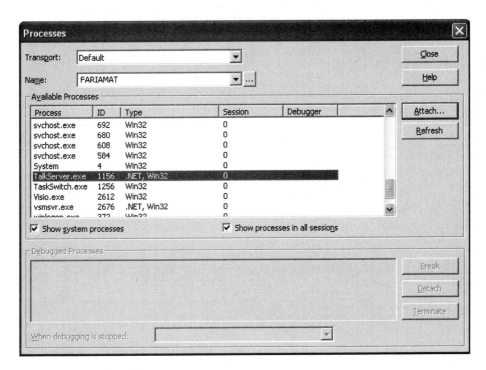

Figure 5-8. Finding the service

If you're running the service under a system account, you must select the "Show system processes" check box, or the service won't appear in the list. When you find the TalkService, select it and click Attach. Finally, in the Attach to Process window (Figure 5-9), select the Common Language Runtime check box to debug the code as a CLR application, and click OK.

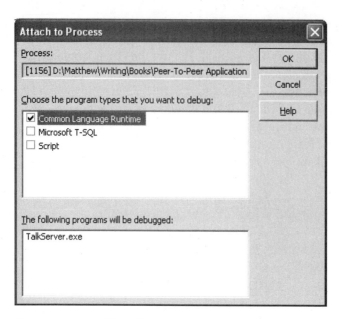

Figure 5-9. Attaching the Visual Studio .NET debugger to a service

Trace messages will now appear in the Debug window (as shown in Figure 5-10), and Visual Studio .NET will be able to work its usual debugging magic with breakpoints, single-stepping, and variable watches.

Figure 5-10. The trace output in Visual Studio .NET

The Last Word

This chapter dove into threading intricacies and the heavy lifting you need to manage concurrent access with the coordination server. Many of these concepts are important for any type of application, but this chapter placed a special focus on the trade-offs and design decisions of Talk .NET so that you can develop a better idea of how to structure a peer-to-peer system. Of course, though we've taken Talk .NET through several stages in evolution, it probably isn't production-ready. To actually deploy it in the real world, you would need to spend much more time profiling and tweaking the code.

In the next chapter, we'll take peer-to-peer systems with Remoting in an entirely new direction and consider how to build a task manager for distributed computing.

CHAPTER 6

Building a Distributed Task Manager

THE REMOTING FRAMEWORK developed over the last few chapters isn't limited to messenger-style applications. In fact, it may be better suited for an entirely different type of application: a distributed supercomputer.

One of the best-known examples of this type of application is SETI@Home, which harnesses the power of idle personal computers to digest large amounts of astronomical data in search of unusual signals. SETI@Home, like the messenger application we've created, isn't a pure peer-to-peer application—it depends on a central server that plays a key role in coordinating the entire system, and it doesn't make use of any peer interaction. Nevertheless, the bulk of the actual work is performed at the edges of the network, by ordinary peers.

This type of distributed processing works well with the Remoting architecture because it doesn't require frequent interaction across the network. Typically, peers will run independently to perform their work, and messages will only be exchanged when starting or completing a task. Thus, the higher-level object abstraction that Remoting uses is perfectly suitable. In fact, inventing a proprietary messaging format and communication protocol for this sort of system might just be overkill.

In this chapter you'll look at how to build your own peer-to-peer task processor system for specific tasks and how to extend the system to handle dynamically defined task types. Along the way, you'll also consider how .NET code-access security allows you to build a better sandbox and execute user-supplied code without risking the threat of Trojans, viruses, and worms.

Distributed Computing Issues

Distributed computing (also described as grid computing, parallelism, and clustering) isn't suitable for all tasks. For example, an operation that takes a relatively short amount of time may actually be lengthened by the overhead needed to send network messages to other peers—not to mention the additional work needed to divide the problem into multiple chunks and reassemble the answer.

Most significantly, distributed computing increases the overall complexity of the system and often makes it more fragile. That's because distributed computing raises other issues that aren't encountered if a single process is doing the same work. These problems include

- How to handle communication errors.

- How to track free workers and in-progress tasks.

- How to deal with a worker that doesn't respond in a timely fashion.

- How to allocate work intelligently, depending on the perceived complexity of the problem and the computing resources (or communication speed) of the worker.

Most developers think of distributed computing as a way to break a single problem down into multiple pieces that can be worked on, independently, by multiple machines. This is the ideal scenario, but not the only case. In some instances, you might use a distributed-computing framework just to remove a bottleneck for a highly computational task on a server. For example, a web service that receives task requests could deliver these requests to a task manager. The task manager would then send each task to a separate computer. The overall throughput of the system would increase, but each individual task wouldn't be broken down or reassembled. We'll examine this pattern, which is often easier to manage in the enterprise world, toward the end of this chapter.

If you want to shorten the time taken to complete individual tasks, rather than simply improve the overall throughput of an application, you'll need to take advantage of *parallelism* by dividing each task into multiple pieces. Some problems are much more suitable for this approach than others. For example, in the next section you'll consider a work manager that calculates prime number lists. In this case, the problem (searching a range of values for prime numbers) is one that can easily be subdivided into smaller pieces, like many search and analysis tasks. However, some tasks can only be performed with *all* the data. One example is the encryption of a large amount of information with cipher-block streaming. In this case, each block of data is encrypted using information from the preceding block, and it's impossible to encrypt the data separately (although distributed computing is used with other cryptography problems, such as cracking unbreakable ciphers).

Parallelism also introduces a new kind of fragility because the overall process is only as successful as its weakest link. If you have a worker that goes offline in the middle of a task, or operates very slowly, the whole task will be held back. To avoid this problem, you can store statistics about peers and use the most reliable ones wherever possible. You might also want to regularly poll a worker to retrieve its progress so you can cancel a slow-running task and reschedule it elsewhere. Or you may want to simply assign a task multiple times (if you have a large pool of workers) and use the first received task results. This approach might seem wasteful, but in a large environment, it provides increased robustness through redundancy.

Finally, note that some tasks aren't well suited for any type of distributed computing. These include operations that perform simple tasks with large amounts of data, in which case the overhead required to transmit the information might not be worth the relatively minor benefits of parallelism. Generally, tasks that make heavy use of computation (for example, CPU-intensive calculations) are the best choices for distributed computing.

> **NOTE** *For more information about new initiatives in distributed computing, you may be interested in visiting* http://www.globus.org, *which is a research project aimed at developing tools for grid computing on a large scale. They currently provide a toolkit for Java and are considering the promise of .NET. Another worthwhile site is* http://www.gridforum.org, *which is a community of researchers and developers working on emerging issues in grid computing.*

In the next few sections, we'll create a distributed work system that's designed to solve a single problem: finding prime numbers. For maximum speed, it uses multiple workers in a single operation and assembles their results with a work manager.

Defining the Task Interface

The first step, as with the messaging application in Chapter 4, is to define the objects used to transmit messages and the common interfaces that are exposed through Remoting. In this example, we'll need three interfaces: a task worker, a work manager, and a task requester. In the actual implementation, the task worker and task requester interfaces will be implemented by the same application so that all peers can perform *and* request work, but this isn't a requirement.

Figure 6-1 shows how messages will be processed in our system.

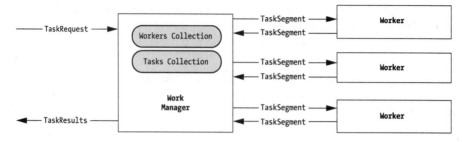

Figure 6-1. The work request process

Figure 6-2 shows a slightly simplified view of steps that would occur with a request and a single worker. It works like this:

1. The work manager receives a TaskRequest object.

2. The work manager stores a Task object internally in a collection.

3. The work manager divides the work into segments and sends available workers a TaskSegment object with a part of the work.

4. When the workers finish, they send back the TaskSegment with the result information added.

5. When all task segments have been received, the work manager compiles the information into a TaskResults object and sends it to the client.

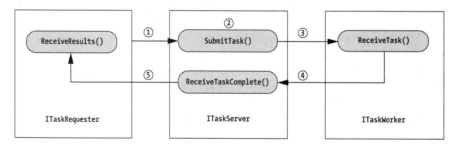

Figure 6-2. The order of work request steps

The TaskComponent Interfaces

The ITaskServer interface defines methods for registering and unregistering peers, for receiving a task request, and for receiving a task-completed notification. Optionally, you might want to add a method such as ReceiveTaskCancel(), which would allow a worker to signal that it's unable to finish processing the assigned task (possibly because it's shutting down).

```
Public Interface ITaskServer

    ' These methods allow workers to register and unregister with the server.
    Function AddWorker(ByVal callback As ITaskWorker) As Guid
    Sub RemoveWorker(ByVal workerID As Guid)

    ' This method is called to send a task-complete notification.
    Sub ReceiveTaskComplete(ByVal taskSegment As TaskSegment, _
      ByVal workerID As Guid)

    ' This method is used to register a task.
    Function SubmitTask(ByVal taskRequest As TaskRequest) As Guid

End Interface
```

The ITaskWorker interface defines a single method for receiving a task assignment. In addition, you might want to add a CancelTask() method, which allows the server to cancel a task (perhaps if the worker is taking too long and another peer is faster), and a CheckTaskRunning() method, which would allow the server to regularly poll the worker to verify that work is still underway.

```
Public Interface ITaskWorker

    ' The server calls this to submit a task to a client.
    Sub ReceiveTask(ByVal task As TaskSegment)

End Interface
```

Finally, the ITaskRequester defines a single method for receiving the final task results. You could add an additional method here to send a failure notification if a problem occurs midway through the process (for example, a worker application disconnects without finishing its work and there are no other available workers to assign the segment to).

```
Public Interface ITaskRequester

    Sub ReceiveResults(ByVal results As TaskResults)

End Interface
```

These interfaces are all coded in a separate DLL, called the TaskComponent. In addition, two delegates are defined, which are used on the server side to easily launch certain methods asynchronously:

```
Public Delegate Sub ReceiveTaskDelegate(ByVal taskSegment As TaskSegment)
Public Delegate Sub ReceiveResultsDelegate(ByVal results As TaskResults)
```

Message Objects

The next step is to define the objects that route task information around the network. These include the following:

- TaskRequest, which identifies the initial task parameters.

- TaskSegment, which identifies the task parameters for a portion of the task, and the task results for that segment once it's complete.

- TaskResults, which contain the aggregated results from all task segments, which are delivered to the client who made the initial request.

All of these classes are task-specific. In other words, you must customize them with different properties depending on the type of task your system is designed to tackle. In addition, the server uses a Task object to store information about requested and in-progress tasks.

The TaskRequest, TaskSegment, and TaskResults classes are all defined in the TaskComponent assembly because they're a necessary part of the interface between the remote components. The Task class, however, is not defined here, because it's only used by the server, and it can be modified without affecting other parts of the system.

The message objects are serializable, include default constructors, and use public variables. This allows them to be adapted for use with a web service, if needed.

The TaskRequest defines a range of numbers (between FromNumber and ToNumber). This is the range of values that will be searched for prime numbers. In addition, the TaskRequest indicates the ITaskRequester client that should be notified when the prime number list has been calculated.

```
<Serializable()> _
Public Class TaskRequest

    Public Client As ITaskRequester
    Public FromNumber As Integer
    Public ToNumber As Integer
```

```
Public Sub New(ByVal client As ITaskRequester, ByVal fromNumber As Integer, _
    ByVal toNumber As Integer)
    Me.Client = client
    Me.FromNumber = fromNumber
    Me.ToNumber = toNumber
End Sub


Public Sub New()
    ' Default constructor.
End Sub


End Class
```

The TaskSegment class resembles TaskRequest, with a few additions. It now stores a TaskID and SequenceNumber. The SequenceNumber is used when reassembling segments to ensure that the answers are ordered properly. The TaskSegment class also identifies the GUID of the worker who has been assigned this task, and a Primes integer array that will hold the results when the TaskSegment is sent back to the server.

```
<Serializable()> _
Public Class TaskSegment

    Public TaskID As Guid
    Public SequenceNumber As Integer
    Public FromNumber As Integer
    Public ToNumber As Integer
    Public WorkerID As Guid

    ' This holds the task results.
    Public Primes() As Integer

    Public Sub New(ByVal taskID As Guid, ByVal fromNumber As Integer, _
        ByVal toNumber As Integer, ByVal sequenceNumber As Integer)
        Me.TaskID = taskID
        Me.FromNumber = fromNumber
        Me.ToNumber = toNumber
        Me.SequenceNumber = sequenceNumber
        Me.WorkerID = WorkerID
    End Sub
```

```
        Public Sub New()
            ' Default constructor.
        End Sub

End Class
```

The TaskResults class stores information about the full range of numbers (the same information used in the TaskRequest) as well as the list of prime numbers (as an array of integers named Primes).

```
<Serializable()> _
Public Class TaskResults

        Public Primes() As Integer
        Public FromNumber As Integer
        Public ToNumber As Integer

        Public Sub New(ByVal fromNumber As Integer, ByVal toNumber As Integer, _
            ByVal results() As Integer)
            Me.Primes = results
            Me.FromNumber = fromNumber
            Me.ToNumber = toNumber
        End Sub

        Public Sub New()
            ' Default constructor.
        End Sub

End Class
```

The Task Logic

It also makes sense to define the task processing logic in a separate component. For convenience, we'll add this logic to the TaskComponent.

There are many different mathematical methods for finding primes in a range of numbers (as well as methods for testing probable primes). One historical method that's often cited for finding small primes (those less than 10,000,000) is the *sieve of Eratosthenes*, invented by Eratosthenes in about 240 B.C. In this method, you begin by making a list of all the integers in a range of numbers. You then strike out the multiples of all primes less than or equal to the square root of the maximum number. The numbers that are left are the primes.

In this chapter, we won't go into the theory that proves the sieve of Eratosthenes works or show the fairly trivial code that performs it. However, the full code is presented with the online examples for this chapter, and it takes this form:

```
Public Class Eratosthenes

    Public Shared Function FindPrimes(ByVal fromNumber As Integer, _
      ByVal toNumber As Integer) As Integer()
        ' (Code omitted.)
    End Function

End Class
```

The sieve of Eratosthenes is an excellent test for the distributed work manager because it can take quite a long amount of time, and it depends solely on the CPU speed of the computer. Calculating a list of primes between 1,000,000 and 5,000,000 might take about ten minutes on an average computer.

> **TIP** *For more information about the sieve of Eratosthenes, see* `http://primes.utm.edu/links/programs/sieves/Eratosthenes`, *which contains a wealth of resources about prime-number searching and the math involved.*

Creating the Work Manager

The work manager follows a similar pattern to the coordination server developed for the Talk .NET system over the last two chapters. Perhaps the most important detail is the information that the work manager stores in its memory, which includes the collections shown here:

```
Private Workers As New Hashtable()
Private Tasks As New Hashtable()
```

The Workers collection tracks information about the registered peers and how to reach them using WorkerRecord objects. These objects are indexed by the WorkerID. The Tasks collection holds a collection of Task objects, which represent the ongoing, currently scheduled tasks. Objects in the Tasks collection are indexed by TaskID. To write more error-proof code, you could replace the worker and task hashtables with custom dictionary collections that can only hold WorkerRecord and Task objects respectively. These custom dictionary collections would derive from System.Collections.DictionaryBase.

The work manager can also use private variables to store global preferences. In this fairly simple example, we'll only use one custom setting: an integer that sets the maximum number of workers that can be assigned to a task. This helps to ensure that other workers will be free to serve new requests. It also prevents a task from being broken into so many separate pieces that the communication time begins to become a factor.

```
Private MaxWorkers As Integer
```

The MaxWorkers settings is read from a configuration file when the server object is created:

```
Public Sub New()
    MyBase.New()

    ' Retrieve configuration settings.
    MaxWorkers = Int32.Parse(ConfigurationSettings.AppSettings("MaxWorkers"))
End Sub
```

For our test, we'll allow three maximum workers:

```
<?xml version="1.0" encoding="utf-8" ?>
<configuration>
    <appSettings>
        <add key="MaxWorkers" value="3" />
    </appSettings>

    <system.runtime.remoting>
        <!-- Remoting settings omitted. -->
    </system.runtime.remoting>
</configuration>
```

The work manager also uses the trace component used in the messenger application, which shows a window with trace messages that indicate what actions the server has performed.

Tracking Workers

The server provides an AddWorker() method that allows peers to register themselves in the Workers collection, and a RemoveWorker() method that allows peers to remove themselves. The following is the code for these methods:

```
Public Function AddWorker(ByVal callback As TaskComponent.ITaskWorker) _
  As System.Guid Implements TaskComponent.ITaskServer.AddWorker

    Dim Worker As New WorkerRecord(callback)
    SyncLock Workers
        Workers(Worker.WorkerID) = Worker
    End SyncLock
    Trace.Write("Added worker " & Worker.WorkerID.ToString())
    Return Worker.WorkerID

End Function

Public Sub RemoveWorker(ByVal workerID As System.Guid) _
  Implements TaskComponent.ITaskServer.RemoveWorker

    SyncLock Workers
        Workers.Remove(workerID)
    End SyncLock
    Trace.Write("Removed worker " & workerID.ToString())

End Sub
```

Note that the RemoveWorker() method assumes that the worker has finished all its tasks before exiting. Clearly, it would make sense to add a check to this code that looks for outstanding TaskSegments registered to this worker and tries to reassign them.

Workers are stored as WorkerRecord objects, as shown in the following example. Each worker has a globally unique identifier (GUID), which is generated automatically when the WorkerRecord class is instantiated. This allows workers to be identified uniquely on a network, without needing to assign them preexisting names (like a user alias). It's a technique you'll use again in later peer-to-peer examples in this book.

```
Public Class WorkerRecord

    Private _WorkerID As Guid = Guid.NewGuid()
    Private _WorkerReference As ITaskWorker
    Private _TaskAssigned As Boolean = False

    Public ReadOnly Property WorkerID() As Guid
        Get
            Return _WorkerID
        End Get
    End Property
```

```
Public ReadOnly Property ITaskWorker() As ITaskWorker
    Get
        Return _WorkerReference
    End Get
End Property

Public Property TaskAssigned() As Boolean
    Get
        Return _TaskAssigned
    End Get
    Set(ByVal Value As Boolean)
        _TaskAssigned = Value
    End Set
End Property

Public Sub New(ByVal worker As ITaskWorker)
    _WorkerReference = worker
End Sub

End Class
```

The WorkerRecord also provides a TaskAssigned property, which is initially set to False. In our simple example, a worker can be assigned at most one task. A more sophisticated worker might be able to hold a queue of task requests and deal with them one by one. In this case, you would replace the TaskAssigned Boolean variable with a TasksAssigned integer count. When assigning a task, the server would look for peers that have the lowest number of assigned tasks first.

Tasks

When the server receives a TaskRequest, it creates a new Task object. The Task object stores the original Task data, along with additional information, including

- The GUID, which the Task class generates automatically.

- A collection that contains WorkerRecords for the workers that are processing the segments of this task.

- A hashtable with an entry for each TaskSegment result. These entries are indexed by sequence number.

The Task class code is shown here:

```vbnet
Public Class Task

    Private _TaskID As Guid = Guid.NewGuid()

    ' The original task information.
    Private _Request As TaskRequest

    ' Holds WorkerRecord objects.
    Private _WorkersInProgress As New ArrayList()

    ' Holds partial prime lists, indexed by sequence number.
    Private _TaskResults As New Hashtable()

    Public ReadOnly Property TaskID() As Guid
        Get
            Return _TaskID
        End Get
    End Property

    Public ReadOnly Property Request() As TaskRequest
        Get
            Return _Request
        End Get
    End Property

    Public Property Workers() As ArrayList
        Get
            Return _WorkersInProgress
        End Get
        Set(ByVal Value As ArrayList)
            _WorkersInProgress = Value
        End Set
    End Property

    Public Property Results() As Hashtable
        Get
            Return _TaskResults
        End Get
        Set(ByVal Value As Hashtable)
            _TaskResults = Value
        End Set
    End Property
```

```
Public Function GetJoinedResults() As Integer()
    ' (Code omitted.)

End Function


Public Sub New(ByVal taskRequest As TaskRequest)
    _Request = taskRequest
End Sub


End Class
```

The Task class also contains a GetJoinedResults() method that steps through the hashtable or results and combines all values into a large array, which can then be returned to the client. Each entry in the hashtable is an array of primes that represents the solution for part of the original requested range. The code uses the fact that the entries in the results hashtable are indexed by their sequence number. Thus, as long as all the segments are present, they can be reassembled in order by starting with sequence number 0, regardless of the actual order in which the results were received.

```
Public Function GetJoinedResults() As Integer()

    ' Count the number of primes.
    Dim NumberOfPrimes As Integer
    Dim SegmentResults() As Integer
    Dim i As Integer
    For i = 0 To _TaskResults.Count - 1
        SegmentResults = CType(_TaskResults(i), Integer())
        NumberOfPrimes += SegmentResults.Length
    Next

    ' Create the whole array.
    Dim Results(NumberOfPrimes - 1) As Integer

    ' Combine the partial results, in order.
    Dim Pos As Integer
    For i = 0 To _TaskResults.Count - 1
        SegmentResults = CType(_TaskResults(i), Integer())
        SegmentResults.CopyTo(Results, Pos)
        Pos += SegmentResults.Length
    Next

    Return Results

End Function
```

Dispatching Tasks

The bulk of the work manager logic takes place in the SubmitTask() method, which receives a task request, breaks it into segments, and assigns it. The first step is to examine the request information and verify that it's valid.

```
' Validate task request.
If taskRequest.FromNumber > taskRequest.ToNumber Then
    Throw New ArgumentException("First number must be smaller than the second.")
End If
```

Note that the error condition leads to an exception. That means that SubmitTask() shouldn't be implemented as a one-way method, or the client will not receive this information.

Next, the code judges the range of numbers. If the range is very small, it decides to only send the request to one worker. Otherwise, it uses the full number of maximum workers allowed by MaxWorkers.

```
' Calculate if the task can benefit from parallelism.
Dim TotalRange As Integer = taskRequest.ToNumber - taskRequest.FromNumber
Dim MaxWorkersForTask As Integer
If TotalRange < 10000 Then
    MaxWorkersForTask = 1
Else
    MaxWorkersForTask = MaxWorkers
End If
```

> **TIP** *Depending on your design, it might make most sense to encapsulate the logic for validating a task and evaluating the Task range with dedicated methods in the Task class. This would be particularly useful if you wanted the work manager to manage more than one type of task. In this case, you would create a generic interface (possibly named ITask) that you would implement in all your Task classes.*

Assuming these two steps succeed, a new Task object is created.

```
' Create the task.
Dim Task As New Task(taskRequest)
```

Next, the code searches for free workers. It attempts to use as many workers as there are available (up to the specified maximum), and it takes the first available workers it finds. This may include the worker making the request, which is perfectly reasonable. The workers are added to the Tasks.Workers collections and immediately marked as assigned.

```
Dim Worker As WorkerRecord

' This lock ensures that the server won't try to allocate two different
' tasks to the same worker if the requests arrive simultaneously.
SyncLock Workers
    ' Try to find workers for this task.
    Dim Item As DictionaryEntry
    For Each Item In Workers
        Worker = CType(Item.Value, WorkerRecord)
        If Not Worker.TaskAssigned Then
            Worker.TaskAssigned = True
            Task.Workers.Add(Worker)
        End If
        If Task.Workers.Count >= MaxWorkersForTask Then Exit For
    Next
End SyncLock
```

Next, a quick check is made to ensure that there's at least one worker, or an exception will be thrown.

```
If Task.Workers.Count = 0 Then
    Throw New ApplicationException("No free workers. Try again later.")
End If
```

The work of dividing the task into segments begins next. First, a calculation is made to determine an average range for numbers. For example, if there's a total range of 100,000 and three workers to handle it, the average range is 33,333. The first two workers will receive this range of numbers, while the last will receive everything that remains (in this case 33,334 items). Once the segment is constructed, it's sent asynchronously to the worker by calling the worker's ReceiveTask() method.

```
Trace.Write("Trying to assign " & Task.Workers.Count.ToString() & _
    " worker(s) for task " & Task.TaskID.ToString())

' Calculate segment sizes.
Dim Segment As TaskSegment
Dim LowerBound As Integer = taskRequest.FromNumber
Dim AverageRange As Integer = Math.Floor(TotalRange / Task.Workers.Count)
Dim i As Integer
```

```
' Divide the task into segments, and dispatch each segment.
' This code will be skipped if there's only one segment because
' (WorkersToUse.Count - 2) will equal 0.
Dim ReceiveTask As ReceiveTaskDelegate
For i = 0 To Task.Workers.Count - 2
    Segment = New TaskSegment(Task.TaskID, LowerBound, _
                                LowerBound + AverageRange, i)
    LowerBound += AverageRange + 1
    Worker = CType(Task.Workers(i), WorkerRecord)
    Segment.WorkerID = Worker.WorkerID
    ReceiveTask = New ReceiveTaskDelegate(AddressOf _
        Worker.ITaskWorker.ReceiveTask)
    ReceiveTask.BeginInvoke(Segment, Nothing, Nothing)
Next

' Create the last segment to get the remaining numbers.
 Segment = New TaskSegment(Task.TaskID, LowerBound, taskRequest.ToNumber, i)
 Worker = CType(Task.Workers(Task.Workers.Count - 1), WorkerRecord)
 Segment.WorkerID = Worker.WorkerID

 ReceiveTask = New ReceiveTaskDelegate(AddressOf Worker.ITaskWorker.ReceiveTask)
 ReceiveTask.BeginInvoke(Segment, Nothing, Nothing)
```

Finally, the Task object is stored in the Tasks collection.

```
' Store the Task object.
SyncLock Tasks
    Tasks.Add(Task.TaskID, Task)
End SyncLock

Trace.Write("Created and assigned task " & Task.TaskID.ToString() & ".")
```

Completing Tasks

The work manager's ReceiveTaskComplete() method is the last part of the
ITaskServer interface. It receives completed TaskSegment objects, adds them
to the corresponding Task (from the in-memory Tasks collection), and then
marks the worker as available. If the number of received results equals the number of task segments, the task is declared complete. A notification message is
sent to the original task requester with the list of primes, and the task is removed
from memory.

```
Public Sub ReceiveTaskComplete(ByVal taskSegment As TaskSegment, _
  ByVal workerID As System.Guid) _
  Implements TaskComponent.ITaskServer.ReceiveTaskComplete

    Trace.Write("Received result sequence #" & _
      taskSegment.SequenceNumber.ToString() & " for task " & _
      taskSegment.TaskID.ToString() & ".")

    Dim Task As Task = CType(Tasks(taskSegment.TaskID), Task)
    Task.Results.Add(taskSegment.SequenceNumber, taskSegment.Primes)

    ' Free up worker.
    Dim Worker As WorkerRecord = CType(Workers(taskSegment.WorkerID), _
      WorkerRecord)
    Worker.TaskAssigned = False

    ' Check if this is the final submission.
    If Task.Results.Count = Task.Workers.Count Then

        SyncLock Tasks
            Trace.Write("Task " & Task.TaskID.ToString() & " completed.")
            Dim Primes() As Integer = Task.GetJoinedResults()
            Dim Results As New TaskResults(Task.Request.FromNumber, _
              Task.Request.ToNumber, Primes)
            Dim ReceiveResults As New ReceiveResultsDelegate( _
              AddressOf Task.Request.Client.ReceiveResults)
            ReceiveResults.BeginInvoke(Results, Nothing, Nothing)

            ' Remove task.
            Tasks.Remove(Task.TaskID)
        End SyncLock

    End If

End Sub
```

You might choose to implement the ReceiveTaskComplete() method as
a one-way method for maximum performance because the worker doesn't need
to receive any information or exceptions that might be raised on the server.

Creating the Task Worker

The peer application performs two functions: It allows a user to submit task requests, and it performs prime number calculations when instructed to by the server.

To encourage users to run the worker component continuously, it uses a system tray interface. When the application is first started, it loads a system tray icon. Users can right-click the system tray icon to receive a menu with options for exiting the application or submitting new tasks, as shown in Figure 6-3. Another option would be to implement the worker as a Windows service that starts automatically when the computer boots up.

Figure 6-3. The worker in the system tray

The System Tray Interface

Creating a system tray application is quite easy. First, we create a Component class that holds the logic for the ContextMenu and NotifyIcon controls. All component classes have a design-time surface where you can create and store these objects, much like the component tray when designing a form. This allows you to configure the menu properties quickly using designers, rather than code it all manually in your startup class.

The skeleton for this class is shown here:

```
Public Class Startup
    Inherits System.ComponentModel.Component
    Friend WithEvents mnuContext As System.Windows.Forms.ContextMenu
    Friend WithEvents mnuShowStatus As System.Windows.Forms.MenuItem
    Friend WithEvents mnuSeparator As System.Windows.Forms.MenuItem
    Friend WithEvents mnuExit As System.Windows.Forms.MenuItem

    Friend WithEvents TrayIcon As System.Windows.Forms.NotifyIcon

    ' This is the object that provides the client-side remotable interface.
    Private Client As New ClientProcess()
```

```
' This is the main status form. We create it here to ensure that there's
' ever only one instance.
Private frm As New MainForm()

Public Sub New()
    frm.Client = Client
    InitializeComponent()
End Sub

Private Sub InitializeComponent()
    ' (Designer code omitted.)
End Sub


' (Event handlers go here.)
End Class
```

On startup, the code creates our component, ensures the NotifyIcon is visible, and logs in to the server through the remotable ClientProcess.

```
Public Shared Sub Main()

    Dim Startup As New Startup()
    Startup.TrayIcon.Visible = True

    ' Create the new remotable client object.
    Startup.Client.Login()

    ' Prevent the application from exiting prematurely.
    System.Windows.Forms.Application.Run()

End Sub
```

The NotifyIcon has an attached context menu, which is immediately available. The menu items allow the user to exit the application or access the main window:

```
Private Sub mnuShowStatus_Click(ByVal sender As Object, _
  ByVal e As System.EventArgs) Handles mnuShowStatus.Click

    frm.Show()

End Sub
```

```
Private Sub mnuExit_Click(ByVal sender As Object, ByVal e As System.EventArgs) _
   Handles mnuExit.Click

    If Client.Status = BackgroundStatus.Processing Then
        MessageBox.Show("A background task is still in progress.", "Cannot Exit")
    Else
        Try
            Client.LogOut()
        Catch
            ' Ignore error that might occur if server no longer exists.
        End Try

        ' Clear the system tray icon manually.
        ' Otherwise, it may linger until the user moves the mouse over it.
        TrayIcon.Visible = False

        System.Windows.Forms.Application.Exit()
    End If

End Sub
```

The ClientProcess

The ClientProcess class follows a similar model to the chat client in our earlier Talk .NET example. It calls server methods to request a new task and receives task-complete notifications or task requests. If it receives information that the main form needs to access, it raises an event. In addition, it includes two read-only properties, which provide the server-generated GUID and the current status (which indicates if the worker is currently carrying out a prime number search). The possible status values are provided in an enumeration:

```
Public Enum BackgroundStatus
    Processing
    Idle
End Enum
```

Note that the ClientProcess class works both as a task worker (by implementing ITaskWorker) and as a TaskRequester (by implementing ITaskRequester). Here's the essential code, without the remotable methods:

```
Public Class ClientProcess
    Inherits MarshalByRefObject
    Implements ITaskWorker, ITaskRequester
```

```
' This event occurs when work begins or ends on the background thread.
Public Event BackgroundStatusChanged(ByVal sender As Object, _
    ByVal e As BackgroundStatusChanged)


' This event occurs when the prime number series is received
' (answer to a query).
Public Event ResultsReceived(ByVal sender As Object, _
    ByVal e As ResultsReceivedEventArgs)


' The reference to the server object.
Private Server As ITaskServer


' The server-assigned ID.
Private _ID As Guid
Public ReadOnly Property ID() As Guid
    Get
        Return _ID
    End Get
End Property


' Indicates whether prime number work is being carried out.
Private _Status As BackgroundStatus = BackgroundStatus.Idle
Public ReadOnly Property Status() As BackgroundStatus
    Get
        Return _Status
    End Get
End Property


Public Sub New()

    ' Configure the client channel for sending messages and receiving
    ' the server callback.
    RemotingConfiguration.Configure("TaskWorker.exe.config")

    ' Create the proxy that references the server object.
    Server = CType(Activator.GetObject(GetType(ITaskServer), _
        "tcp://localhost:8000/WorkManager/TaskServer"), ITaskServer)

End Sub


Public Sub Login()
    ' Register the current worker with the server.
    _ID = Server.AddWorker(Me)
End Sub
```

```
Public Sub LogOut()
    Server.RemoveWorker(ID)
End Sub


' This override ensures that if the object is idle for an extended
' period, it won't lose its lease and be garbage collected.
Public Overrides Function InitializeLifetimeService() As Object
    Return Nothing
End Function


' Submits client's request to the server.
Public Sub FindPrimes(ByVal fromNumber As Integer, ByVal toNumber As Integer)
    Server.SubmitTask(New TaskRequest(Me, fromNumber, toNumber))
End Sub


<System.Runtime.Remoting.Messaging.OneWay()> _
Public Sub ReceiveTask(ByVal task As TaskComponent.TaskSegment) _
  Implements TaskComponent.ITaskWorker.ReceiveTask
    ' (Code omitted.)
End Sub


<System.Runtime.Remoting.Messaging.OneWay()> _
Public Sub ReceiveResults(ByVal results As TaskComponent.TaskResults) _
  Implements TaskComponent.ITaskRequester.ReceiveResults
    ' (Code omitted.)
End Sub


End Class
```

The remotable ReceiveTask() and ReceiveResults() methods are both implemented as one-way methods so that the server won't be put on hold while the client deals with the information. The ReceiveTask() method performs all of its work directly in the method body, and then returns the completed segment to the server. An event is fired to notify the client form when the processing status changes.

```
_Status = BackgroundStatus.Processing
' Raise an event to alert the form that the background thread is processing.
RaiseEvent BackgroundStatusChanged(Me, _
  New BackgroundStatusChanged(BackgroundStatus.Processing))


' Find the prime numbers and submit the list to the server.
task.Primes = Erastothenes.FindPrimes(task.FromNumber, task.ToNumber)
Server.ReceiveTaskComplete(task, ID)
```

```
' Raise an event to alert the form that the background thread is finished.
_Status = BackgroundStatus.Idle
RaiseEvent BackgroundStatusChanged(Me, _
    New BackgroundStatusChanged(BackgroundStatus.Idle))
```

Alternatively, you could implement a separate thread to do this work, which would then call ReceiveTaskComplete() when finished. This would give the client the ability to cancel, prioritize, or otherwise monitor the thread as needed.

The ReceiveResults() method simply raises an event to the client with the list of primes:

```
' Raise an event to notify the form.
RaiseEvent ResultsReceived(Me, New ResultsReceivedEventArgs(results.Primes))
```

Here's the code detailing the two custom EventArgs objects used by the ClientProcess:

```
Public Class ResultsReceivedEventArgs
    Inherits EventArgs

    Private _Primes() As Integer
    Public Property Primes() As Integer()
        Get
            Return _Primes
        End Get
        Set(ByVal Value As Integer())
            _Primes = Value
        End Set
    End Property

    Public Sub New(ByVal primes() As Integer)
        _Primes = primes
    End Sub

End Class

Public Class BackgroundStatusChanged
    Inherits EventArgs

    Private _Status As BackgroundStatus
    Public Property Status() As BackgroundStatus
        Get
            Return _Status
        End Get
```

```
        Set(ByVal Value As BackgroundStatus)
            _Status = Value
        End Set
    End Property

    Public Sub New(ByVal status As BackgroundStatus)
        Me.Status = status
    End Sub
End Class
```

The Main Form

The main form allows the user to submit new tasks and see if the local worker is currently occupied with a task segment. The form is shown in Figure 6-4.

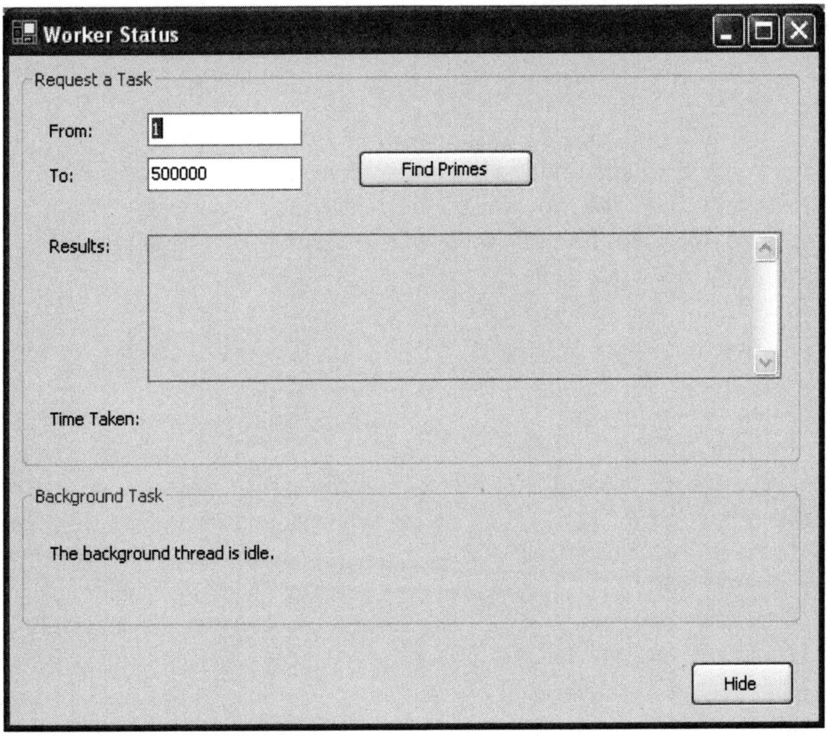

Figure 6-4. The main form

The form code is quite straightforward. When the user clicks the Find Primes button, the start time is recorded and the ClientProcess.FindPrimes() method is called, which will forward the request to the server. If there's an error (for example, the server can't find any available workers), it will appear in the interface immediately.

```
Private StartTime As DateTime

Private Sub cmdFind_Click(ByVal sender As System.Object, _
    ByVal e As System.EventArgs) Handles cmdFind.Click

    txtResults.Text = ""
    lblTimeTaken.Text = ""

    Try
        StartTime = DateTime.Now
        Client.FindPrimes(txtFrom.Text, txtTo.Text)
    Catch Err As Exception
        MessageBox.Show(Err.ToString())
    End Try

End Sub
```

The form handles both the BackgroundStatusChanged and the ResultsReceived events, and updates the interface accordingly. However, before the update is performed, the code must be marshaled to the correct user-interface thread. To accomplish this goal, we reuse the UpdateControlText object introduced in the last chapter.

```
Public Class UpdateControlText

    Private NewText As String

    ' The reference is retained as a generic control,
    ' allowing this helper class to be reused in other scenarios.
    Private ControlToUpdate As Control

    Public Sub New(ByVal newText As String, ByVal controlToUpdate As Control)
        Me.NewText = newText
        Me.ControlToUpdate = controlToUpdate
    End Sub

    ' This method must execute on the user-interface thread.
    Public Sub Update()
        Me.ControlToUpdate.Text = NewText
    End Sub

End Class
```

When the background status changes, a label control is modified accordingly:

```
Private Sub Client_BackgroundStatusChanged(ByVal sender As Object, _
    ByVal e As TaskWorker.BackgroundStatusChanged) _
    Handles Client.BackgroundStatusChanged

    Dim NewText As String
    If e.Status = BackgroundStatus.Idle Then
        NewText = "The background thread has finished processing its " & _
                  "prime number query, and is now idle."
    ElseIf e.Status = BackgroundStatus.Processing Then
        NewText = "The background thread has received a new " & _
                  "prime number query, and is now processing it."
    End If

    Dim ThreadsafeUpdate As New UpdateControlText(NewText, lblBackgroundInfo)

    ' Invoke the update on the user-interface thread.
    Me.Invoke(New MethodInvoker(AddressOf ThreadsafeUpdate.Update))

End Sub
```

When results are received, the array of prime numbers is converted to a long string, which is used to fill a text box. A StringBuilder object is used to quickly build up the string. This operation is much faster than string concatenation, and the difference is dramatic. If you run the same code without using a StringBuilder, you'll notice that the Time Taken label is updated long before the prime number list appears.

```
Private Sub Client_ResultsReceived(ByVal sender As Object, _
    ByVal e As TaskWorker.ResultsReceivedEventArgs) Handles Client.ResultsReceived

    Dim NewText As String
    NewText = DateTime.Now.Subtract(StartTime).ToString()
    Dim ThreadsafeUpdate As New UpdateControlText(NewText, lblTimeTaken)

    ' Invoke the update on the user-interface thread.
    Me.Invoke(New MethodInvoker(AddressOf ThreadsafeUpdate.Update))

    Dim Builder As New System.Text.StringBuilder()
    Dim Prime As Integer
    For Each Prime In e.Primes
        Builder.Append(Prime.ToString() & " ")
```

```
Next
NewText = Builder.ToString()
ThreadsafeUpdate = New UpdateControlText(NewText, txtResults)

' Invoke the update on the user-interface thread.
Me.Invoke(New MethodInvoker(AddressOf ThreadsafeUpdate.Update))

End Sub
```

There are a couple of additional form details that aren't shown here. For example, if the user attempts to close the form, you need to make sure that it isn't disposed, only hidden. You can see all the details in the code download provided for this chapter.

Figure 6-5 shows a prime number query that was satisfied by multiple clients.

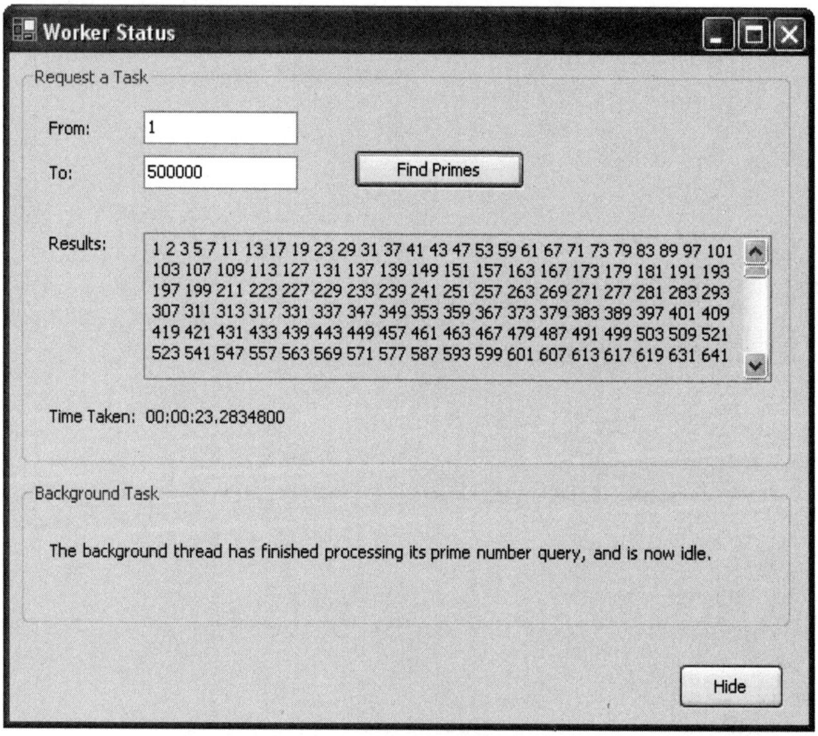

Figure 6-5. A completed prime number query

Figure 6-6 shows the server log for the operation.

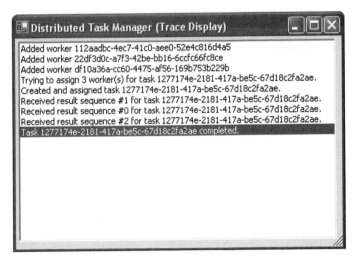

Figure 6-6. *The server trace transcript*

> **TIP** *If you run multiple instances of the TaskWorker on the same computer, you'll be able to test the system, but the processing speed won't increase. That's because all workers are still competing for the resources of the same computer.*

Enhancing the Work Manager

Distributed computing is easy with .NET Remoting, but it's difficult to do well. In order to manage the system, you need a dedicated work manager that must be coded very carefully, or it could weaken the entire system.

Many potential enhancements to the work-manager system deal with improving the work manager itself. The next few sections describe several possibilities.

Queuing

Currently, tasks are allocated as soon as they are received, much as messages were immediately sent with the first version of the Talk .NET coordination server. With a queued work manager, new task requests would be stored in memory. A dedicated work manager thread would periodically scan the queued tasks and allocate them to workers. One advantage of this approach is that it would allow the work manager to hold on to submitted tasks that can't be fulfilled right away (because there are no available workers). This approach would also allow you to deal with worker cancellations.

Fortunately, this design is easy to implement. In fact, you've already seen it, in Chapter 5 with an asynchronous message delivery! This design can be adapted almost exactly to the work manager coordinator.

You might also want to use the worker manager queuing thread to monitor currently assigned tasks. In this case, you could remove an assigned task if a peer doesn't respond after a long amount of time, and assign it to a different worker. If the task is extremely important and the system is working over a fast network, you might even want to add a GetProgress() method in the worker, which the server could call periodically to verify that a task is properly underway.

Queuing could also be applied in the worker itself. In this scenario, work segments would be added to a collection in memory. A separate thread would perform the actual work and would retrieve a new task segment as soon as the current one is finished.

> **NOTE** *For a demonstration of queuing in action, refer to the revamped coordination server in Chapter 5, or the file transfer application that we'll develop in Chapter 9.*

Performance Scoring

Currently, the work manager assigns work to the first available workers. This means that in a system with lots of extra capacity, the workers registered near the top of the collection will serve the most requests.

If you have peers of widely different abilities or connection speeds, you might want to assign work more intelligently. In this case, the server needs to track information about each worker. This information would probably be stored in the WorkerRecord object, although you could create another class and store it in a different hashtable (indexed by a worker ID) to reduce tread contention.

There are several questions you need to answer with performance scoring:

- What statistics will you measure?

- How often will you retrieve the statistics?

- How will you combine the statistics to arrive at a single performance metric?

- How will the performance metric influence the work assignment or worker choice?

For example, you might decide to track the peer's uptime, the number of task segments the peer has processed, the average response time for completing a task segment, and so on. Then, you need to provide a property that combines these details to arrive at a single number. There's no magic formula here—you may need to tweak this calculation based on experience. Here's an example that combines this information with different weighting

```
Performance Score = Total Uptime In Minutes - (Average Task Time In Minutes) * 50
```

In this case, the higher the performance score, the better. The average task time is weighted by a factor of 50 representing its importance relative to the total uptime.

Finally, now that you have this information, you need to optimize your work-assignment algorithm. There are two basic choices here:

- Sort the collection of available workers by performance score. Then, take the workers with the best performance score, and use only them.

- Use the workers as normal, but adjust the amount of work given to them so that the best performing workers receive the greatest share of the work. For example, in the prime number example, a better performing worker would receive a larger range of numbers.

The first approach is best suited to the prime number example. The second approach works well when you have a problem with a high degree of parallelism (for example, a task that's being divided into dozens of task segments).

Writing Directly to a Result Store

In the distributed prime number example, all communication flows through the central work manager. In some cases, you may be able to reduce the amount of communication by using peers that store their results directly. This technique is primarily useful when you're using a distributed-computing framework to remove a processing bottleneck but aren't dividing individual tasks into multiple segments.

For example, consider a web service that allows clients to upload graphic projects that will be rendered on the server and stored on a hard drive. This task is extremely CPU-intensive, so you're unlikely to perform it inside the web-service method itself. Instead, the web service might forward the request to a back-end work manager. The client would check for the completed file at a later date.

In this scenario, the work manager doesn't necessarily need to receive the results from the peers because it doesn't need to contact the client directly or reassemble multiple task segments. The workers will still send back a task-complete acknowledgement to the work manager in order to confirm that the work was completed and that it doesn't need to be resubmitted. However, the workers can store the results directly in a database, file, or some other sort of permanent storage.

To support this design, the task request message would need to contain information about how the task results should be serialized. To ensure maximum flexibility, you could define an abstract class to use like this:

```
<Serializable()> _
Public MustInherit Class ResultStore
End Class
```

Following is an example result store that contains the information needed to store results in a database:

```
<Serializable()> _
Public Class DatabaseStore
    Inherits ResultStore

    Public DatabaseConnection As String
    Public Table As String
    Public TaskIDFieldName As String
    Public ClientIDFieldName As String
    Public ResultFieldName As String

End Class
```

Now the work manager would create a DatabaseStore method and send it to the appropriate worker with the task request. The worker would complete the task and then store it directly in the specified location.

A Generic Task Client

In the prime number work manager, the work manager system is tightly bound to the type of problem (in this case, calculating prime numbers). The message formats are hard-coded to use certain properties that only make sense in this context. Then the task-submission logic implements the task-specific code needed to divide the range of prime numbers into shorter lists, and so on. This limits the flexibility of the system.

You might be able to create a more flexible system by creating a work manager that supports multiple types of tasks, defining a generic interface for all task objects, and moving some of the code into the task object itself. However, the task server and workers would still need to reference the assemblies for all the types of tasks.

What if there were a way for a requester to define a new type of task *with* a request? This would allow you to create a distributed computer that could tackle any client-defined problem, without needing to modify and redeploy the software. In fact, this is possible with .NET, but it isn't suitable in all situations.

The basic concept is for the task requester to submit a .NET assembly (as an array of bytes) with the task. The worker would then save this file to disk, and load the task processor using reflection. The worker only needs to know the name of the class, which it uses to instantiate the task-specific object. It could call methods in a generic task interface (for example, IGenericTask.DoTask()) to perform its work. The data would be returned as a variable-sized byte array, which only the client would be able to interpret.

Here's a snippet of code that creates an object in an assembly, knowing only its name and an interface that it supports:

```
' Load an assembly from a file.
Dim TaskAssembly As System.Reflection.Assembly
TaskAssembly = System.Reflection.Assembly.LoadFrom("PrimeNumberTest.dll")

' Instantiate a class from the assembly.
Dim TaskProcess As IGenericTask
TaskProcess = CType(TaskAssembly.CreateInstance("TaskProcessor"), IGenericTask)

' (You can now call TaskProcess.DoTask() to perform the task.)
```

> **TIP** *The Assembly.LoadFrom() method provides several useful overloaded versions. One version takes a URI that points to a remote assembly (possibly an assembly, which can include a Universal Naming Convention (UNC) path to an assembly on another computer, or a URL to an assembly on a web server). This version is particularly useful because the assembly is transparently copied to the local GAC, where it's cached. If you use LoadFrom() in this way to instantiate an assembly that already exists in the GAC, the local copy is used, thereby saving time.*

To make this example even more generic, the DoTask() method uses a byte array for all input parameters and the return value, which allows you to store any type and length of data.

```
<Serializable()> _
Public Class TaskRequest
```

```
    Public Client As ITaskRequester
    Public InputData() As Byte
    Public OutputData() As Byte

End Class
```

The easiest way to convert the real input and output values into a byte array is to use a memory stream and a BinaryWriter. Here's the code you would use to call the prime number test component generically. It's included with the online examples for this chapter in the DynamicAssemblyLoad project.

```
Dim ms As New MemoryStream()
Dim w As New BinaryWriter(ms)

' Write the parameters to the memory stream.
w.Write(FromValue)
w.Write(ToValue)

' Convert the memory stream to a byte array.
Dim InputData() As Byte = ms.ToArray()

' Call the task, generically.
Dim OutputData() As Byte = TaskProcess.DoTask(InputData)

' Convert the returned values (the list of primes) using a BinaryReader,
' and display them.
ms = New MemoryStream(OutputData)
Dim r As New BinaryReader(ms)
Do Until ms.Position = ms.Length
    Console.WriteLine(r.ReadInt32())
Loop
```

Of course, this approach sacrifices some error-checking ability for the sake of being generic. If the caller doesn't encode parameters in the same way that the task processor decodes them, an error will occur.

A Configurable Sandbox

As it stands, the generic task client is a perfect tool for distributing a malicious virus on a broad scale. Once an assembly is saved to a user's local hard drive, it has full privileges and can take any action from calculating prime numbers to deleting operating system files. In other words, an attacker could define a malicious task, and your system would set to work executing it automatically!

Fortunately, there's a solution. You need to build your own code *sandbox* and carefully restrict what the assembly can do. This is the approach taken by the peer-to-peer .NET Terrarium learning game. It allows you to restrict a dynamically loaded assembly so that it can't perform any actions other than the ones you allow. The code for this task is somewhat lengthy, but it works remarkably well. We'll examine the code you need piece by piece.

All the changes are implemented in the worker application. The goal is to create a way that the worker can identify user-supplied assemblies, and assign them less permissions before executing them. In order to create this design, you'll need to create a custom-evidence class, a membership condition, and a policy level.

First of all, you need to create a serializable Evidence class that will be used to identify assemblies that should be granted lesser permission. This class doesn't require any functionality because it acts as a simple marker.

```
<Serializable()> _
Public NotInheritable Class SandboxEvidence
End Class
```

Next, you need to create a MembershipCondition class that implements IMembershipCondition. This class is responsible for implementing a Check() method that scans a collection of evidence and returns True, provided it finds an instance of SandboxEvidence. (In other words, the SandboxMembership Condition class checks whether an assembly should be sandboxed.)

The abbreviated code is shown here. It leaves out some of the methods you must include for XML serialization. However, because you don't need to store this membership condition (it is implemented programmatically), these methods simply throw a NotImplementedException.

```
<Serializable()> _
Public NotInheritable Class SandboxMembershipCondition
    Implements IMembershipCondition

    Public Function Check(ByVal ev As Evidence) As Boolean _
      Implements IMembershipCondition.Check

        Dim Evidence As Object
        For Each Evidence In ev
            If TypeOf Evidence Is SandboxEvidence Then
                Return True
            End If
        Next
        Return False
```

```
End Function

' (Other methods omitted.)

End Class
```

Now you have the required ingredients to create a safe sandbox. The first step is to determine what permissions sandboxed code should be granted. In this case, we'll only allow it the Execute permission. This allows it to perform calculations, allocate memory, and so on, but doesn't allow it to access the file system, a database, or any other system resource.

```
' Create a permission set with the permissions the dynamically loaded assembly
' should have.
Dim SandBoxPerms As New NamedPermissionSet("Sandbox", PermissionState.None)
SandBoxPerms.AddPermission(New SecurityPermission(SecurityPermissionFlag.Execution))
```

Now that you've defined the permissions, you need to create a policy that will apply them. A policy level is essentially a tree of code groups. At runtime, the .NET security infrastructure will examine each code group. When it finds a code group with a membership condition that matches the evidence provided with the assembly, it takes the permission set from the code group and uses it for all the code that executes.

In this case, you need a policy tree with two groups:

- A group that matches the SandboxEvidence and grants the limited SandBoxPerms permission set.

- A group that matches all other code and grants full privileges.

In addition, you need a root group that contains both these groups and defines a "first match" rule. This organization is shown in Figure 6-7 and Figure 6-8.

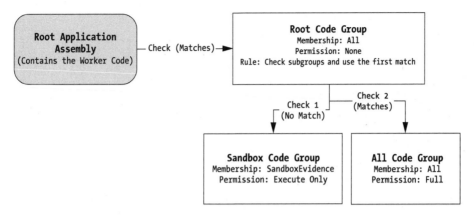

Figure 6-7. Granting all permissions to the worker assembly

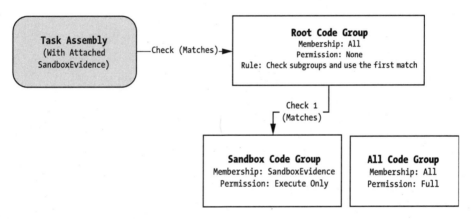

Figure 6-8. Granting reduced permissions to the task assembly

The code you need is shown here:

```
Dim Policy As PolicyLevel = PolicyLevel.CreateAppDomainLevel()
Policy.AddNamedPermissionSet(SandBoxPerms)

' The policy collection automatically includes an "everything" and
' a "nothing" permission set. We need to use these.
Dim None As NamedPermissionSet = Policy.GetNamedPermissionSet("Nothing")
Dim All As NamedPermissionSet = Policy.GetNamedPermissionSet("Everything")

Dim SandboxCondition As New SandboxMembershipCondition()
Dim AllCondition As New AllMembershipCondition()

' The default group grants nothing.
Dim RootCodeGroup As New FirstMatchCodeGroup(AllCondition, _
  New PolicyStatement(None))
```

```
' Code with the SandboxEvidence is given execute permission only.
Dim SandboxCodeGroup As New UnionCodeGroup(SandboxCondition, _
  New PolicyStatement(SandBoxPerms))

' All other code will be given full permission.
Dim AllCodeGroup As New UnionCodeGroup(AllCondition, New PolicyStatement(All))

' Add these membership conditions.
RootCodeGroup.AddChild(SandboxCodeGroup)
RootCodeGroup.AddChild(AllCodeGroup)
Policy.RootCodeGroup = RootCodeGroup
```

Finally, you set the policy to the current application domain using the SetAppDomainPolicy() method. This method can only be called once.

```
' Set this policy into action for the current application.
AppDomain.CurrentDomain.SetAppDomainPolicy(Policy)
```

You can then load the task assembly—but with a twist. When you load it, you'll specify a SandboxEvidence object that will identify the assembly as one that needs to run with reduced permissions.

```
' Create the evidence that identifies assemblies that should be sandboxed.
Dim Evidence As New Evidence()
Evidence.AddHost(New SandboxEvidence())

' Load an assembly from a file.
' We specify the evidence to use as an extra parameter.
Dim TaskAssembly As System.Reflection.Assembly
TaskAssembly = System.Reflection.Assembly.LoadFrom("PrimeNumberTest.dll", _
  Evidence)

' (Instantiate the class as before.)
```

> **NOTE** *You can test this code using the DynamicAssemblyLoad project included with the samples for this chapter. If you add any restricted code to the task processor (for example, an attempt to access the file system), a security exception will be thrown when you execute it.*

Toward a Pure Peer-to-Peer Task Manager

The distributed computing example in this chapter relied on a central component to coordinate work. However, this isn't incompatible with the peer-to-peer programming philosophy. That's because a peer in the prime number system can act both as a worker *and* a task requester. The next step is to allow a peer to play all three roles: worker, requester, and coordinator, for its own tasks.

One way to implement this is to reduce the role of the central component, as you'll see in the third part of this book. For example, you could replace the work manager with a basic discovery server. A peer that wants to request a task would then query the server, which could return a list containing a subset of available workers. The peer would then contact these peers to begin a new task. In this scenario, you would need to use a two-stage commit protocol. First, the peer would contact workers and ask if they were available. If the worker is available, it would respond "yes" and make itself unavailable for any other requests for a brief time period while it waits for an assignment from the requester (possibly five minutes). Next, the requester peer would deliver task segments to all the workers it had reserved. (See Figure 6-9.)

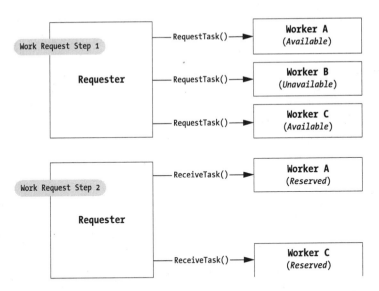

Figure 6-9. The two-stage request process with a decentralized work manager

Of course, decentralization has its sacrifices, and a fully decentralized task processor might not be what you want at all. Without a central authority, it's easy for a malicious (or just plain greedy) peer to monopolize network resources. Also, it's difficult to modify the rules for prioritizing tasks and determine how to subdivide them into task segments, because every peer would need to be updated. For those reasons, a hybrid design such as the one developed in this chapter may be the most effective and practical.

The Last Word

In this chapter, we considered the design of a distributed work manager. This type of application promises vastly improved performance, but introduces new complications and requires much more work than a stand-alone application. However, the benefits increase as the pool of available workers increases and the task load mounts. SETI@Home, the largest public-distributed computing project in terms of computing power, reached a record 71 teraflops per second on September 26, 2001. By comparison, the fastest individual computer in the world, IBM's ASCI White, runs at 12.3 teraflops per second. ASCI White costs over $100 million, while SETI@Home cost an estimated $500,000 to develop.

Distributed computing is highly dependent on the problem domain. Some approaches work well for certain types of problems, and some tasks are inherently more suited to distributed computing than others. Most distributed supercomputers have their own individual approaches, which are customized based on the task and type of data. In the future, it's likely that broader standards and a consistent framework will emerge from communities such as the Global Grid Forum (http://www.gridforum.org) and Globus (http://www.globus.org). For a list of some current large-scale distributed applications with their performance information, visit http://www.aspenleaf.com/distributed/distrib-projects.html.

Part Three

Peer-to-Peer with a Discovery Server

CHAPTER 7

Networking Essentials

So far, we've used the Remoting infrastructure to communicate between applications. However, peer-to-peer applications often need to work at a lower level and take networking, sockets, and broadcasts into their own hands.

In this chapter, we'll cover the essentials of network programming with .NET. We'll start by reviewing the basics of physical networks and network protocols such as the Internet Protocol (IP), Transmission Control Protocol (TCP), and User Datagram Protocol (UDP), and then consider the support that's built into the System.Net namespace. We'll also present sample applications that demonstrate how you can stream data across a network with a TCP or UDP connection. All of this is in preparation for the peer-to-peer file-sharing application we'll develop over the next two chapters.

Network Basics

A network is defined simply as a group of devices connected by communication links. A traditional local area network (LAN) connects devices over a limited area, such as a company website or an individual's house. Multiple local area networks are connected into a wide area network (WAN) using a variety of technologies. In fact, the Internet is nothing more than a high-speed backbone that joins together millions of LAN networks.

Networks are made up of four key physical components (not including the cabling), as described here:

- A network interface card (NIC) is the adapter that connects a device to a LAN. In a personal computer, all traffic flows through the network card.

- A hub connects multiple devices in a LAN. Essentially, traffic received by the hub is forwarded to every device connected to the hub.

- A switch connects multiple hubs or devices. It works like a hub, but with intelligence. Traffic received by a hub is forwarded to a destination node based on a lookup table stored in the switch. In the past, switches were most often used to connect hubs, but the low cost of switches and their superior performance means that many modern networks connect devices directly to switches.

- A router connects multiple subnets. Each subnet may consist of connected devices, hubs, and switches.

Figure 7-1 shows a sample network diagram that puts these parts into perspective.

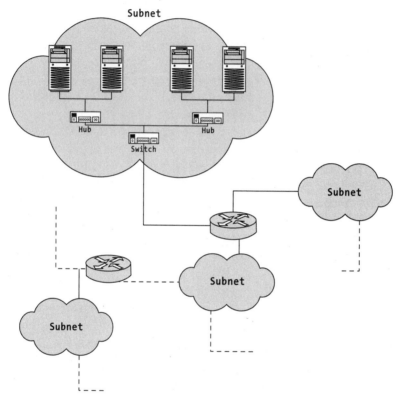

Figure 7-1. The network hierarchy

Programming tasks rarely require any understanding of the physical makeup of a network. What's much more important are the protocols used to encode information sent over a network link. Understanding the technology used to transfer information around a network can be difficult, because there are layers upon layers of different protocols that work in conjunction. At the transport level, most of the computers or devices connected to the network use the *Ethernet Protocol*. Ethernet defines the electrical signals that devices use to communicate on the wire. Other layers are built on top of the transport protocol, as shown in Figure 7-2.

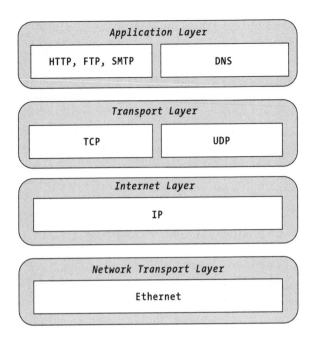

Figure 7-2. The network protocol stack

This diagram simplifies life slightly by concentrating on the protocols with which you'll need to work when programming a peer-to-peer application. For example, it doesn't mention other network-level technologies for data linking, such as frame relay, or Internet-layer protocols such as the Internet Control Message Protocol (ICMP), which is used to manage and report errors between devices on a network and the Internet Group Management Protocol (IGMP), which is used to join multicast groups.

Each of the layers in Figure 7-2 plays a critical role in networking; you'll be introduced to them over the next few sections.

Internet Protocol

The Internet Protocol (IP) is an addressing protocol that's one of the cornerstones of the modern Internet. With IP, every device on a network is assigned a unique 32-bit (four bytes) numeric address, called the IP address. Usually, the address is represented in a dotted quad notation, as in 192.145.0.1. Each of these four values represents one byte of the IP address, and can thus be a number from 0 to 255.

According to IP, nodes on a network must send information using *IP datagrams*. Each datagram contains the actual data that's being sent and an IP header. The IP header is the important part—it allows the maze of switches and routers in between the source and the destination to direct the message appropriately. The IP header contains quite a bit of information, but the most important details are as follows:

- The time to live (in hops). For example, if a message only has five hops to live, it can only cross five routers before it will be discarded. Of course, the IP packet might take several independent paths, each one of which will be limited to five hops.

- The IP address of the device that sent the message.

- The IP address of the device that should receive the message.

Of course, you'll never need to create an IP header or break your data into separate IP packets on your own because the .NET and Windows infrastructure will handle these lower-level tasks for you. In this book, we won't analyze the IP header in detail or explain how routers and subnets route and filter messages. There are numerous books dedicated to networking technology.

IP Addresses

One less obvious fact about IP is that the IP address itself reveals some information about the device. Every IP address is made up of two pieces: a portion that identifies the network (and possibly the subnet of the network), and a portion that identifies the device in the network. The number of bytes allocated to each part depends on the type of network that's being used. Here's how it works:

- If the first value in the IP address is from 1–126, it's a class A network address.

- If the first value in the IP address is from 128–191, it's a class B network address.

- If the first value in the IP address is from 192–223, it's a class C network address.

The difference between these types of networks is the number of nodes they can accommodate. Class A addresses are used for extremely large networks that can accommodate over 16 million nodes. With a class A network, the first byte in the IP address is used to define the network and the remaining three bytes identify the host. It's only possible to have 126 class A networks worldwide, so only extremely large companies such as AT&T, IBM, and HP have class A networks. Thus, in the IP address 120.24.0.10, the number 120 identifies the network and the remaining values identify the device.

Class B addresses use the first two bytes to describe the network. There can be about 16,000 class B networks worldwide, each with a maximum of 65,534 devices. Thus, in the IP address 150.24.0.10, the value 150.24 identifies the network, and the 0.10 identifies the device.

Finally, class C networks use the first three bytes to describe a network. That leaves only one byte to identity the device. As a result, class C networks can hold only 254 devices. Most companies that request an IP address will be assigned a class C IP address. If more devices are required, multiple class C networks can be used.

Note that this list leaves out some valid IP addresses because they have special meanings. Here's a summary of special IP addresses:

- 127.0.0.0 is a loopback address that always refers to the local network.

- 127.0.0.1 is a loopback address that refers to the current device.

- IP addresses that start with a number from 224–239 are used for multicasting.

- IP addresses that start with 240–255 are reserved for testing purposes.

Chapter 1 introduced the problem that the world is running out of IP addresses. In fact, there are already more devices connected to the Internet than there are available IP addresses. To compensate for this problem, devices that aren't connected to the Internet (or access the Internet through a gateway computer) can be given private IP addresses. Private IP addresses aren't globally unique. They're just unique within a network. All classes of networks reserve some values for private IP addresses, as follows:

- In a class A network, any address beginning with 10 is private.

- In a class B network, any address beginning with 172.16–172.31 is private.

- In a class C network, any address beginning with 192.168.0–192.168.255 is private.

Of course, a computer that's sheltered from the Internet doesn't *need* to use a private IP address—just about any IP address would do. Unfortunately, computers without an IP address can be difficult or impossible to contact from another network. This is one of the headaches of peer-to-peer programming.

> **NOTE**   *The current version of the Internet Protocol is known as IPv4. At some point, IPv6 will replace IPv4. Among other improvements, IPv6 will enlarge the pool of available addresses, because every address will use 128 bits (16 bytes) instead of 32 bits.*

Tracing, Pinging, and More

For a behind-the-scenes look at networking, you can use some of the command-line utilities that are included with the Windows operating system. One well-known utility is ping.exe, which contacts a device at a specified IP address using the ICMP protocol, and sends four test packets requesting a response. If the remote device receives the ping request, it will normally echo the packets back. Each packet is 32 bytes in size and is given 128 hops to live.

For example entering this at the command line:

```
ping 127.0.0.1
```

might elicit this response:

```
Pinging 127.0.0.1 with 32 bytes of data:

Reply from 127.0.0.1: bytes=32 time<1ms TTL=128
Reply from 127.0.0.1: bytes=32 time<1ms TTL=128
Reply from 127.0.0.1: bytes=32 time<1ms TTL=128
Reply from 127.0.0.1: bytes=32 time<1ms TTL=128

Ping statistics for 127.0.0.1:
    Packets: Sent = 4, Received = 4, Lost = 0 (0% loss),
Approximate round trip times in milli-seconds:
    Minimum = 0ms, Maximum = 0ms, Average = 0ms
```

The ping utility can be used to test if a remote host is online, although it may not succeed, depending on the firewall. For example, many heavily trafficked sites ignore ping requests because they're wary of being swamped by a flood of simultaneous pings that will tie up the server, thereby creating a denial-of-service attack.

To study the low-level communication in more detail, you can use an interesting utility called tracert.exe. It attempts to contact the host specified in the IP address, and indicates the route that was taken.

This tracert request simply uses the local loopback alias:

```
tracert 127.0.0.1
```

It receives the following unremarkable response:

```
Tracing route to localhost [127.0.0.1]
over a maximum of 30 hops:


  1    <1 ms    <1 ms    <1 ms  localhost [127.0.0.1]

Trace complete.
```

The following tracert request, however, contacts a Microsoft web server. Note that we've used a domain name instead of the IP address. You can use either interchangeably with all of the command-line utilities discussed in this section. However, many IP addresses will not have a DNS entry (particularly if the computer isn't a web server).

```
tracert www.yahoo.com
```

Here's the result:

```
Tracing route to www.yahoo.akadns.net [64.58.76.177]
over a maximum of 30 hops:

  1    26 ms    23 ms    23 ms  tlgw11.bloor.phub.net.cable.rogers.com
[24.114.131.1]
  2    23 ms    23 ms    24 ms  10.1.67.1
  3    26 ms    23 ms    23 ms  gw02.bloor.phub.net.cable.rogers.com
[66.185.83.157]
  4    25 ms    23 ms    23 ms  gw01.wlfdle.phub.net.cable.rogers.com
[66.185.80.6]
  5    28 ms    23 ms    24 ms  gw02.wlfdle.phub.net.cable.rogers.com
[66.185.80.142]
  6    48 ms    47 ms    47 ms  dcr1-so-3-1-0.NewYork.cw.net [206.24.207.85]
  7    51 ms    53 ms    53 ms  dcr1-loopback.Washington.cw.net [206.24.226.99]
  8    52 ms    52 ms    53 ms  bhr1-pos-0-0.Sterling1dc2.cw.net [206.24.238.34]
  9    51 ms    53 ms    52 ms  csr03-ve242.stng01.exodus.net [216.33.98.219]
 10    57 ms    54 ms    52 ms  216.35.210.122
 11    55 ms    53 ms    53 ms  www8.dcx.yahoo.com [64.58.76.177]

Trace complete.
```

In this case, 11 routers are crossed en route to the Yahoo! web server, which isn't bad! As with the ping test, a tracecert can fail if a firewall prevents it.

Another interesting utility is arp.exe, which can display the media access control (MAC) address and IP address of the current computer. (The MAC address is a unique hexadecimal value hard-coded in the network card.)

Here's a sample arp request:

```
arp -a
```

And here's the command-line response:

```
Interface: 24.114.131.60 -- 0x10003
  Internet Address      Physical Address       Type
    24.114.131.1        00-00-77-95-5d-5b      dynamic
```

Alternatively, you can use ipconfig.exe to retrieve just IP information for the current computer.

Finally, you can use route.exe to determine how outgoing requests are routed from your computer. Enter the following at the command line to see a list of address ranges and where the request will be forwarded:

```
route print
```

In the display below, requests for the local computer (IP address 24.114.131.0) are routed to the loopback alias 127.0.0.1. All other requests are dispatched to the gateway at 24.114.131.60.

```
===========================================================================
Active Routes:
Network Destination        Netmask          Gateway        Interface  Metric
          0.0.0.0          0.0.0.0      24.114.131.1    24.114.131.60     30
     24.114.131.0  255.255.255.128    24.114.131.60    24.114.131.60     30
    24.114.131.60  255.255.255.255       127.0.0.1         127.0.0.1     30
   24.255.255.255  255.255.255.255    24.114.131.60    24.114.131.60     30
        127.0.0.0        255.0.0.0       127.0.0.1         127.0.0.1      1
        224.0.0.0        240.0.0.0    24.114.131.60    24.114.131.60     30
  255.255.255.255  255.255.255.255    24.114.131.60    24.114.131.60      1
Default Gateway:       24.114.131.1
===========================================================================
Persistent Routes:
  None
```

Transmission Control Protocol and User Datagram Protocol

Transmission Control Protocol (TCP) and User Datagram Protocol (UDP) are two higher-level protocols that depend on IP. When you program an application, you won't create IP datagrams directly. Instead, you'll send information using TCP or UDP.

TCP is a connection-oriented protocol that has built-in flow control, error correction, and sequencing. Thanks to these features, you won't need to worry about resending information if a data collision occurs. You also won't have to worry about resolving any one of the numerous possible network problems that could occur as information is segmented into packets and then transported and reassembled in its proper sequence at another computer. As a result, TCP is a fairly complex protocol with a certain amount of overhead built-in. However, it's also the favorite of most network programmers, and it's the protocol we'll use to transfer files with the application developed in the next two chapters.

> **TIP**   *If an unrecoverable error occurs with TCP and retransmission cannot solve it, an error will be propagated up the stack until it appears in your code as a .NET exception. You can catch and respond to this exception accordingly.*

UDP is a connectionless protocol for transferring data. It doesn't guarantee that messages will be received in sequence, that messages won't be lost, or that only one copy of a given message will be received. As a result, UDP is quite fast, but it requires a significant amount of work from the application programmer if you need to send important data. One reason UDP might be used in a peer-to-peer application is to support peer discovery. This is because UDP allows you to send messages to multiple nodes on the network at once, without necessarily knowing their IP address. This is possible through broadcasting and multicasting, two technologies introduced later in this chapter.

Ports

Both TCP and UDP introduce the concept of ports. Port numbers don't correspond to anything physical—they're simply a method for differentiating different application endpoints on the same computer. For example, if you're running a web server, your computer will respond to requests on port 80. Another application might use port 8000. Ports map connections to applications.

Port numbers are divided into three categories:

- Ports from 0–1023 are well-known system ports. They should only be used by a privileged system process (for example, part of the Windows operating system), not your application code.

- Ports from 1024–49151 are registered user ports. Your server applications can use one of these ports, although you may want to check that your choice doesn't conflict with a registered port number for an application that could be used on your server.

- Ports from 49152–65525 are dynamic ports. They're often used for ports that are allocated at runtime (for example, a local port a client might use when contacting a server).

The Internet Assigned Numbers Authority (IANA) assigns registered ports. For a list of defined port numbers, refer to `http://www.iana.org/assignments/port-numbers`.

Remember, every transmission over TCP or UDP involves two port numbers: one at the server end and one at the client end. The server port is generally the more important one. It's fixed in advance, and the server usually listens to it continuously. The client port is used to receive data sent from the server, and it can be chosen dynamically when the connection is initiated. A combination of port number and IP address makes an endpoint, or *socket,* as shown in Figure 7-3.

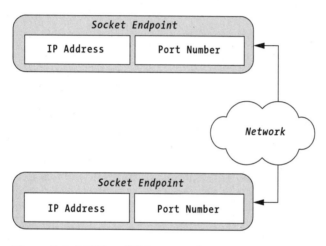

Figure 7-3. A TCP or UDP connection

Finally, it's worth noting that although only one application can use a port at a time, an application can serve multiple clients through the same port—in fact, with .NET, it's easy.

> **NOTE** *An endpoint in a TCP connection is called a stream socket. An endpoint in a UDP connection is called a datagram socket. There's one other type of socket that we won't use in this book, which is the lower-level raw socket, which bypasses both TCP and UDP.*

Application-Level Protocols

Several higher-level protocols are common in the Internet world. These are called application protocols, and the interesting fact is that they're built *on top* of TCP or UDP.

For example, the File Transfer Protocol (FTP), Hypertext Transfer Protocol (HTTP), and e-mail protocols (SMTP, POP3, and IMAP) all use TCP to establish connections and send messages. They simply define a grammar of recognized messages. For example, FTP defines commands such as STOR (upload a file) and QUIT (close the connection). These commands, however, are nothing special—they're really just ASCII-formatted strings that are sent over a TCP connection. You could easily create your own FTP-like protocol by defining some string constants and relying on the TCP to perform all the heavy lifting.

Similarly, some application-level protocols are based on UDP. They include Trivial File Transfer Protocol (TFTP), Lightweight Directory Access Protocol (LDAP), and DNS (the protocol used to transfer domain name information). In this case, the low-bandwidth features of UDP are preferred to the connection-centric ones of TCP.

This brings our exploration of core networking concepts to a close. In the next section, you'll consider how these protocols are used in .NET code.

Networking in .NET

The .NET Framework includes two namespaces designed for network programming: System.Net and System.Net.Sockets. The System.Net namespace includes several classes that won't interest peer-to-peer programmers, including abstract base classes and types used to set Windows authentication credentials. However, there are also several noteworthy types:

- IPAddress represents a numeric IP address.

- IPEndPoint represents a combination of an IPAddress and port number. Taken together, these constitute a socket endpoint.

- Dns provides shared helper methods that allow you to resolve domain names (for example, you can convert a domain name into a number IP address, and vice versa).

- IPHostEntry associates a DNS host name with an array of IPAddress objects. Usually, you'll only be interested in retrieving the first IP address (in fact, in most cases there will only be one associated IP address).

- The FileWebRequest and FileWebResponse classes are useful when downloading a file from a URI (such as *file://ComputerName/ShareName/ FileName*). However, we won't use these classes in this book.

- The HttpWebRequest and HttpWebResponse classes are useful when downloading a web page from a web server. However, we won't use these classes in this book.

The System.Net.Sockets class includes the types you'll need for socket programming with TCP or UDP. This namespace holds the most important functionality for the peer-to-peer programmer, including the following class types:

- TcpListener is used on the server side to listen for connections.

- TcpClient is used on the server and client side to transfer information over a TCP connection. Usually, you'll transmit data by reading and writing to the stream returned from TcpClient.GetStream().

- UdpClient is used on the server and client to transfer information over a UDP connection, using methods such as Send() and Receive().

- Socket represents the Berkeley socket used by both TCP and UDP. You can communicate using this socket directly, but it's usually easier to use the higher-level TcpClient and UdpClient classes.

- SocketException represents any error that occurs at the operating system level when attempting to establish a socket connection or send a message.

- NetworkStream is used with TCP connections. It allows you to send and receive data using a convention .NET stream, which is quite handy.

In the remainder of this chapter, we'll consider some of these essential types and create a few sample programs that show networking in action.

The Dns Class

On the Internet, publicly accessible IP addresses can be mapped to host names. For example, the IP address 207.46.134.222 maps to http://www.microsoft.com, and you can use either the domain name or the IP address when accessing the site in a browser.

In some cases, you'll need to retrieve the IP address for a domain name, or vice versa. This task is performed seamlessly in a web browser, and it can also be accomplished using the nslookup.exe command-line utility. In order to retrieve this information, your computer must access a DNS server. If the DNS server you contact cannot resolve the name by examining the values in its cache, it will forward the request to a DNS root server.

In .NET, you can perform this task quite easily using the Dns class, which provides a small set of shared methods. For example, the following code snippet retrieves an IPHostEntry for a specific domain name and then displays the first linked IP address.

```
Dim IP As IPHostEntry
IP = Dns.GetHostByName("www.microsoft.com")


' Displays "207.46.249.27".
Console.WriteLine(IP.AddressList(0).ToString())
```

The following code performs the reverse task:

```
Dim IP As IPHostEntry
IP = Dns.GetHostByAddress("207.46.249.27")


' Displays "microsoft.com".
Console.WriteLine(IP.HostName)
```

Finally, you can use the Dns.GetHostName() method to retrieve the host name of the current computer, which you can then convert into the local numeric IP address.

```
Dim IP As IPHostEntry
IP = Dns.GetHostByName(Dns.GetHostName())


' Displays the IP address for the current computer.
Console.WriteLine(IP.AddressList(0).ToString())
```

Network Streams

In .NET, you can send data over a TCP connection using the NetworkStream class, which follows the standard .NET streaming model. That means that you can write data to a NetworkStream in the same way that you would write bytes to a file. (It also means you can chain a CryptoStream onto your network stream for automatic encryption.)

The NetworkStream class differs slightly from other .NET streams because it represents a buffer of data that's just about to be sent or has just been received. On the sender's side, the buffer is emptied as data is sent across the network. On the recipient's side, the buffer is emptied as data is read into the application.

Because of this behavior, the NetworkStream class is not seekable, which means you cannot use the Seek() method or access the Length or Position properties. In addition, the NetworkStream class adds a few useful properties:

- Writeable and Readable indicate whether the NetworkStream supports write and read operations, respectively.

- Socket contains a reference to the underlying socket that's being used for data transmission.

- DataAvailable is a Boolean flag that's set to True when there's incoming data in the stream that you have not yet read.

The Write() and Read() methods allow you to copy byte arrays to and from the NetworkStream, but to simplify life you'll probably use the BinaryWriter and BinaryReader classes that are defined in the System.IO namespace. These classes can wrap any stream, and automatically convert common .NET types (such as strings, integers, and dates) into an array of bytes.

One good rule of thumb is to use the same approach for writing to a file as you do when reading it. For example, if you use the BinaryWriter to write data, use the BinaryReader to retrieve it, instead of the NetworkStream.Read() methods. This prevents you from introducing problems if you don't decode data the same way you encode it. For example, by default the BinaryWriter encodes data to binary using UTF-8 encoding. If you use Unicode to decode it, a problem could occur.

> **TIP** *Keep in mind that when you read more than one byte at a time, the method will not return until all the data is read. For example, if you use BinaryReader.ReadString(), the method will not return until it reaches the end of the string.*

The BinaryReader class also helps to add type safety to the NetworkStream. For example, if you use BinaryReader.ReadString() and the data in the stream doesn't correspond to a string, an exception will be thrown immediately.

Communicating with TCP

TCP connections require a three-stage handshaking mechanism:

1. First, the server must enter listening mode by performing a *passive open*. At this point, the server will be idle, waiting for an incoming request.

2. A client can then use the IP address and port number to perform an *active open*. The server will respond with an acknowledgment message in a predetermined format that incorporates the client sequence number.

3. Finally, the client will respond to the acknowledgment. At this point, the connection is ready to transmit data in either direction.

In .NET, you perform the passive open with the server by using the TcpListener.Start() method. This method initializes the port, sets up the underlying socket, and begins listening, although it doesn't block your code. After this point, you can call the Pending() method to determine if any connection requests have been received. Pending() examines the underlying socket and returns True if there's a connection request. You can also call AcceptTcpClient() at any point to retrieve the connection request, or block the application until a connection request is received.

When AcceptTcpClient() returns, it provides a TcpClient object that can be used to retrieve and send data. The easiest approach is to create a NetworkStream by calling the TcpClient.GetStream() method. After this, communication is simply a matter of reading and writing to a stream, and it can be performed in more or less the same way you would access a file on your computer's hard drive.

The following example shows a console server that waits for a TCP connection request on port 11000. When a connection request is received, it accepts it automatically and starts a new thread to listen for data received from the client. When a message is received, a BinaryReader is used to retrieve it, and the message is displayed in the console window. At the same time, the main application thread loops continuously, prompting the user for input, and sends input strings to the client using a BinaryWriter.

```
Imports System.Net
Imports System.Net.Sockets
Imports System.IO
Imports System.Threading

Module TcpServerConsole

    Private Stream As NetworkStream

    Public Sub Main()
```

```vb
' Create a new listener on port 11000.
Dim Listener As New TcpListener(11000)

' Initialize the port and start listening.
Listener.Start()

Console.WriteLine("* TCP Server *")
Console.WriteLine("Waiting for a connection...")

Try
    ' Wait for a connection request
    ' and return a TcpClient initialized for communication.
    Dim Client As TcpClient = Listener.AcceptTcpClient()
    Console.WriteLine("Connection accepted.")
    Console.WriteLine(New String("-", 40))
    Console.WriteLine()

    ' Retrieve the network stream.
    Stream = Client.GetStream()

    ' Create a new thread for receiving incoming messages.
    Dim ReceiveThread As New Thread(AddressOf ReceiveData)
    ReceiveThread.IsBackground = True
    ReceiveThread.Start()

    ' Create a BinaryWriter for writing to the stream.
    Dim w As New BinaryWriter(Stream)

    ' Loop until the word QUIT is entered.
    Dim Text As String
    Do
        Text = Console.ReadLine()

        ' Send the text to the remote client.
        If Text <> "QUIT" Then w.Write(Text)

    Loop Until Text = "QUIT"

    ' Terminate the receiving thread.
    ReceiveThread.Abort()

    ' Close the connection socket.
    Client.Close()
```

```
                ' Close the underlying socket (stop listening for new requests).
                Listener.Stop()

            Catch Err As Exception
                Console.WriteLine(Err.ToString())
            End Try

        End Sub


    Private Sub ReceiveData()

        ' Create a BinaryReader for the stream.
        Dim r As New BinaryReader(Stream)

        Do
            ' Display any received text.
            Try
                If Stream.DataAvailable Then
                    Console.WriteLine(("*** RECEIVED: " + r.ReadString()))
                End If

            Catch Err As Exception
                Console.WriteLine(Err.ToString())
            End Try
        Loop

    End Sub

End Module
```

This demonstrates one important aspect of socket programming with
.NET—you can write and read data asynchronously.

The client code uses the TcpClient.Connect() method to initiate the connection. After that point, the stream is retrieved from the GetStream() method,
and the code is almost identical.

```
Imports System.Net
Imports System.Net.Sockets
Imports System.IO
Imports System.Threading


Module TcpClientConsole

    Private Stream As NetworkStream
```

```vbnet
Public Sub Main()

    Dim Client As New TcpClient()

    Try
        ' Try to connect to the server on port 11000.
        Client.Connect(IPAddress.Parse("127.0.0.1"), 11000)
        Console.WriteLine("* TCP Client *")
        Console.WriteLine("Connection established.")
        Console.WriteLine(New String("-", 40))
        Console.WriteLine()

        ' Retrieve the network stream.
        Stream = Client.GetStream()

        ' Create a new thread for receiving incoming messages.
        Dim ReceiveThread As New Thread(AddressOf ReceiveData)
        ReceiveThread.IsBackground = True
        ReceiveThread.Start()

        ' Create a BinaryWriter for writing to the stream.
        Dim w As New BinaryWriter(Stream)

        ' Loop until the word QUIT is entered.
        Dim Text As String
        Do
            Text = Console.ReadLine()

            ' Send the text to the remote client.
            If Text <> "QUIT" Then w.Write(Text)

        Loop Until Text = "QUIT"

        ' Close the connection socket.
        Client.Close()

    Catch Err As Exception
        Console.WriteLine(Err.ToString())
    End Try

End Sub


Private Sub ReceiveData()
```

```
' Create a BinaryReader for the stream.
Dim r As New BinaryReader(Stream)

Do
    ' Display any received text.
    Try
        If Stream.DataAvailable Then
            Console.WriteLine(("*** RECEIVED: " + r.ReadString()))
        End If

    Catch Err As Exception
        Console.WriteLine(Err.ToString())
    End Try
Loop

End Sub

End Module
```

Figure 7-4 shows both parts of the applications as they interact.

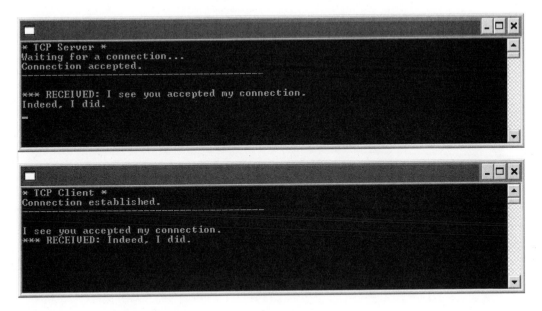

Figure 7-4. Sending data over TCP

Handling Multiple Connections

Newcomers to network programming often wonder how they can handle more than one simultaneous request, and they sometimes assume that multiple server reports are required. This isn't the case—if it were, a small set of applications could quickly exhaust the available ports.

Instead, server applications handle multiple requests with the same port. This process is almost completely transparent because the underlying TCP architecture in Windows automatically identifies messages and routes them to the appropriate object in your code. Connections are uniquely identified based on four pieces of information: the IP address and server port, and the IP address and client port. For example, Figure 7-5 shows a server with connections to two different clients. The server endpoint is the same, but the connections are uniquely identified at the operating system level based on the client's IP address and port number.

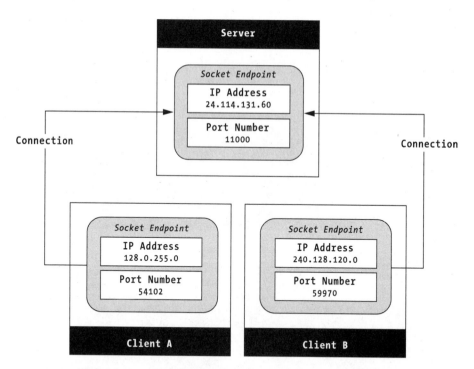

Figure 7-5. Multiple TCP connections

Remember, unless you specify otherwise, the client's port is chosen dynamically from the set of available ports when the connection is created. That means that you could create a client that opens multiple connections to the same server. On the server side, each connection would be dealt with uniquely, because each connection would have a different client port number.

Of course, to handle simultaneous connections you'll need to use multi-threading. Here's an outline of the basic pattern you would use on the server:

```
Dim Listener As New TcpListener(11000)
Dim Client As TcpClient

' Initialize the port and start listening.
Listener.Start()

Do
    ' Wait for a connection request
    ' and return a TcpClient initialized for communication.
    Client = Listener.AcceptTcpClient()

    ' Create a new object to handle this connection.
    Dim Handler As New MyTcpClientHandler(Client)

    ' Start this object working on another thread.
    Dim HandlerThread As New Thread(AddressOf Handler.Process())
    HandlerThread.Start()
Loop

' Close the underlying socket (stop listening for new requests).
Listener.Stop()
```

In addition, the main listener thread would probably use some sort of collection to track in-progress connections. Chapter 9 presents a complete example of a multithreaded server and client, with a file-sharing application that uses TCP connections to transfer file data.

Communicating with UDP

In UDP, no connection needs to be created. As a result, there's no differentiation between client and server, and no listener class. Data can be sent immediately once the UdpClient object is created. However, you cannot use the NetworkStream to send messages with UDP. Instead, you must write binary data directly using the Send() and Receive() methods of the UdpClient class. Every time you use the Send() method, you specify three parameters: a byte array, the length of the byte array, and the IPEndPoint for the remote computer where the message will be sent.

The following example rewrites the earlier TCP demonstration to use UDP. Because UDP does not make any distinction between client and server, we only need one application: a generic client that can both send and receive messages.

When the console application is started, it prompts you for the IP address and remote port where messages should be sent, and the local port that will be polled for incoming messages. Here's the complete code:

```
Imports System.Net
Imports System.Net.Sockets
Imports System.IO
Imports System.Threading
Imports System.Text


Module UdpClientConsole

    ' The port used to listen for incoming messages.
    Private LocalPort As Integer

    Public Sub Main()

        ' Set up ports.
        Console.Write("Remote IP: ")
        Dim IP As String = Console.ReadLine()

        Console.Write("Remote port: ")
        Dim Port As String = Console.ReadLine()

        ' Define the IP and port where messages are sent.
        Dim RemoteEndPoint As New IPEndPoint(IPAddress.Parse(IP), _
          Int32.Parse(Port))

        Console.Write("Local port: ")
        LocalPort = Int32.Parse(Console.ReadLine())
        Console.WriteLine(New String("-", 40))
        Console.WriteLine()

        ' Create a new thread for receiving incoming messages.
        Dim ReceiveThread As New Thread(AddressOf ReceiveData)
        ReceiveThread.IsBackground = True
        ReceiveThread.Start()

        Dim Client As New UdpClient()

        Try
```

```
                ' Loop until the word QUIT is entered.
                Dim Text As String
                Dim Data() As Byte
                Do
                    Text = Console.ReadLine()

                    ' Send the text to the remote client.
                    If Text <> "QUIT" Then
                        ' Encode the data to binary manually using UTF8 encoding.
                        Data = Encoding.UTF8.GetBytes(Text)

                        ' Send the text to the remote client.
                        Client.Send(Data, Data.Length, RemoteEndPoint)
                    End If

                Loop Until Text = "QUIT"

        Catch Err As Exception
            Console.WriteLine(Err.ToString())
        End Try

    End Sub


Private Sub ReceiveData()

    Dim Client As New UdpClient(LocalPort)

    Dim Data() As Byte
    Dim Text As String

    Do
        Try
            ' Receive bytes.
            Data = Client.Receive(Nothing)

            ' Try to convert bytes into a message using UTF8 encoding.
            Text = Encoding.UTF8.GetString(Data)

            ' Display the retrieved text.
            Console.WriteLine("*** RECEIVED: " & Text)
```

```
        Catch Err As Exception
            Console.WriteLine(Err.ToString())
        End Try
    Loop

End Sub

End Module
```

Note that the code passes a null reference (Nothing) to the UdpClient.Receive() method. This instructs it to retrieve any message that has been received on the listening port. Alternatively, you could supply an IPEndPoint representing a remote client. In this case, the Receive() method would only retrieve data sent by that client.

If you start two instances of the UDP test application, you might have an exchange such as the one shown in Figure 7-6. In this example, both instances are on the local computer. They differ only in the port that they're using.

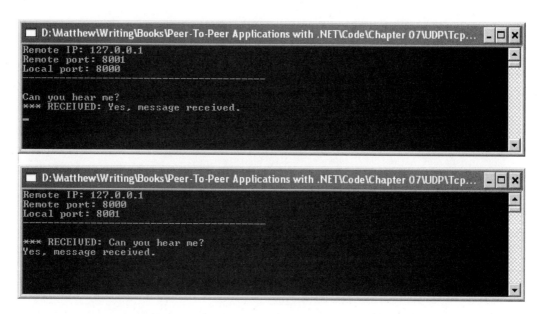

Figure 7-6. Sending data over UDP

Broadcasts and Multicasts

UDP provides one feature that TCP doesn't: the ability to send broadcasts and multicasts.

Broadcasts are network messages that are sent to all devices on the local subnet. When a client receives a broadcast, it decides whether the message is of interest or should be discarded. The architecture of broadcast messages makes them quite bandwidth-intensive, because a separate copy of the message is sent to each device. For this reason, routers always block broadcast messages, and they can never reach outside their own portion of the network.

To send a broadcast message, you use an IP address that identifies the network and has all host bits set to 1. In other words, if the network is identified by the first three bytes (142.128.0), you would send a broadcast to all machines on this network by sending a UDP message to the IP address (142.128.0.255). Even without knowing the network portion of an IP address, you can set all bits to 1, and use the broadcast address 255.255.255.255, which will attempt to contact every reachable computer (but, once again, it will be blocked by all routers).

Here's a snippet of code for use in sending a simple broadcast message:

```
Dim IP As String = "255.255.255.255"
Dim Port As String = 8800

Dim RemoteEndPoint As New IPEndPoint(IPAddress.Parse(IP), _
  Int32.Parse(Port))

Dim Client As New UdpClient()
Dim Data() As Byte = System.Text.Encoding.UTF8.GetBytes("Broadcast Message")

' Send the broadcast message.
Client.Send(Data, Data.Length, RemoteEndPoint)
```

Broadcasting would be highly inefficient if it were implemented with TCP, because the broadcaster would be flooded with acknowledgment messages from every recipient. As it is, broadcast messages with UDP still aren't that bandwidth-friendly. A much more efficient protocol is *multicasting*. Multicasting provides a way to define "groups" of computers with a multicasting IP address. Devices can join this group, in which case they'll receive all multicast messages, or leave it at will. Even better, multicast messages can cross router boundaries and flow freely across the Internet. Unfortunately, multicasting still isn't supported by all network hardware.

Multicast addresses range from 224.0.0.0 to 239.255.255.255. However, not all of these addresses are available (some have special meanings, and others are scope-relative, which means they cannot cross a router). You can register a multicast port for your application from the IANA, which is responsible for assigning all multicast ports. See http://www.iana.org/assignments/multicast-addresses for current assignments. Alternatively, you can use the predefined multicast address 224.0.0.1 to access all computers on a subnet. (You can also use a machine and device capabilities (MADCAP) server to request a dynamically assigned multicast address that will be used for a limited period of time, although this technique is beyond the scope of this book.)

Here's the code you would use to send a multicast message on the local subnet of the network:

```
Dim IP As String = "224.0.0.1"
Dim Port As String = 8800

Dim RemoteEndPoint As New IPEndPoint(IPAddress.Parse(IP), _
    Int32.Parse(Port))

Dim Client As New UdpClient()
Dim Data() As Byte = System.Text.Encoding.UTF8.GetBytes("Multicast Message")

' Send the broadcast message.
Client.Send(Data, Data.Length, RemoteEndPoint)
```

In .NET, a client can join a multicast group using the UdpClient.JoinMulticastGroup() method, and unsubscribe using the DropMultiCastGroup() method. Thus, before you can receive the multicast message shown earlier, you would need to use this code:

```
Dim Client As New UdpClient(LocalPort)
Client.JoinMulticastGroup(IPAddress.Parse("224.0.0.1"))
```

Both broadcasting and multicasting could be used to support peer-to-peer discovery, although they have several weaknesses. Broadcasting is bandwidth-intensive, and can't propagate beyond a local network. Multicasting is much more efficient, but isn't supported by all ISPs.

The Last Word

The technology that allows communication to flow from device to device over the Internet is quite complex, with multiple layers that work together to ensure reliability and scalability. Fortunately, the .NET Framework makes networking programming fairly easy, by encapsulating DNS lookup in a Dns class and providing a .NET implementation of Windows sockets through the TcpListener, TcpClient, and UdpClient. Armed with these techniques, you're ready to create the file-sharing application in Chapter 9. First, though, you need to consider a new method of peer-to-peer discovery: using a web service.

CHAPTER 8

Building a Discovery Web Service

IN THE CLIENT-SERVER WORLD, applications are deployed in a static, well-known environment. Database connection strings, server paths, and other location-specific details rarely change, and can often be hard-coded in configuration files (or even application code). Developers and network administrators work in close contact, and the system runs smoothly, day in and day out.

In a peer-to-peer application, you can't take anything about the environment for granted. The first consideration for any peer-to-peer application is how peers will discover one another on the network and retrieve the information they need to communicate. One approach is to create a complex "switchboard" of messages that routes peer requests around the network in a constant low babble. However, there's another approach that's easier to implement (and easier to make reliable). This approach is to use a hybrid design, with a central component that acts as a repository for peer information.

You've already tackled one such design in the second part of this book, where a central coordinator served stored information about peers in a chat system. However, this approach was tied to the Remoting network pointer (the ObjRef), and required a continuously running server application. This chapter presents an approach that's often more robust and scalable, thus replacing the central coordination component with a stateless web service and a back-end database. We'll use this approach to create a discovery service that will support the file-sharing application described in the next chapter.

The Discovery Service

A discovery service has one key task: to map peer identifiers to peer connectivity information (see Figure 8-1). The peer identifier might be a unique user name or a dynamically generated identifier such as a globally unique identifier (GUID). The connectivity information includes all the details needed for another peer to create a direct connection. Typically, this includes an IP address and port number, although this information could be wrapped up in a higher-level construct. For example, the coordination server that we used in the Remoting chat application stores a proxy (technically, an ObjRef) that encapsulates the IP address and port number as well as other details such as the remote class type and version.

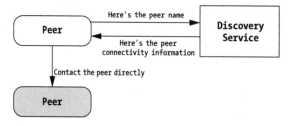

Figure 8-1. The discovery pattern

In addition, a discovery service might provide information about the resources a peer provides. For example, in the file-sharing application demonstrated in the next chapter, a peer creates a query based on a file name or keyword. The server then responds with a list of peers that can satisfy that request. In order to provide this higher-level service, the discovery service needs to store a catalog of peer information, as shown in Figure 8-2. This makes the system more dependent on its central component, and it limits the ways that you can search, because the central component must expect the types of searches and have all the required catalogs. However, if your searches are easy to categorize, this approach greatly improves performance and reduces network bandwidth.

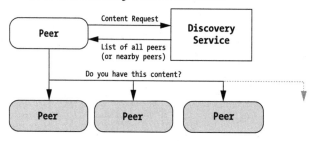

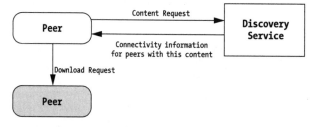

Figure 8-2. The effect of indexing content with a discovery service

Stateful and Stateless Discovery Services

Discovery services can be divided into two categories: stateful and stateless. The coordination component in Part Two was a *stateful* server; in other words, it runs continuously and stores all information directly in memory. This approach is fast for an off-the-cuff solution, but it presents a few shortcomings, including the following:

- Long-running applications sometimes fail.

- If the server needs to be restarted, all the information about active peers will be lost. This may be a minor issue if the peers are able to dynamically log back in, or it may be a more severe disruption.

- It's not efficient to store a large amount of information in memory. As the amount of information increases (for large systems, or for systems in which other resources need to be centrally indexed), the performance of the central server worsens.

- Stateful applications can be called simultaneously by multiple clients. As you saw in Chapter 5, you can deal with this by using threading code, but the issues are sometimes subtle and mistakes can lead to errors that are difficult to diagnose.

In this chapter we'll use a *stateless* server, which retains no in-memory information. Instead, information is serialized into a back-end database. This has the advantage of allowing more complex searches and reducing concurrency problems because databases are extremely efficient at handling large volumes of data and large numbers of simultaneous users. The discovery logic is coded using a .NET web service, which springs to life when called and is destroyed immediately after it returns the requested information.

Overall, you'll find that the discovery service is more efficient for large systems. However, it does impose some additional requirements. The central server will need to run a reliable database engine (in our example, SQL Server), and Internet Information Server (IIS), which hosts all web services. Fortunately, IIS is built-in to Windows 2000, Windows XP, and Windows Server 2003.

> **TIP** *If you don't have an instance of SQL Server, you can use a scaled-down version for free. It's called Microsoft Data Engine (MSDE), and it's included with all versions of Visual Studio .NET. The key limitations are that it will only support five simultaneous connections, and it doesn't include graphical tools for designing a database. For more information, refer to the Visual Studio .NET Help files.*

In the next few sections, we'll present a whirlwind review of web services and then dive directly into a full-scale example by developing the discovery service we'll need to use with the file-sharing application described in the next chapter.

Web Service Essentials

As a .NET programmer, you've probably already heard more than a little about Microsoft's favorite new innovation, the hotly hyped web services. Web services play much the same role as components exposed through Remoting: They're packages for business code that you want to execute on another computer. Unlike Remoting, web services use the ASP.NET engine, require IIS, and stress interoperability with other platforms through open standards such as SOAP, which is used to communicate with a web service, and Web Services Description Language (WSDL), which is used to describe the functionality provided by a web service.

Here's a short list of the key differences between Microsoft's two new distributed technologies, Remoting and web services:

- Remoting has the option of using faster communication through TCP/IP connections and the BinaryFormatter. Web services only support SOAP message formatting, which uses larger XML text messages.

- Web services support open standards that target cross-platform use, such as SOAP and WSDL. This allows third-party clients (such as a Java application) to interact with them.

- Web services only support a small set of .NET types for parameters or return values. You can use your own custom classes, but they can only include data members. Property procedures, constructor logic, methods, and so on, cannot be used.

- Web services don't require a component host application. Instead, this functionality is provided by the ASP.NET engine and IIS.

- Web services are requested much like a web page over an HTTP channel. This allows web-service requests to cross most firewalls. Of course, the same is possible with Remoting, as long as you configure your component accordingly.

- Web services are always stateless. That means they can't run asynchronously in the background or perform tasks continuously. Instead, they're created to serve a single client request and are destroyed immediately when the request ends. Remoting components don't have this limitation, as long as they're client-activated or Singleton objects (such as the Talk .NET coordination server in Chapter 4).

- Web services can use some powerful ASP.NET features, such as caching, process recycling, web-farm server clustering, and application state.

It's sometime said that Remoting always performs better than web services, because it can use binary formatting and the TCP/IP protocol, rather than larger SOAP messages and the HTTP protocol. This is true to a point, but this minor advantage can be countered by some of the built-in ASP.NET services, such as caching. It's also true that the restricted nature of web services simplifies design issues. It's generally easier to create a high-performance stateless object such as a web service than a stateful coordination object that needs to make heavy use of threads and synchronization codes.

Most .NET programmers have already heard more than enough about the promise of .NET web services. In this chapter, we'll cover the most important essentials in an abbreviated form, so that we can get back to peer-to-peer programming as quickly as possible. You won't learn about background information such as the SOAP and WSDL standards. If you're interested in a more detailed exploration of web services, there are many excellent books available. And if you've already mastered web services, feel free to skip ahead.

The Anatomy of a Web-Service Request

The ASP.NET engine handles a web-service request in much the same way as a web-page request. The only difference is that web-service results are usually formatted in an XML grammar called SOAP, not ordinary HTML.

Here's an overview of the process (shown in Figure 8-3):

1. A client sends a SOAP-formatted request to a web service.

2. IIS receives the request, determines that it's for ASP.NET, and invokes the ASP.NET engine.

3. ASP.NET creates the web-services object.

4. ASP.NET runs the requested method with the supplied information.

5. ASP.NET destroys the web-services object.

6. ASP.NET returns the web-services result in a SOAP-formatted message over HTTP.

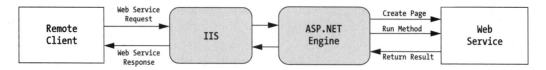

Figure 8-3. Serving a web-service request with ASP.NET

ASP.NET uses a pool of worker threads to handle multiple concurrent requests efficiently. A new, distinct web-service object is created for each request, ensuring that you don't need to worry about creating your own custom threading code.

The Least You Need to Know About IIS

IIS is the software a computer needs to serve web requests, whether they're for ordinary HTML pages or ASP.NET web pages and web services. IIS performs two key functions:

- It exposes directories on your hard drive as virtual web directories over HTTP. For example, you might map the path *C:\MyWeb* to http://[ComputerName]/PublicWeb. Now, the web services and web pages in *C:\MyWeb* can be accessed through HTTP in a web browser, using addresses that start with http://[ComputerName]/PublicWeb.

- Using file extensions, IIS maps web requests to the application that can handle them. For example, ASP.NET pages (*.aspx* files) and web services (*.asmx* files) are registered to the ASP.NET worker process. When IIS receives a web request for one of these file types, it invokes the ASP.NET engine, which handles the rest of the work.

IIS also imposes its own security controls, which you can customize. For example, by default, IIS will not allow a client to browse the list of files contained in a virtual directory. You can also use IIS to authenticate the user by demanding Windows authentication credentials, although this technique is of little use in a peer-to-peer application because the clients won't have Windows user accounts on the server.

IIS is included with the Windows 2000, Windows XP, and Windows Server 2003 operating systems, but isn't automatically installed. To install it, follow these steps:

1. Click the Start button, and select Settings ➤ Control Panel.

2. Choose Add or Remove Programs, and click Add/Remove Windows Components.

3. Find Internet Information Server in the list, select it, and click Next to install the appropriate files.

You can test if IIS is installed by requesting the page `http://localhost/localstart.asp` in your web browser. *Localstart.asp* is an ordinary ASP file that's stored in the root directory of your computer's website. Localhost is an alias that always refers to the IP address 127.0.0.1. This is known as the loopback address, because it always refers to the current computer. If your request works and you see the IIS Help page in your browser, IIS is installed correctly.

Typically, the root website `http://localhost` is mapped to the directory *c:\intepub\wwwroot*. You can create new virtual directories using the IIS Manager administrative utility. Just select Internet Information Server from the Administrative Tools section of the Control Panel, and follow these steps:

1. Right-click the Default Web Site item (under your computer in the tree), and choose New ➤ Virtual Directory to start the Virtual Directory wizard. Click Next.

2. Enter the alias, which is the name of the new virtual directory you want to create, and click Next.

3. Choose the physical directory that will be exposed. Click Next to continue.

4. The next window allows you to adjust the permissions granted to the virtual directory. The default settings allow clients to run ASP.NET pages and web services, but they can't make any modifications or upload files. This is the recommended configuration.

5. Click Next, and then Finish to end the wizard. You will see the virtual directory appear in the IIS Manager tree.

It's always a good idea to create a dedicated virtual directory before creating a project in Visual Studio .NET. Otherwise, your project will automatically be placed in a subdirectory of *c:\inetpub\wwwroot*. The discovery service presented in this chapter uses the virtual directory `http://[ComputerName]/Discovery`, which is mapped to the physical directory *C:\Code\P2P\Chapter08\Discovery*.

> **TIP** *Any computer on your network can access a web service using the computer name or IP address of the computer where the web service is hosted. However, if you want to expose a web service on the Internet, you'll probably need to invest in a fixed IP address or enlist the services of a dedicated Internet hosting company. With a fixed IP address, it also becomes possible to register a domain name (for example,* http://www.mysite.com*).*

The Web-Service Class

Like a Remoting component, a web service is, at its simplest, just a collection of methods organized in a class. To expose a method over the Internet, you need to add a <WebMethod> attribute to the method. In addition, it's a common convention to derive from the WebService class, although this isn't required. Both the WebMethod attribute and the WebService class are found in the System.Web.Services namespace.

Here's a sample web service with one method:

```
Public Class MyService

    <WebMethod()> _
    Public Sub MyMethod()
         ' (Code goes here.)
    End Sub

End Class
```

Although web services can include any .NET code, they only support a limited set of .NET types for use as method parameters or return values. Supported types include

- Basic data types such as integers, floating point numbers, Boolean variables, dates and times, strings, and enumerations.

- Arrays of any supported type.

- The ADO.NET DataSet (although this type will probably not be understood by non-.NET clients).

- The XmlNode object, which represents an arbitrary portion of an XML document.

- A custom class or structure. However, only data members will be preserved. All code will be ignored.

There's one nice side to this limitation. It means that you never need to distribute a custom assembly to clients that need to use a web service. Instead, they can download all the information they need about the service.

Remember, all web services are stateless. That means that if you create any member variables, they'll be initialized to default empty values every time a web method is invoked. Similarly, if you create a constructor, it will be called before every method call.

In order to deploy a web service on a website, you need to follow three simple steps:

1. Compile the web service into a *.dll* assembly.

2. Copy the assembly into the *bin* directory of a virtual directory on your server.

3. Add an *.asmx* file extension that will allow you to identify the web service in the virtual directory.

The *.asmx* file is the web-service endpoint. The client cannot access your web-service *.dll* directly—instead, it makes a request for the *.asmx* file, along with information about the method it wants to invoke and the data it's sending. The *.asmx* file simply indicates the class and assembly name for the corresponding web service in a single line of text:

```
<%@ WebService Language="vb" Class="MyService" %>
```

The ASP.NET engine will then instantiate the corresponding class from the *bin* subdirectory and run the requested method.

> **NOTE** *Visual Studio .NET automates this process when you create a web-service project, compiling the web service into an assembly and generating the corresponding .asmx file. These are the only two files you need to deploy.*

The Web-Service Client

As with Remoting, a web-service client communicates with a web service using a proxy. With Remoting, the proxy is generated dynamically at runtime. With web services, the proxy is generated by some tool at design time. In Visual Studio .NET, the proxy is created in a process called "adding a web reference." It's at this point that you specify the location of the web service, and then Visual Studio .NET generates a proxy class that can communicate with it and adds the proxy class to your project.

The proxy class has the same interface as the web service it communicates with. To use a web method, you create an instance of the proxy class and invoke the method of the proxy class. To your code, it seems like using an ordinary local object, but behind the scenes the proxy class creates and sends a SOAP request, waits for a response, and converts the return value into the expected .NET type. If you haven't already used web-service references in your own projects, you'll see how to add one in the next chapter.

Now that we've covered the groundwork, we're ready to begin coding a real-world application. The next section begins by creating a registration database, which we'll expose through a simple .NET web service.

The Registration Database

The registration database stores a list of all the peers that are currently available and the information needed to connect to them. It also uses a basic cataloging system, whereby each peer uploads a catalog of available resources shortly after logging in. When a peer needs a specific resource, it calls a web-service method. The web service attempts to find peers that can provide the resource and returns a list of search matches with the required peer-connectivity information.

In this case, the resources are files that a peer is willing to exchange. The catalog stores file names, but that isn't enough. File names can be changed arbitrarily and have little consistency among users, so searching based on file names isn't a desirable option. Instead, file names are indexed using multiple *content descriptors*. In the case of an MP3 file, these content descriptors might include information such as the artist name, song title, and so on. The file-sharing application can use more than one possible method to retrieve this information, but the most likely choice is to retrieve it from the file. For example, MP3 files include a header that stores song data. A file-sharing application could use this information to create a list of keywords for a file, and submit that to the server. This is the approach taken in our sample registration database.

> **NOTE** *In order to index a file, a peer must understand the file format and know how to extract the required information. The server does not deal with the file data, and can't perform this task.*

Creating the Database

The registration database consists of three tables, as shown in Figure 8.4. These tables include the following:

- The Peers table lists currently connected peers, each of which is assigned a unique GUID. The peer-connectivity information includes the numeric IP address (stored as a string in dotted notation) and port number. The Peers table also includes a LastUpdate time, which allows an expiration policy to be used to remove old peer registration records.

- The Files table lists shared files, the peer that's sharing them, and the date stamp on the file. Each file has a unique GUID, thereby ensuring that they can be tracked individually.

- The Keywords table lists a single-word descriptor for a file. You'll notice that the Keywords table is linked to both the Files table *and* the Peers table. This makes it easier to delete the keywords related to a peer if the peer registration expires, without having to retrieve a list of shared files.

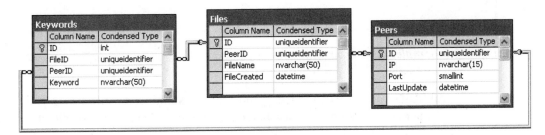

Figure 8-4. The registration database

Figure 8-5 shows the sample data that you would expect in the registration database after a single client has connected and registered two shared files (in this case, recordings of two classical compositions by Debussy).

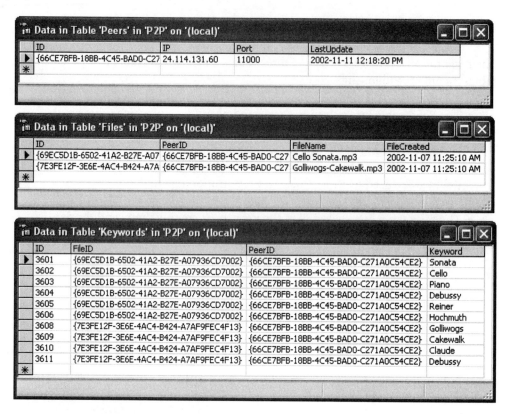

Figure 8-5. Sample registration data

All GUID values are generated by the peer and submitted to the server. This allows the peer to keep track of its shared files and quickly validate download requests, as you'll see in the next chapter.

TIP *If you want to test this database on your own system, you can use the SQL script that's included with the samples for this chapter. It automatically creates the database and the stored procedures described in the next section, provided you are using SQL Server 2000.*

Stored Procedures

The next step is to define a set of stored procedures that encapsulate some of the most common database tasks.

The AddPeer stored procedure inserts a new peer registration record in the database. RefreshPeer updates the LastUpdated field in the peer record. Every peer must call this method periodically to prevent their registration record from expiring.

```
CREATE Procedure AddPeer
(
    @ID    uniqueidentifier,
    @IP    nvarchar(15),
    @Port smallint
)
AS
INSERT INTO Peers
(
    ID, IP, Port, LastUpdate
)
VALUES
(
    @ID, @IP, @Port, GETDATE()
)
GO



CREATE Procedure RefreshPeer
(
    @ID    uniqueidentifier
)
AS
UPDATE Peers SET LastUpdate=GETDATE() WHERE ID=@ID
GO
```

Two more stored procedures, AddFile and AddKeyword, allow new catalog information to be added to the database.

```
CREATE Procedure AddFile
(
    @ID           uniqueidentifier,
    @PeerID       uniqueidentifier,
    @FileName     nvarchar(50),
    @FileCreated  datetime
)
AS
INSERT INTO Files
(
    ID, PeerID, FileName, FileCreated
)
VALUES
(
    @ID, @PeerID, @FileName, @FileCreated
```

```
)
GO


CREATE Procedure AddKeyword
(
    @FileID    uniqueidentifier,
    @PeerID    uniqueidentifier,
    @Keyword   nvarchar(50)
)
AS
INSERT INTO Keywords
(
    FileID, PeerID, Keyword
)
VALUES
(
    @FileID, @PeerID, @Keyword
)
GO
```

Finally, a DeletePeersAndFiles stored procedure handles the unregistration process, removing related records from the Files, Peers, and Keywords tables. The DeleteFiles stored procedure provides a similar function, but leaves the peer record intact. Its primary use is when updating the catalog.

```
CREATE Procedure DeletePeerAndFiles
(
    @ID    uniqueidentifier
)
AS
DELETE FROM Files WHERE PeerID = @ID
DELETE FROM Peers WHERE ID = @ID
DELETE FROM Keywords WHERE PeerID = @ID
GO


CREATE Procedure DeleteFiles
(
    @ID    uniqueidentifier
)
AS
```

```
DELETE FROM Files WHERE PeerID = @ID
DELETE FROM Keywords WHERE PeerID = @ID
GO
```

The database doesn't include a stored procedure for performing queries, because this step is easier to accomplish with a dynamically generated SQL statement that uses a variable number of WHERE clauses.

Creating the Database Class

The next step is to create a class that encapsulates all the data-access logic. The web service will then make use of this class to perform database tasks, rather than connect with the database directly. This separation makes it easier to debug, enhance, and optimize the data-access logic.

For maximum reusability, the data-access code could be implemented as a separate assembly. In our example, however, it's a part of the web service project.

The database code includes a Peer and SharedFile class, which models a row from the Peers and Files tables, respectively. The SharedFile class also includes information about the related peer.

```
Public Class Peer
    Public Guid As Guid
    Public IP As String
    Public Port As Integer
End Class

Public Class SharedFile
    Public Guid As Guid
    Public FileName As String
    Public FileCreated As Date
    Public Peer As New Peer()
    Public Keywords() As String
End Class
```

Neither of these classes uses full property procedures, because they aren't fully supported in a web service. If you were to add property procedure code, it might be used on the server side. However, it would be ignored on the client side, thus limiting its usefulness.

The database code could be separated into multiple classes (for example, a PeersDB, FilesDB, and KeywordsDB database). However, because there's a relatively small set of tasks that will be performed with the registration database, you can implement all methods in a single class without any confusion. Here's the basic framework for the class:

```
Public Class P2PDatabase

    Private ConnectionString As String

    Public Sub New()
        ConnectionString = ConfigurationSettings.AppSettings("DBConnection")
    End Sub

    Public Sub AddPeer(ByVal peer As Peer)
        ' (Code omitted.)
    End Sub

    Public Sub RefreshPeer(ByVal peer As Peer)
        ' (Code omitted.)
    End Sub

    Public Sub DeletePeerAndFiles(ByVal peer As Peer)
        ' (Code omitted.)
    End Sub

    Public Sub AddFileInfo(ByVal files() As SharedFile, ByVal peer As Peer)
        ' (Code omitted.)
    End Sub

    Public Function GetFileInfo(ByVal keywords() As String) As SharedFile()
        ' (Code omitted.)
    End Function

End Class
```

When a P2PDatabase instance is created, the connection string is retrieved from a configuration file. This will be the configuration associated with the application that's using the P2PDatabase class. In our example, this is the *web.config* file used by the web service.

```
<?xml version="1.0" encoding="utf-8" ?>

<configuration>
  <appSettings>
    <add key="DBConnection"
         value="Data Source=localhost;Initial Catalog=P2P;user ID=sa" />
```

```
        </appSettings>
    <system.web>
        <!-- Other settings omitted. -->
    </system.web>
</configuration>
```

The actual database code is quite straightforward. The basic pattern is to create a command for the corresponding stored procedure, add the required information as parameters, and execute the command directly. For example, here's the code used to register, update, and remove peer information:

```
Public Sub AddPeer(ByVal peer As Peer)

    ' Define command and connection.
    Dim con As New SqlConnection(ConnectionString)
    Dim cmd As New SqlCommand("AddPeer", con)
    cmd.CommandType = CommandType.StoredProcedure

    ' Add parameters.
    Dim param As SqlParameter
    param = cmd.Parameters.Add("@ID", SqlDbType.UniqueIdentifier)
    param.Value = peer.Guid
    param = cmd.Parameters.Add("@IP", SqlDbType.NVarChar, 15)
    param.Value = peer.IP
    param = cmd.Parameters.Add("@Port", SqlDbType.SmallInt)
    param.Value = peer.Port

    Try
        con.Open()
        cmd.ExecuteNonQuery()
    Finally
        con.Close()
    End Try

End Sub

Public Sub RefreshPeer(ByVal peer As Peer)

    ' Define command and connection.
    Dim con As New SqlConnection(ConnectionString)
    Dim cmd As New SqlCommand("RefreshPeer", con)
    cmd.CommandType = CommandType.StoredProcedure
```

```vb
        ' Add parameters.
        Dim param As SqlParameter
        param = cmd.Parameters.Add("@ID", SqlDbType.UniqueIdentifier)
        param.Value = peer.Guid

        Try
            con.Open()
            cmd.ExecuteNonQuery()
        Finally
            con.Close()
        End Try

    End Sub

    Public Sub DeletePeerAndFiles(ByVal peer As Peer)

        ' Define command and connection.
        Dim con As New SqlConnection(ConnectionString)
        Dim cmd As New SqlCommand("DeletePeerAndFiles", con)
        cmd.CommandType = CommandType.StoredProcedure

        ' Add parameters.
        Dim param As SqlParameter
        param = cmd.Parameters.Add("@ID", SqlDbType.UniqueIdentifier)
        param.Value = peer.Guid

        Try
            con.Open()
            cmd.ExecuteNonQuery()
        Finally
            con.Close()
        End Try

    End Sub
```

> **NOTE** *Even if you're new to ADO.NET coding, the previous code sample is fairly self-explanatory. There are numerous books dedicated to the basics of ADO.NET programming, including several titles from Apress.*

Note that if an error occurs, the connection is closed, but the error isn't handled. Instead, it's allowed to propagate back to the caller (in this case, the web service), which will handle it accordingly. Another option would be to catch all errors and throw a higher-level exception, such as an ApplicationException, with the original exception wrapped inside.

The code for the AddFileInfo() method is lengthier because it adds multiple records: one new file record, and one keyword record for each keyword string in the File.Keywords array. All the work is performed with the same open connection, thereby reducing the overhead required for the whole process. The AddFileInfo() method also clears the current registration information before it begins by calling the DeleteFiles stored procedure. This ensures that the same peer can't accidentally register the same file twice.

```
Public Sub AddFileInfo(ByVal files() As SharedFile, ByVal peer As Peer)

    ' Define commands and connection.
    Dim con As New SqlConnection(ConnectionString)
    Dim cmdDelete As New SqlCommand("DeleteFiles", con)
    cmdDelete.CommandType = CommandType.StoredProcedure

    Dim cmdFile As New SqlCommand("AddFile", con)
    cmdFile.CommandType = CommandType.StoredProcedure

    Dim cmdKeyword As New SqlCommand("AddKeyword", con)
    cmdKeyword.CommandType = CommandType.StoredProcedure

    Dim param As SqlParameter

    Try
        con.Open()

        ' Delete current registration information.
        param = cmdDelete.Parameters.Add("@ID", SqlDbType.UniqueIdentifier)
        param.Value = peer.Guid
        cmdDelete.ExecuteNonQuery()

        Dim File As SharedFile
        For Each File In files

            ' Add parameters.
            cmdFile.Parameters.Clear()
            param = cmdFile.Parameters.Add("@ID", SqlDbType.UniqueIdentifier)
            param.Value = File.Guid
            param = cmdFile.Parameters.Add("@PeerID", SqlDbType.UniqueIdentifier)
```

```
                    param.Value = peer.Guid
                    param = cmdFile.Parameters.Add("@FileName", SqlDbType.NVarChar, 50)
                    param.Value = File.FileName
                    param = cmdFile.Parameters.Add("@FileCreated", SqlDbType.DateTime)
                    param.Value = File.FileCreated

                    cmdFile.ExecuteNonQuery()

                    ' Add keywords for this file.
                    ' Note that the lack of any keywords isn't  considered
                    ' to be an error condition (although it could be).
                    Dim Keyword As String
                    For Each Keyword In File.Keywords
                        cmdKeyword.Parameters.Clear()
                        param = cmdKeyword.Parameters.Add("@FileID", _
                                SqlDbType.UniqueIdentifier)
                        param.Value = File.Guid
                        param = cmdKeyword.Parameters.Add("@PeerID", _
                                SqlDbType.UniqueIdentifier)
                        param.Value = peer.Guid
                        param = cmdKeyword.Parameters.Add("@Keyword", _
                                SqlDbType.NVarChar, 50)
                        param.Value = Keyword
                        cmdKeyword.ExecuteNonQuery()
                    Next
                Next

        Finally
            con.Close()
        End Try

    End Sub
```

Finally, the GetFileInfo() method creates a dynamic SQL query based on a list of search keywords. The query joins the Files, Peers, and Keywords tables in order to retrieve all the required peer-connectivity and file information. For each keyword, a WHERE clause is appended to the SQL expression. For maximum performance, this process is performed with a StringBuilder object instead of through ordinary string concatenation.

```vb
Public Function GetFileInfo(ByVal keywords() As String) As SharedFile()

    ' Build dynamic query string.
    Dim DynamicSQL As New System.Text.StringBuilder( _
     "SELECT DISTINCT Files.ID AS FileID, Peers.ID AS PeerID, " & _
     "FileName, FileCreated, IP, Port " & _
     "FROM Files, Keywords, Peers " & _
     "WHERE Files.ID = keywords.FileID AND Files.PeerID = Peers.ID AND ")

    Dim i As Integer
    For i = 1 To keywords.Length
        DynamicSQL.Append("Keyword LIKE '%" + keywords(i - 1) + "%' ")
        If Not (i = keywords.Length) Then DynamicSQL.Append("OR ")
    Next

    ' Define command and connection.
    Dim con As New SqlConnection(ConnectionString)
    Dim cmd As New SqlCommand(DynamicSQL.ToString(), con)
    Dim r As SqlDataReader
    Dim Files As New ArrayList()

    Try
        con.Open()
        r = cmd.ExecuteReader()
        Do While (r.Read())
            Dim File As New SharedFile()
            File.Guid = r("FileID")
            File.FileName = r("FileName")
            File.FileCreated = r("FileCreated")
            File.Peer.IP = r("IP")
            File.Peer.Port = r("Port")
            File.Peer.Guid = r("PeerID")
            Files.Add(File)
        Loop
    Finally
        con.Close()
    End Try

    ' Convert the generic ArrayList to an array of SharedFile objects.
    Return CType(Files.ToArray(GetType(SharedFile)), SharedFile())

End Function
```

Results from the query are retrieved using a DataReader. Each time a matching file is found, a new SharedFile object is created and added to an ArrayList. Once all the matching files are found, the ArrayList is converted to a strongly typed SharedFile array, and returned.

> **TIP** *You might want to use the SQL statement SET ROWCOUNT before you execute the query. This way, you can limit the total number of requests and ensure that the discovery service won't be swamped by returning tens of thousands of results to a poorly worded query. For example, the SQL statement SET ROWCOUNT 100 caps search results to the first 100 rows that match the query.*

The Discovery Service

Now that the actual data-access logic has been written, the actual discovery web service will need very little code. For the most part, its methods simply wrap the P2PDatabase component. All exceptions are caught, logged, and suppressed, so that sensitive information will not be returned to the client, who is in no position to correct low-level database errors anyway.

A typical interaction with the discovery service goes as follows:

1. The client generates a new GUID to identify itself, records its current IP address and port, and calls Register() with this information.

2. The client inspects the files that it's sharing, creates the keywords lists, and calls PublishFiles() to submit the catalog.

3. After this point, the client calls RefreshRegistration() periodically, to prevent its login information from expiring.

4. Optionally, the client calls SearchForFile() with any queries.

5. The client ends the session by calling Unregister().

The complete web-service code is shown here:

```
Public Class DiscoveryService
    Inherits System.Web.Services.WebService
```

```vbnet
' This object will be created with each new method request.
' (This isn't a problem because P2PDatabase is stateless.)
Private DB As New P2PDatabase()

<WebMethod()> _
Public Function Register(ByVal peer As Peer) As Boolean

    Try
        DB.AddPeer(peer)
        Return True
    Catch
        Return False
    End Try

End Function

<WebMethod()> _
Public Function RefreshRegistration(ByVal peer As Peer) As Boolean

    Try
        DB.RefreshPeer(peer)
        Return True
    Catch err As Exception
        Trace.Write(err.ToString)
        Return False
    End Try

End Function

<WebMethod()> _
Public Sub Unregister(ByVal peer As Peer)

    Try
        DB.DeletePeerAndFiles(peer)
    Catch err As Exception
        Trace.Write(err.ToString)
    End Try

End Sub

<WebMethod()> _
Public Function PublishFiles(ByVal files() As SharedFile, _
  ByVal peer As Peer) As Boolean
```

```
     Try
          DB.AddFileInfo(files, peer)
          Return True
     Catch err As Exception
          Trace.Write(err.ToString)
          Return False
     End Try

End Function


<WebMethod()> _
Public Function SearchForFile(ByVal keywords() As String) As SharedFile()

     Try
          Return DB.GetFileInfo(keywords)
     Catch err As Exception
          Trace.Write(err.ToString)
          Dim EmptyArray() As SharedFile = {}
          Return EmptyArray
     End Try

End Function



End Class
```

To improve performance, you might consider using ASP.NET caching. However, as queries are likely to differ quite a bit, and the list of keywords stored in the database can grow dramatically, it's difficult to implement an effective caching strategy.

There's one function that the web service doesn't provide: removing expired peer information. In Chapter 5, you saw how this type of work can be performed on a dedicated thread. However, as web services are stateless, it's not easy to run other code asynchronously. Instead, you would need to create a separate component that runs on the server (perhaps a Windows service), and periodically scans the database for Peer records beyond a certain age limit. It would then remove these records using the DeletePeerAndFiles stored procedure. This logic is easy to implement and could be added to the P2PDatabase class.

Testing the Discovery Service

Once you've completed the service, you can load the corresponding *.asmx* page into Internet Explorer to see an automatically generated test page that lists the web methods exposed by this web service (see Figure 8-6). However, you won't be able to test them directly because they require a client that can create and configure the custom Peer and SharedFile objects.

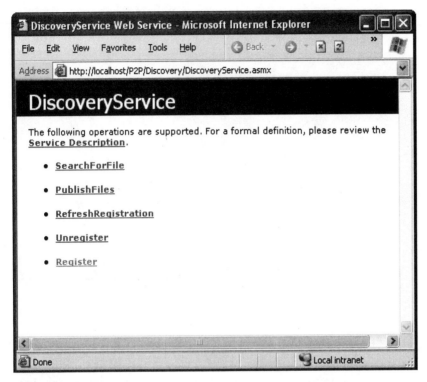

Figure 8-6. Viewing web-service methods in Internet Explorer

To put the directory service to a real test, you need to build a dedicated client application, such as the one presented in the next chapter. In this case, you'll probably want to debug your web service and client application at the same time. To do so, right-click the project name in the Solution Explorer, and select Properties. Then, navigate to the Configuration Properties → Debugging node, and choose "Wait for an external process to connect" (as shown in Figure 8-7). Now, when you run your web-service project, Visual Studio .NET will load the debugging symbols and wait for a client request. You can use the full set of debugging tools to watch the web service as it reacts, including breakpoints, variable watches, and the command window.

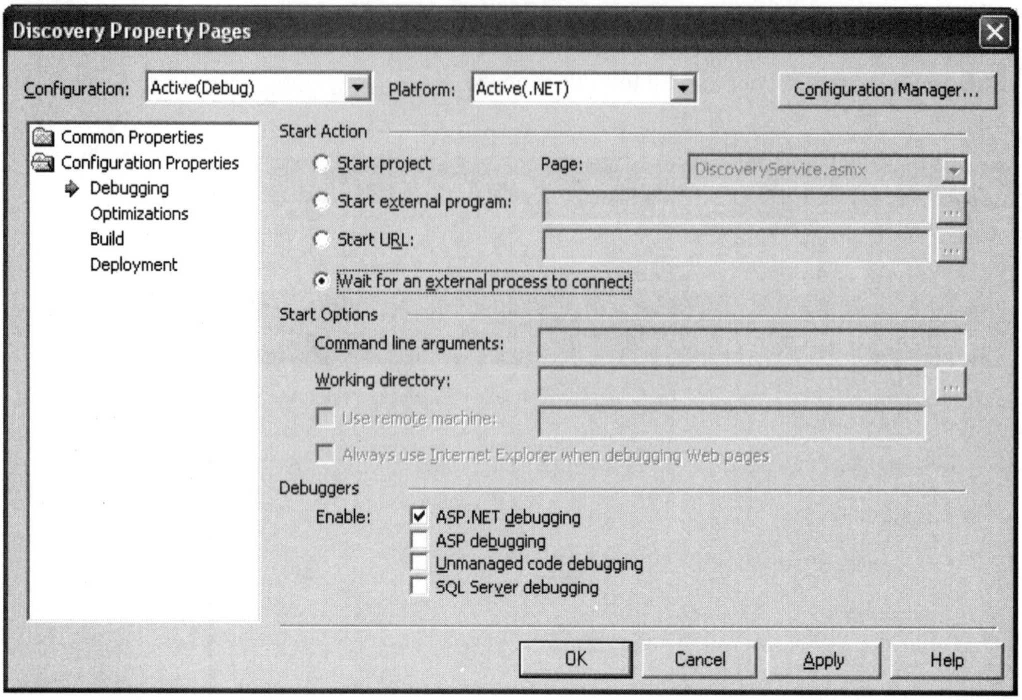

Figure 8-7. Configuring web-service debugging

The Last Word

This chapter laid the groundwork for the ambitious file-sharing application that we'll develop in the next chapter. Here you learned how to use the .NET web-service functionality and a back-end database to create a highly scalable registry service. Best of all, the code is carefully separated into multiple layers through stored procedures and a dedicated database component, thereby ensuring that it can be easily altered and extended in the future.

It's important to realize that the discovery process isn't standardized in peer-to-peer applications. There are many other ways you can organize or customize a registration database. For example, the registration database used in this example stores enough data for peers to make direct TCP/IP connections. However, if you wanted to use some other type of communication protocol, you might store different information. Chapter 10 develops a discovery service that uses Remoting. It simply serializes ObjRef objects to a binary database field. A peer can then read this information, reconstruct a proxy object, and use it directly through the .NET Remoting platform services.

CHAPTER 9

Building a
File Sharer

IN THE LAST CHAPTER, you learned how to catalog peers and resources with a
discovery web service. In this chapter, we'll develop a sophisticated file-sharing
application that uses the discovery service.

The file-sharing client is a lengthy example, and it will take the entire
chapter to dissect the code. This complexity is a result of the multiple roles that
a peer-to-peer application must play. A peer-to-peer client needs to periodically
submit registration information to a central web service, serve files to hordes
of eager peers, and retrieve more files from a different set of peers on the
network—potentially all at once. The only way to handle these issues is with
careful, disciplined threading code.

An Overview of FileSwapper

The FileSwapper application is built around a single form (see Figure 9-1). This
form uses multiple tables and allows users to initiate searches, configure settings, and monitor uploads and downloads.

FileSwapper divides its functionality into a small army of classes, including
the following:

- SwapperClient, which is the main form class. It delegates as much work as
  possible to other classes and uses a timer to periodically update its login
  information with the discovery service.

- Global, which includes the data that's required application-wide (for
  example, registry settings).

- App, which includes shared methods for some of the core application
  tasks such as Login(), Logout(), and PublishFiles(), and also provides
  access to the various application threads.

- KeywordUtil and MP3Util, which provide a few shared helper methods for
  analyzing MP3 files and parsing the keywords that describe them.

- RegistrySettings, which provides access to the application's configuration settings, along with methods for saving and loading them.

- ListViewItemWrapper, which performs thread-safe updating of a ListViewItem.

- Search, which contacts the discovery service with a search request on a separate thread (allowing long-running searches to be easily interrupted).

- FileServer and FileUpload, which manage the incoming connections and transfer shared files to interested peers.

- FileDownloadQueue and FileDownloadClient, which manage in-progress downloads from other peers.

- Messages, which defines constants used for peer-to-peer communication.

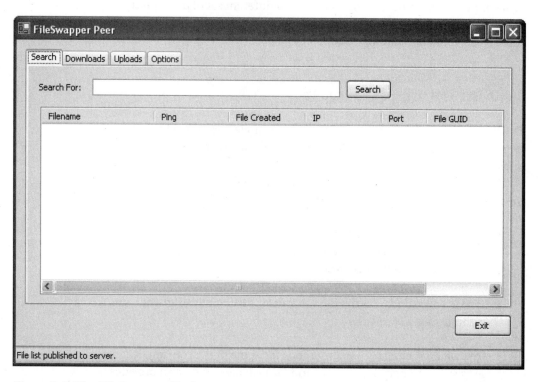

Figure 9-1. The FileSwapper display

The file-transfer process is fairly easy. Once a peer locates another peer that has an interesting file, it opens a direct TCP/IP connection and sends a download request. Conceptually, this code is quite similar to some of the examples shown in Chapter 7. However, the application is still fairly complex because it needs to handle several tasks that require multithreading at once. Because every peer acts as both a client and a server, every application needs to simultaneously monitor for new incoming connections that are requesting files. In addition, the application must potentially initiate new outgoing connections to download other files. Not only does the client need to perform uploading and downloading at the same time, but it also needs to be able to perform multiple uploads or downloads at once (within reason). In order to accommodate this design, a separate thread needs to work continuously to schedule new uploads or downloads as required.

Figure 9-2 shows a simplified view of threads in the FileSwapper application. Note that for the most part, independent threads run code in separate objects to prevent confusion. However, this isn't a requirement, and a single object could be executed on multiple threads or a single thread could run the code from multiple objects.

The full FileSwapper application can be downloaded with the code for this chapter. In this chapter, we'll walk through all the threading and networking code, but omit more trivial details such as namespace imports and the automatically generated Windows designer code. We'll begin by examining some of the building blocks such as the classes used to register the peer, to read configuration information, and to process MP3 files. Next, you'll look at the code for searching available peers. Finally, you'll see the multithreaded code for handling simultaneous uploads and downloads over the network.

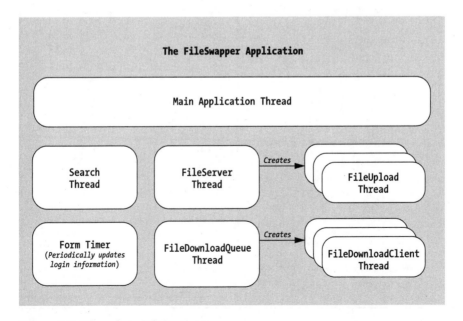

Figure 9-2. Threads in FileSwapper

The Discovery Service Web Reference

The FileSwapper requires a web reference to the discovery service in order to work. To add this, right-click the project name in the Solution Explorer, and choose Add Web Reference. Type the full path to the virtual directory and web service *.asmx* file in the Address field of the Add Web Reference window. When you press Enter, the list of web-service methods from the Internet Explorer test page will appear, as shown in Figure 9-3.

Click Add Reference to generate the proxy class and add it to your project. The proxy class should not be manually modified once it's created, and so it isn't shown in the Solution Explorer. However, you can examine it by choosing Project ➤ Show All Files from the Visual Studio .NET window. The proxy class is always named *Reference.vb*, as shown in Figure 9-4. We won't consider the proxy class code in this book, although it makes interesting study if you'd like to understand a little more about how web services convert .NET objects into SOAP messages and back.

If you need to change a web service, you must recompile it and then update the client's web reference. To do so, right-click the web-service reference in the Solution Explorer, and choose Update Web Reference.

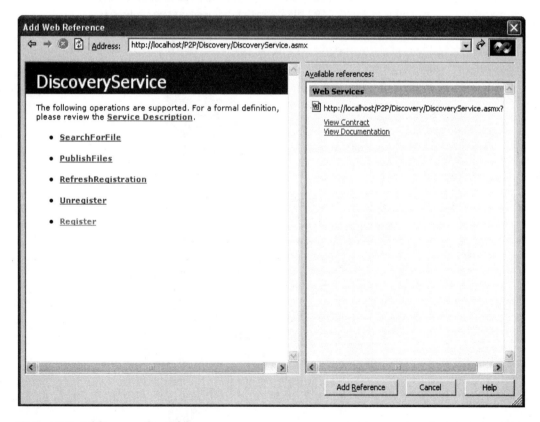

Figure 9-3. Adding a web reference

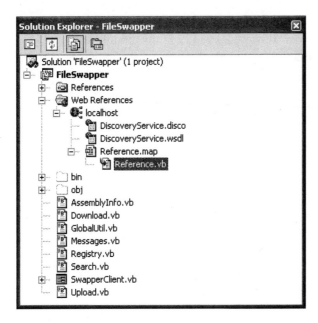

Figure 9-4. The hidden proxy class

In the remainder of this chapter, we'll walk through the FileSwapper code class-by-class, and discuss the key design decisions.

> **TIP** *If you click on a web reference in the Solution Explorer, you can find a property called Url Behavior in the Properties window. This property is set to static by default, in which case a fixed URL is set for the discovery service and added to the generated proxy class code. If you change the Url Behavior property to dynamic, an application setting will be added to the client application's configuration file with the web-service URL. This way, if you move the web service to another server you only need to change the configuration file, rather than recompile the client application.*

Global Data and Tasks

The FileSwapper application uses two classes that consist of shared members: Global and App. These classes act like global modules and are available from any location in the FileSwapper code. That means that you don't need to create an instance of these classes—instead, their properties and methods are always available and you can access them through the class name.

The Global class stores data that's required by multiple objects in the application. As with any application, it's always best to keep the amount of global data to a minimum. A large number of global variables usually indicates a poor structure that really isn't object-oriented. All the data in the Global class is held using public shared variables, making it widely available. For example, any code in the application can use the Global.Identity property to access information about the current computer's IP address and port number settings.

Here's the full code for the Global class:

```
Public Class Global

    ' Contains information about the current peer.
    Public Shared LoggedIn As Boolean = False
    Public Shared Identity As New Peer()

    ' Lists files that are available for other peers.
    Public Shared SharedFiles() As SharedFile

    ' Provides access to configuration settings that are stored in the registry.
    Public Shared Settings As New RegistrySettings()

End Class
```

Though these variables are always available, some of them still need to be set at startup before they contain any useful information. For example, the Identity, SharedFiles, and Settings variables all begin in a default, empty state.

The App class also relies on shared variables to store a common set of information. It actually stores references to three separate objects, each of which will be executed on an independent thread. Using the App class, your startup code can easily initialize the threads on startup and abort them when the application is about to end. The App class also includes a private shared variable that references the web-service proxy. This ensures that no other part of the application can access the discovery service directly—instead, the application must call one of the App class methods.

Here's the outline for the App class, with all its public and private member variables:

```
Public Class App

    ' Holds a reference to the web-service proxy.
    Private Shared Discovery As New DiscoveryService()
```

```
Public Shared SearchThread As Search
Public Shared DownwnloadThread As FileDownloadQueue
Public Shared UploadThread As FileServer

' (Code omitted.)
```

End Class

The App class also defines five higher-level methods that deal with registration. First, the App.Login() method retrieves the IP address of the current computer, configures the Global.Identity property accordingly, and logs in to the discovery web service.

```
Public Shared Sub Login()
    Global.Identity.Guid = Guid.NewGuid
    Global.Identity.IP = _
      Dns.GetHostByName(Dns.GetHostName).AddressList(0).ToString()

    Global.LoggedIn = Discovery.Register(Global.Identity)
End Sub
```

The App.Logout() method uses the Global.Identity information to unregister the peer, provided the peer is currently logged in. Similarly, the App.Refresh Login() method resubmits the Global.Identity information to prevent the peer from expiring from the discovery service.

```
Public Shared Sub Logout()
    If Global.LoggedIn Then Discovery.Unregister(Global.Identity)
End Sub

Public Shared Sub RefreshLogin()
    If Global.LoggedIn Then
        Discovery.RefreshRegistration(Global.Identity)
    End If
End Sub
```

The App.PublishFiles() method (shown next) examines files in the local share path and creates a catalog, which it assigns to the Global.SharedFiles variable. The PublishFiles() method retrieves the share path from the directory specified in the registry and examines the file extension to determine the type of file. Depending on the application settings, non-MP3 files may be ignored. Temporary files (files with the extension *.tmp*) are always ignored because they most likely correspond to an in-progress download. Here's the code for the PublishFiles() method:

```
Public Shared Function PublishFiles() As Boolean
    Try
        Dim Dir As New DirectoryInfo(Global.Settings.SharePath)
        Dim Files() As FileInfo = Dir.GetFiles()
        Dim FileList As New ArrayList()
        Dim File As FileInfo
        Dim IsMP3 As Boolean

        For Each File In Files
            IsMP3 = Path.GetExtension(File.Name).ToLower() = ".mp3"

            If Path.GetExtension(File.Name).ToLower() = ".tmp" Then
                ' Ignore all temporary files.
            ElseIf (Not IsMP3) And Global.Settings.ShareMP3Only Then
                ' Ignore non-MP3 files depending on setting.
            Else
                Dim SharedFile As New SharedFile()
                SharedFile.Guid = Guid.NewGuid()
                SharedFile.FileName = File.Name
                SharedFile.FileCreated = File.CreationTime

                If IsMP3 Then
                    SharedFile.Keywords = MP3Util.GetMP3Keywords(File.FullName)
                Else
                    ' Determine some other way to set keywords,
                    ' perhaps by file name or file
                    ' type.
                    ' The default (no keywords) will prevent the
                    ' file from appearing in a search.
                End If

                FileList.Add(SharedFile)
            End If
        Next

        Global.SharedFiles = CType(FileList.ToArray(GetType(SharedFile)), _
            SharedFile())
        Return Discovery.PublishFiles(Global.SharedFiles, Global.Identity)

    Catch Err As Exception
        MessageBox.Show(Err.ToString())
    End Try
End Function
```

If you're using non-MP3 files, you'll need to add code to determine a set of valid keywords. This code might parse the file name or look for data inside the file. In the case of MP3 files, the code retrieves the tag data using the utility methods shown in the next section.

Finally, the App.SearchForFile() method simply wraps the web method of the same name:

```
Public Shared Function SearchForFile(ByVal keywords() As String) As SharedFile()
    Return Discovery.SearchForFile(keywords)
End Function
```

Utility Functions

There are three utility classes in the FileSwapper: RegistrySettings, MP3Util, and KeywordUtil. All of them use shared methods to provide helper functions.

The first class, RegistrySettings, wraps access to the Windows registry. It allows the application to store and retrieve machine-specific information. You could replace this class with code that reads and writes settings in an application configuration file, but the drawback would be that multiple users couldn't load the same client application file from a network (as they would end up sharing the same configuration file).

The RegistrySettings class provides five settings as public variables and two methods. The Load() method retrieves the values from the specified key and configures the public variables. The Save() method stores the current values in the appropriate locations. The RegistrySettings class also hard-codes several pieces of information, including the first-run defaults (which are used if no preexisting registry information is found), and the path used for storing registry settings (*HKEY_LOCAL_MACHINE\Software\FileSwapper\Settings*). This information could also be drawn from an application configuration file.

```
Public Class RegistrySettings

    Public SharePath As String
    Public ShareMP3Only As Boolean
    Public MaxUploadThreads As Integer
    Public MaxDownloadThreads As Integer
    Public Port As Integer

    Public Sub Load()
        Dim Key As RegistryKey
        Key = Microsoft.Win32.Registry.LocalMachine.CreateSubKey( _
            "Software\FilesSwapper\Settings")
```

```
        SharePath = Key.GetValue("SharePath", Application.StartupPath)
        Port = CType(Key.GetValue("LocalPort", "8000"), Integer)
        ShareMP3Only = CType(Key.GetValue("OnlyShareMP3", "True"), Boolean)
        MaxUploadThreads = CType(Key.GetValue("MaxUploadThreads", "2"), Integer)
        MaxDownloadThreads = CType(Key.GetValue("MaxDownloadThreads", "2"), _
            Integer)
    End Sub

    Public Sub Save()
        Dim Key As RegistryKey
        Key = Microsoft.Win32.Registry.LocalMachine.CreateSubKey( _
            "Software\FilesSwapper\Settings")

        Key.SetValue("SharePath", SharePath)
        Key.SetValue("LocalPort", Port.ToString())
        Key.SetValue("OnlyShareMP3", ShareMP3Only.ToString())
        Key.SetValue("MaxUploadThreads", MaxUploadThreads.ToString())
        Key.SetValue("MaxDownloadThreads", MaxDownloadThreads.ToString())
    End Sub

End Class
```

> **TIP** *Instead of including a Load() and Save() method, you could create property procedures for the RegistrySettings class that perform this work. Then, whenever you set a property, the value will be committed, and whenever you access a value, it will be retrieved from the registry. This adds additional overhead, but it's minor.*

The MP3Util class provides the functionality for retrieving MP3 tag data from a file. The class provides two shared functions. The first, GetMP3Keywords(), opens a file, looks for the 128-byte ID3v2 tag that should be found at the end of the file, and verifies that it starts with the word "TAG". If so, individual values for the artist, album, and song title are retrieved using the second method, GetTagData(), which converts the binary data to a string using ASCII encoding information. All the retrieved data is delimited with spaces and combined into a long string using a StringBuilder. This string is then parsed into a list of keywords.

```vbnet
Public Class MP3Util

    Public Shared Function GetMP3Keywords(ByVal filename As String) As String()
        Dim fs As New FileStream(filename, FileMode.Open)

        ' Read the MP3 tag.
        fs.Seek(0 - 128, SeekOrigin.End)
        Dim Tag(2) As Byte
        fs.Read(Tag, 0, 3)

        If Encoding.ASCII.GetString(Tag).Trim() = "TAG" Then

            Dim KeywordString As New StringBuilder()
            ' Title.
            KeywordString.Append(GetTagData(fs, 30))
            ' Artist.
            KeywordString.Append(" ")
            KeywordString.Append(GetTagData(fs, 30))
            ' Album.
            KeywordString.Append(" ")
            KeywordString.Append(GetTagData(fs, 30))
            ' Year.
            KeywordString.Append(" ")
            KeywordString.Append(GetTagData(fs, 4))

            fs.Close()
            Return KeywordUtil.ParseKeywords(KeywordString.ToString())

        Else
            fs.Close()
            Dim EmptyArray() As String = {}
            Return EmptyArray
        End If
    End Function

    Public Shared Function GetTagData(ByVal stream As Stream, _
      ByVal length As Integer) As String
        Dim Bytes(length - 1) As Byte
        stream.Read(Bytes, 0, length)

        Dim TagData As String = Encoding.ASCII.GetString(Bytes)
```

```
    ' Trim nulls.
    Dim TrimChars() As Char = {" ", vbNullChar}
    TagData = TagData.Trim(TrimChars)
    Return TagData
  End Function

End Class
```

> **NOTE** *The GetTagData() includes a very important final step, which removes all null characters from the string. Without this step, the string will contain embedded nulls. If you try to submit this data to the discovery web service, the proxy class will throw an exception, because it won't be able to format the strings into a SOAP message.*

The final utility class is KeywordUtil. It includes a single shared method—ParseKeywords()—that takes a string which contains a list of keywords, and splits it into words wherever a space, comma, or period is found. This step is performed using the built-in String.Split() method. Thus, if you index an MP3 file that has the artist "Claude Debussy," the keyword list will include two entries: "Claude" and "Debussy". This allows a peer to search with both or only one of these terms.

At the same time that ParseKeywords() splits the keyword list, it also removes extraneous strings, such as noise words ("the", "for", "and", and so on). You may want to add additional noise words to improve its indexing. In addition, strings that include only a delimiter are removed (for example, a string containing a single blank space). This is necessary because the String.Split() method doesn't deal well with multiple spaces in a row. To make the processing logic easy, keywords are added into an ArrayList on the fly and converted into a strongly typed string array when the process is complete.

```
Public Class KeywordUtil

    Private Shared NoiseWords() As String = {"the", "for", "and", "or"}
    Public Shared Function ParseKeywords(ByVal keywordString As String) _
      As String()
        ' Split the list of words into an array.
        Dim Keywords() As String
        Dim Delimeters() As Char = {" ", ",", "."}
        Keywords = keywordString.Split(Delimeters)
```

```
        ' Add each valid word into an ArrayList.
        Dim FilteredWords As New ArrayList()
        Dim Word As String
        For Each Word In Keywords
            If Word.Trim() <> "" And Word.Length > 1 Then
                If Array.IndexOf(NoiseWords, Word.ToLower()) = -1 Then
                    FilteredWords.Add(Word)
                End If
            End If
        Next

        ' Convert the ArrayList into a normal string array.
        Return FilteredWords.ToArray(GetType(String))
    End Function

End Class
```

Thread-Safe ListViewItem Updates

The FileSwapper is a highly asynchronous application that provides real-time status information for many tasks. In several places in code, a user-interface operation needs to be marshaled to the user-interface thread in order to prevent potential errors. This is usually the case when updating one of the three main ListView controls in the FileSwapper: the upload status display, the download status display, and the search-result listing.

For the first two cases, there's a direct mapping between threads and ListView items. For example, every concurrent upload requires exactly one ListViewItem to display ongoing status information. To simplify the task of creating and updating the ListViewItem, FileSwapper includes a wrapper class called ListViewItemWrapper. ListViewItemWrapper performs two tasks. When it's first instantiated, it creates and adds a ListViewItem on the correct thread using the private AddListViewItem() procedure. Second, when a user calls the ChangeStatus() method, it updates the status column of a ListViewItem on the correct thread using the private RefreshListViewItem() procedure. In order to use these subroutines with the Control.Invoke() method, they cannot take any parameters. Thus, the information required to create or update the ListViewItem must be stored in temporary private variables, such as RowName and RowStatus.

Here's the complete code for the ListViewItemWrapper:

```vbnet
Public Class ListViewItemWrapper

    Private ListView As ListView
    Private ListViewItem As ListViewItem

    ' These variables are used to store temporary information required when a call
    ' is marshaled to the user-interface thread.
    Private RowName As String
    Private RowStatus As String

    Public Sub New(ByVal listView As ListView, ByVal rowName As String, _
      ByVal rowStatus As String)
        Me.ListView = listView
        Me.RowName = rowName
        Me.RowStatus = rowStatus

        ' Marshal the operation to the user-interface thread.
        listView.Invoke(New MethodInvoker(AddressOf AddListViewItem))
    End Sub

    ' This code executes on the user-interface thread.
    Private Sub AddListViewItem()
        ' Create new ListView item.
        ListViewItem = New ListViewItem(RowName)
        ListViewItem.SubItems.Add(RowStatus)
        ListView.Items.Add(ListViewItem)
    End Sub

    Public Sub ChangeStatus(ByVal rowStatus As String)
        Me.RowStatus = rowStatus

        ' Marshal the operation to the user-interface thread.
        ListView.Invoke(New MethodInvoker(AddressOf RefreshListViewItem))
    End Sub

    ' This code executes on the user-interface thread.
    Private Sub RefreshListViewItem()
        ListViewItem.SubItems(1).Text = RowStatus
    End Sub

End Class
```

The ListViewItemWrapper is a necessity in our peer-to-peer application, because the downloading and uploading operations won't be performed on the main application threads. However, you'll find that this class is useful in many Windows applications. Any time you need to create a highly asynchronous interface, it makes sense to use this control wrapper design pattern.

The Main Form

We've now covered enough of the FileSwapper code to examine the main form, which acts as the hub of the application.

When the main form first loads, it reads the registry, updates the configuration window with the retrieved settings, starts the other threads, and then logs in, as shown here:

```
Private Sub SwapperClient_Load(ByVal sender As Object, _
  ByVal e As System.EventArgs) Handles MyBase.Load

    Me.Show()
    Me.Refresh()

    ' Read the registry.
    Global.Settings.Load()
    txtSharePath.Text = Global.Settings.SharePath
    txtPort.Text = Global.Settings.Port
    chkMP3Only.Checked = Global.Settings.ShareMP3Only
    txtUploads.Text = Global.Settings.MaxUploadThreads
    txtDownloads.Text = Global.Settings.MaxDownloadThreads

    ' Create the search, download, and upload objects.
    ' They will create their own threads.
    App.SearchThread = New Search(lstSearchResults)
    App.DownwnloadThread = New FileDownloadQueue(lstDownloads)
    App.UploadThread = New FileServer(lstUploads)
    App.UploadThread.StartWaitForRequest()

    ' Start the login process.
    Global.Identity.Port = Global.Settings.Port
    DoLogin()

End Sub
```

The login is actually a multiple step procedure. First, the peer information is submitted with the App.Login() method. Next, the file catalog is created and submitted with the App.PublishFiles() method. Finally, the timer is enabled to automatically update the login information as required.

While the peer is sending data to the discovery web service, the mouse pointer is changed to an hourglass, and the text in the status bar panel is updated to reflect what's taking place.

```
Private Sub DoLogin()

    Me.Cursor = Cursors.WaitCursor

    ' Log in.
    pnlState.Text = "Trying to log in."
    App.Login()
    If Not Global.LoggedIn Then
        pnlState.Text = "Not logged in."
        Return
    End If

    ' Submit list of files.
    pnlState.Text = "Sending file information..."
    If App.PublishFiles() Then
        pnlState.Text = "File list published to server."
    Else
        pnlState.Text = "Could not publish file list."
    End If

    ' Refresh login information every five minutes.
    tmrRefreshRegistration.Start()

    Me.Cursor = Cursors.Default

End Sub
```

The timer fires every 300,000 milliseconds (every five minutes) to update the login information:

```
Private Sub tmRefreshRegistration_Tick(ByVal sender As System.Object, _
    ByVal e As System.EventArgs) Handles tmrRefreshRegistration.Tick

    App.RefreshLogin()

End Sub
```

Currently, no steps are taken to refresh the published file list, although you can add this functionality easily using a timer, or by monitoring the file system for changes.

When the form closes, the client is automatically logged out, and the threads are terminated:

```
Private Sub SwapperClient_Closed(ByVal sender As Object, _
  ByVal e As System.EventArgs) Handles MyBase.Closed


        App.Logout()
        App.DownwnloadThread.Abort()
        App.SearchThread.Abort()
        App.UploadThread.Abort()


End Sub
```

In this case, the code is actually not aborting the thread directly. Instead, it's calling a custom Abort() method that's provided in each of the threaded classes. The code in this method then terminates processing in the most reasonable manner, as you'll see later in this chapter.

To be even more cautious, the FileSwapper also traps the Application.UnhandledException event. This event fires if an exception is about to terminate your application (typically because it isn't handled with a Catch block). You won't be able to stop the application from ending, but you'll be able to perform some last minute cleanup such as attempting to log out of the discovery service, or logging information about the error.

```
Public Sub UnhandledException(ByVal sender As Object, _
  ByVal e As UnhandledExceptionEventArgs)

  ' Log the error.
  Trace.Write(e.ExceptionObject.ToString())

  ' Log out of the discovery service.
  App.Logout()

End Sub
```

This event handler is coded inside the main form and attached shortly after a login:

```
Private Sub SwapperClient_Load(ByVal sender As Object, _
    ByVal e As System.EventArgs) Handles MyBase.Load

    ' (Other code omitted.)
    DoLogin()

    AddHandler AppDomain.CurrentDomain.UnhandledException, _
        AddressOf UnhandledException

End Sub
```

FileSwapper Configuration

The FileSwapper application includes a configuration window (see Figure 9-5)
that allows the registry settings to be configured by the user. This window doesn't
perform any validation, although you could add this code easily.

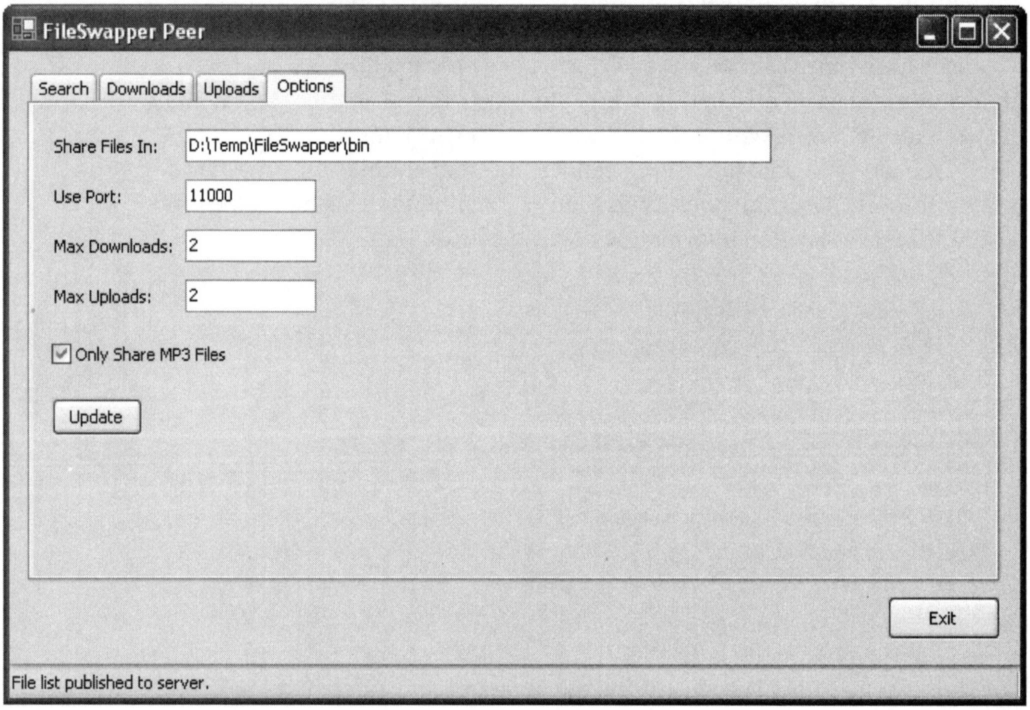

Figure 9-5. FileSwapper configuration settings

When the user clicks the Update() button, these settings are saved in the registry. The peer then logs out and logs back in to the discovery service.

```
Private Sub cmdUpdate_Click(ByVal sender As System.Object, _
  ByVal e As System.EventArgs) Handles cmdUpdate.Click

    Global.Settings.Port = Val(txtPort.Text)
    Global.Settings.SharePath = txtSharePath.Text
    Global.Settings.ShareMP3Only = chkMP3Only.Checked
    Global.Settings.MaxDownloadThreads = Val(txtDownloads.Text)
    Global.Settings.MaxUploadThreads = Val(txtUploads.Text)

    Global.Settings.Save()

    ' Log back in.
    App.Logout()
    Global.Identity.Port = Global.Settings.Port
    DoLogin()

End Sub
```

Searches

The Search class is the first of three custom-threaded objects used by FileSwapper. As part of any search, FileSwapper attempts to contact each peer with a network ping (the equivalent of asking "are you there?"). FileSwapper measures the time it takes for a response and any errors that occur, and then displays this information in the search results. This allows the user to decide where to send a download request, depending on which peer is fastest.

The drawback of this approach is that pinging each peer could take a long time, especially if some peers are unreachable. This in itself isn't a problem, provided the user has some way to cancel a long-running search and start a new one. To implement this approach, the Search class uses custom threading code.

Threading the Search class may seem easy, but it runs into the classic user-interface problem. In order to display the results in the ListView, the user-interface code must be marshaled to the main application thread using the Control.Invoke() method. This isn't difficult, but it is an added complication.

The Search class needs to track several pieces of information:

- The thread it's using to execute the search.

- Its current state (searching, not searching).

- The search keywords.

- The ListView where it should write search results.

- The SearchResults it retrieves.

- The ping times it calculates.

Here's a basic skeleton that shows the private variables used by the Search class:

```
Public Class Search

    ' The thread in which the search is executed.
    Private SearchThread As System.Threading.Thread

    ' The ListView in which results must be displayed.
    Private ListView As ListView

    Private Keywords() As String

    ' The current state.
    Private _Searching As Boolean = False
    Public ReadOnly Property Searching() As Boolean
        Get
            Return _Searching
        End Get
    End Property

    ' The search results and ping times.
    Private SearchResults() As SharedFile
    Private PingTimes As New Hashtable()

    Public Function GetSearchResults() As SharedFile()
        If _Searching = False Then
            Return SearchResults
        Else
            Return Nothing
        End If
    End Function

    Public Sub New(ByVal linkedControl As ListView)
        ListView = linkedControl
    End Sub

    ' (Other code omitted.)

End Class
```

The Search class code uses a thread-wrapping pattern that allows it to manage all the intricate threading details. Essentially, the Search class tracks the thread it's using and performs thread management so the rest of the application doesn't need to. The Search class provides methods such as StartSearch(), which creates and launches the thread, and Abort(), which stops the thread. This is a pattern we'll use again for the file download and upload objects.

```
Public Sub StartSearch(ByVal keywordString As String)
    If _Searching Then
        Throw New ApplicationException("Cancel current search first.")
    Else
        _Searching = True
        SearchResults = Nothing

        ' Parse the keywords using the same logic used when indexing files.
        Keywords = KeywordUtil.ParseKeywords(keywordString)

        ' Create the search thread, which will run the private Search() method.
        SearchThread = New Threading.Thread(AddressOf Search)
        SearchThread.Start()
    End If
End Sub

Public Sub Abort()
    If _Searching Then
        SearchThread.Abort()
        _Searching = False
    End If
End Sub
```

The actual searching code is contained in the private Search() method. The search results are downloaded using the shared App.SearchForFile() method, which passes the request to the discovery web service. The individual peers are pinged using a private PingRecipients() method, which makes use of a separate component. This component isn't shown here, because it requires raw socket code that's quite lengthy.

```
Private Sub Search()
    SearchResults = App.SearchForFile(Me.Keywords)
    _Searching = False

    PingRecipients()
```

```
        Try
            ListView.Invoke(New MethodInvoker(AddressOf UpdateInterface))
        Catch
            ' An error could occur here if the search is canceled and the
            ' class is destroyed before the invoke finishes.
        End Try
    End Sub


    Private Sub PingRecipients()
        PingTimes.Clear()
        Dim File As SharedFile
        For Each File In SearchResults
            Dim PingTime As Integer = PingUtility.Pinger.GetPingTime(File.Peer.IP)
            If PingTime = -1 Then
                PingTimes.Add(File.Guid, "Error")
            Else
                PingTimes.Add(File.Guid, PingTime.ToString() & " ms")
            End If
        Next
    End Sub
```

> **NOTE** *The PingUtility uses the Internet Control Message Protocol (ICMP). As you saw in Chapter 8, not all networks allow ping requests. If a ping attempt fails, the peer's ping time will show an error, but the peer may still be reachable for a file transfer.*

When the results have been retrieved and the ping times compiled, the final results are written to the ListView and the call is marshaled to the correct thread using the Control.Invoke() method.

```
Private Sub UpdateInterface()

    ListView.Items.Clear()
    If SearchResults.Length = 0 Then
        MessageBox.Show("No matches found.", "Error", MessageBoxButtons.OK, _
            MessageBoxIcon.Information)
    Else
        Dim File As SharedFile
        For Each File In SearchResults
            Dim Item As ListViewItem = ListView.Items.Add(File.FileName)
            Item.SubItems.Add(PingTimes(File.Guid).ToString())
            Item.SubItems.Add(File.FileCreated)
```

```
        Item.SubItems.Add(File.Peer.IP)
        Item.SubItems.Add(File.Peer.Port)
        Item.SubItems.Add(File.Guid.ToString())
        Item.SubItems.Add(File.Peer.Guid.ToString())

        ' Store the SharedFile object for easy access later.
        Item.Tag = File
    Next
  End If

End Sub
```

Note that the matching SharedFile object is embedded in each ListViewItem, so that it can be retrieved easily if the user chooses to download the file. This saves you from the work of creating a custom ListViewItem or parsing the text information in the ListViewItem to determine the appropriate settings.

Only one search can run at a time, because the App object provides a single Search variable. When the user clicks the Search button on the SwapperClient form, the current search is aborted immediately, regardless of its state, and a new search is launched based on the current keywords.

```
Private Sub cmdSearch_Click(ByVal sender As System.Object, _
  ByVal e As System.EventArgs) Handles cmdSearch.Click

    If App.SearchThread.Searching Then
        App.SearchThread.Abort()
    End If

    App.SearchThread.StartSearch(txtKeywords.Text)

End Sub
```

Figure 9-6 shows sample search results for a query with the single word "Debussy".

Uploads

The file uploading and downloading logic represents the heart of the FileSwapper application. The user needs the ability not only to perform both of these operations at the same time, but also to serve multiple upload requests or download multiple files in parallel. To accommodate this requirement, we must use a two-stage design, in which one class is responsible for creating new upload or download objects as needed. In the case of an upload, this is the FileServer class. The FileServer waits for requests and creates a FileUpload object for each new file upload. The diagrams in Figure 9-7 show how the FileServer and FileUpload classes interact.

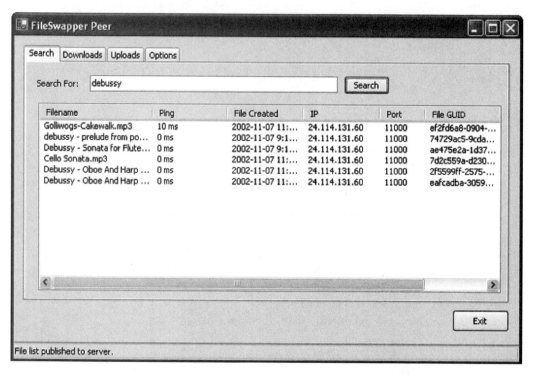

Figure 9-6. A FileSwapper search

The FileServer Class

The FileServer class listens for connection requests on the defined port using a TcpListener. It follows the same pattern as the asynchronous Search class:

- The thread used to monitor the port is stored in a private member variable.

- The thread is created with a call to StartWaitForRequest(), and aborted with a call to Abort(). The actual monitoring code exists in the WaitForRequest() method.

- The ListView that tracks uploads is stored in a private member variable.

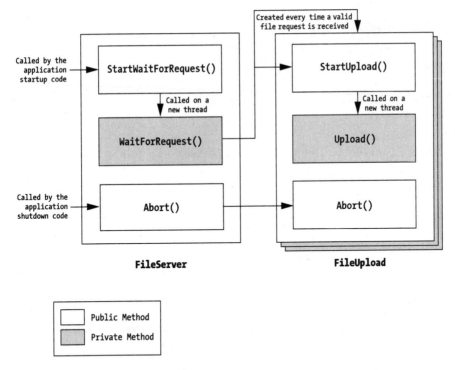

Created every time a valid
file request is received

Called by the
application ——
startup code

StartWaitForRequest()

Called on a
new thread

WaitForRequest()

Called by the
application ——
shutdown code

Abort()

FileServer

StartUpload()

Called on a
new thread

Upload()

Abort()

FileUpload

Public Method
Private Method

Figure 9-7. The uploading process

This framework is shown in the following code listing. One of the differences
you'll notice is that an additional member variable is used to track individual
upload threads. The Abort() method doesn't just stop the thread that's waiting
for connection requests—it also aborts all the threads that are currently transferring files.

```
Public Class FileServer

    ' The thread where the port is being monitored.
    Private WaitForRequestThread As System.Threading.Thread

    ' The TcpListener used to monitor the port.
    Private Listener As TcpListener

    ' The ListView that tracks current uploads.
    Private ListView As ListView

    ' The current state.
    Private _Working As Boolean
    Public ReadOnly Property Working() As Boolean
```

```vbnet
            Get
                Return _Working
            End Get
        End Property


        ' The threads that are allocated to transfer files.
        Private UploadThreads As New ArrayList()

        Public Sub New(ByVal linkedControl As ListView)
            ListView = linkedControl
        End Sub


        Public Sub StartWaitForRequest()
            If _Working Then
                Throw New ApplicationException("Already in progress.")
            Else
                _Working = True

                WaitForRequestThread = New Threading.Thread(AddressOf WaitForRequest)
                WaitForRequestThread.Start()
            End If
        End Sub


        Public Sub Abort()
            If _Working Then
                Listener.Stop()

                WaitForRequestThread.Abort()

                ' Abort all upload threads.
                Dim UploadThread As FileUpload
                For Each UploadThread In UploadThreads
                    UploadThread.Abort()
                Next

                _Working = False
            End If
        End Sub


        Public Sub WaitForRequest()
            ' (Code omitted.)
        End Sub


    End Class
```

The WaitForRequest() method contains some more interesting code. First, it instantiates a TcpListener object and invokes the AcceptTcpClient() method, blocking the thread until it receives a connection request. Once a connection request is received, the code creates a new FileUpload object, starts it, and adds the FileUpload object to the UploadThreads collection.

The WaitForRequest() code doesn't create threads indiscriminately, however. Instead, it examines the Global.MaxUploadThreads setting to determine how many upload threads can exist at any one time. If there's already that number of items in the UploadThreads collection, new requests will receive a busy message instructing them to try again later. The connection will be closed and no new FileUpload object will be created. To ensure that the server is always ready to serve new clients, it automatically scans the UploadThreads collection for objects that have finished processing every time it receives a request. Once it removes these, it decides whether the new request can be accommodated.

> **TIP** *.NET is quite efficient when destroying and creating new threads. However, you could optimize performance even further by reusing upload and download threads and maintaining a thread pool, rather than by creating new threads. One way to do this is to use the ThreadPool class that was introduced in Chapter 5.*

```
Public Sub WaitForRequest()

    Listener = New TcpListener(Global.Settings.Port)
    Listener.Start()
    Do
        ' Block until connection received.
        Dim Client As TcpClient = Listener.AcceptTcpClient()

        ' Check for completed requests.
        ' This will free up space for new requests.
        Dim UploadThread As FileUpload
        Dim i As Integer
        For i = (UploadThreads.Count - 1) To 0 Step -1
            UploadThread = CType(UploadThreads(i), FileUpload)
            If UploadThread.Working = False Then
                UploadThreads.Remove(UploadThread)
            End If
        Next
```

```
        Try
            Dim s As NetworkStream = Client.GetStream()
            Dim w As New BinaryWriter(s)
            If UploadThreads.Count > Global.Settings.MaxUploadThreads Then
                w.Write(Messages.Busy)
                s.Close()
            Else
                w.Write(Messages.Ok)
                Dim Upload As New FileUpload(s, ListView)
                UploadThreads.Add(Upload)
                Upload.StartUpload()
            End If
        Catch Err As Exception
            ' Errors are logged for future reference, but ignored, so that the
            ' peer can continue serving clients.
            Trace.Write(Err.ToString())
        End Try
    Loop

End Sub
```

FileSwapper peers communicate using simple string messages. A peer requests a file for downloading by submitting its GUID. The server responds with a string "OK" or "BUSY" depending on its state. These values are written to the stream using the BinaryWriter. To ensure that the correct values are always used, they aren't hard-coded in the WaitForRequest() method, but defined as constants in a class named Messages. As you can see from the following code listing, FileSwapper peers only support a very limited vocabulary.

```
Public Class Messages

    ' The server will respond to the request.
    Public Const Ok = "OK"

    ' The server has reached its upload limit. Try again later.
    Public Const Busy = "BUSY"

    ' The requested file isn't in the shared collection.
    Public Const FileNotFound = -1

End Class
```

The FileUpload Class

The FileUpload class uses the same thread-wrapping design as the FileServer
and Search classes. The actual file transfer is performed by the Upload() method.
This method is launched asynchronously when the FileServer calls the StartUpload()
method and canceled if the FileServer calls Abort(). A reference is maintained to
the ListView control with the upload listings in order to provide real-time
progress information.

```vb
Public Class FileUpload

    ' The thread where the file transfer takes place.
    Private UploadThread As System.Threading.Thread

    ' The underlying network stream.
    Private Stream As NetworkStream

    ' The current state.
    Private _Working As Boolean
    Public ReadOnly Property Working() As Boolean
        Get
            Return _Working
        End Get
    End Property

    ' The ListView where results are recorded.
    Private ListView As ListView

    Public Sub New(ByVal stream As NetworkStream, ByVal listView As ListView)
        Me.Stream = stream
        Me.ListView = listView
    End Sub

    Public Sub StartUpload()
        If _Working Then
            Throw New ApplicationException("Already in progress.")
        Else
            _Working = True
            UploadThread = New Threading.Thread(AddressOf Upload)
            UploadThread.Start()
        End If
    End Sub
End Sub
```

```
Public Sub Abort()
    If _Working Then
        UploadThread.Abort()
        _Working = False
    End If
End Sub

Private Sub Upload()
    ' (Code omitted)
End Sub
```

```
End Class
```

We'll dissect the code in the Upload() method piece by piece. The first task the Upload() method undertakes is to create a BinaryWriter and BinaryReader for the stream, and then it reads the GUID of the requested file into a string.

```
' Connect.
Dim w As New BinaryWriter(Stream)
Dim r As New BinaryReader(Stream)

' Read file request.
Dim FileRequest As String = r.ReadString()
```

It then walks through the collection of shared files, until it finds the matching GUID.

```
Dim File As SharedFile
Dim Filename
For Each File In Global.SharedFiles
    If File.Guid.ToString() = FileRequest Then
        Filename = File.FileName
        Exit For
    End If
Next
```

> **TIP** *Download requests use a GUID instead of a file name. This design allows you to enhance the FileSwapper program to allow sharing in multiple directories, in which case the file name may no longer be unique. The GUID approach also makes it easy to validate a user request before starting a transfer. This is a key step, which prevents a malicious client from trying to trick a FileSwapper peer into downloading a sensitive file that it isn't sharing.*

If the file isn't found in the collection of shared files, the message constant for file not found (-1) is written to the network stream, and no further action is taken.

```
' Check file is shared.
If Filename = "" Then
    w.Write(Messages.FileNotFound)
```

If the file is found, a new ListViewItem is added to the upload display, using a helper class named ListViewItemWrapper. The ListViewItemWrapper handles the logic needed to create the ListViewItem and change the status text in a thread-safe manner, by marshaling these operations to the correct thread.

```
Else
    ' Create ListView.
    Dim ListViewItem As New ListViewItemWrapper(ListView, Filename, _
        "Initializing")
```

The next step is to open the file and write the file size (in bytes) to the network stream. This information allows the remote peer to determine progress information while downloading the file.

```
Try
    ' Open file.
    Dim Upload As New FileInfo(Path.Combine(Global.Settings.SharePath, _
        Filename))

    ' Read file.
    Dim TotalBytes As Integer = Upload.Length
    w.Write(TotalBytes)
```

Next, the file is opened, and the data is written to the network stream 1KB at a time. The ListViewItem.ChangeStatus method is used to update the status display in the loop, but a time limit is used to ensure that no more than one update is made every second. This reduces on-screen flicker for fast downloads.

```
    Dim TotalBytesRead, BytesRead As Integer

    Dim fs As FileStream = Upload.OpenRead()
    Dim Buffer(1024) As Byte
    Dim Percent As Single
    Dim LastWrite As DateTime = DateTime.MinValue
```

```
            Do
                ' Write a chunk of bytes.
                BytesRead = fs.Read(Buffer, 0, Buffer.Length)
                w.Write(Buffer, 0, BytesRead)
                TotalBytesRead += BytesRead

                ' Update the display once every second.
                If DateTime.Now.Subtract(LastWrite).TotalSeconds > 1 Then
                    Percent = Math.Round((TotalBytesRead / TotalBytes) * 100, 0)
                    LastWrite = DateTime.Now
                    ListViewItem.ChangeStatus(Percent.ToString() & "% transferred")
                End If
            Loop While BytesRead > 0

            fs.Close()
            ListViewItem.ChangeStatus("Completed")

        Catch Err As Exception
            Trace.Write(Err.ToString)
            ListViewItem.ChangeStatus("Error")
        End Try

    End If

    Stream.Close()
    _Working = False
```

In this case, the client simply disconnects when it stops receiving data and notices that the connection has been severed. Alternatively, you could use a special signal (such as a specific byte sequence) to indicate that the file is complete or, more practically, you could precede every 1KB chunk with an additional byte describing the status (last chunk, more to come, and so on). The client would have to remove this byte before writing the data to the file.

Figure 9-8 shows the upload status list with three entries. Two uploads have completed, while one is in progress.

Downloads

The file-downloading process is similar to the file-uploading process. A FileDownloadQueue class creates FileDownloadClient instances to serve new user requests, provided the maximum number of simultaneous downloads hasn't been reached. Download progress information is written directly to the download ListView display, using the thread-safe ListViewItemWrapper. The whole process is diagrammed in Figure 9-9.

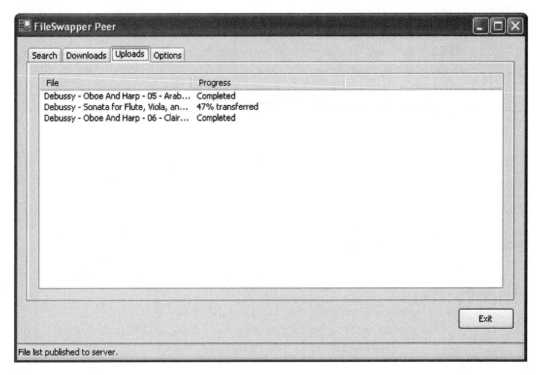

Figure 9-8. FileSwapper uploads

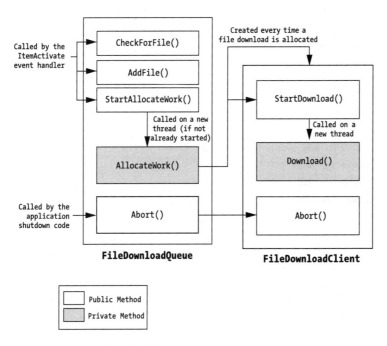

Figure 9-9. The downloading process

A download operation begins when a user double-clicks an item in the ListView search results, thereby triggering the ItemActivate event. The form code handles the event, checks that the requested file hasn't already been submitted to the FileDownloadQueue, and then adds it. This code demonstrates another advantage of using GUIDs to uniquely identify all files on the peer-to-peer network: it allows each peer to maintain a history of downloaded files.

The complete code for the ItemActivate event handler is shown here:

```vb
Private Sub lstSearchResults_ItemActivate(ByVal sender As Object, _
   ByVal e As System.EventArgs) Handles lstSearchResults.ItemActivate

    ' Retrieve information about the requested file.
    Dim File As SharedFile
    File = CType(CType(sender, ListView).SelectedItems(0).Tag, SharedFile)

    ' Check if the file is already downloaded, or in the process of being
    ' downloaded.
    If App.DownwnloadThread.CheckForFile(File) Then
        MessageBox.Show("You are already downloading this file.", "Error", _
            MessageBoxButtons.OK, MessageBoxIcon.Information)

    ' If you comment-out the following lines, you'll be able to test
    ' FileSwapper with a single active instance and download files
    ' from your own computer.
    ElseIf File.Peer.Guid.ToString() = Global.Identity.Guid.ToString() Then
        MessageBox.Show("This is a local file.", "Error", _
            MessageBoxButtons.OK, MessageBoxIcon.Information)

    Else
        ' Add the file to the download queue.
        App.DownwnloadThread.AddFile(File)

        ' Start the download queue thread if necessary (this is only performed
        ' once, the first time you download a file).
        If Not App.DownwnloadThread.Working Then
            App.DownwnloadThread.StartAllocateWork()
        End If

        ' Switch to the Downloads tab to see progress information.
        tbPages.SelectedTab = tbPages.TabPages(1)
    End If

End Sub
```

The FileDownloadQueue Class

The FileDownloadQueue tracks and schedules ongoing downloads. When the user requests a file, it's added to the QueuedFiles collection. If the maximum download thread count hasn't yet been reached, the file is removed from this collection and a new FileDownloadClient object is created to serve the request. All active FileDownloadClient objects are tracked in the DownloadThreads collection.

The FileDownloadQueue class creates new FileDownloadClient objects as needed in its private AllocateWork() method, which it executes on a separate thread. The application requests a new download by calling the StartAllocate Work() method, which creates the thread and invokes the AllocateWork() method asynchronously. The Abort() method stops the work allocation. This is the same design you saw with the FileServer class.

```
Public Class FileDownloadQueue

    ' The thread where downloads are scheduled.
    Private AllocateWorkThread As System.Threading.Thread

    ' The ListView where downloads are tracked.
    Private ListView As ListView

    ' The current state.
    Private _Working As Boolean
    Public ReadOnly Property Working() As Boolean
        Get
            Return _Working
        End Get
    End Property

    ' The collection of files that are waiting to be downloaded.
    Private QueuedFiles As New ArrayList()

    ' The threaded objects that are currently downloading files.
    Private DownloadThreads As New ArrayList()

    Public Sub New(ByVal linkedControl As ListView)
        ListView = linkedControl
    End Sub
```

```
Public Sub StartAllocateWork()
    If _Working Then
        Throw New ApplicationException("Already in progress.")
    Else
        _Working = True

        AllocateWorkThread = New Threading.Thread(AddressOf AllocateWork)
        AllocateWorkThread.Start()
    End If
End Sub

Public Sub Abort()
    If _Working Then
        AllocateWorkThread.Abort()

        ' Abort all download threads.
        Dim DownloadThread As FileDownloadClient
        For Each DownloadThread In DownloadThreads
            DownloadThread.Abort()
        Next

        _Working = False
    End If
End Sub

Private Sub AllocateWork()
    ' (Code omitted.)
End Sub

Public Function CheckForFile(ByVal file As SharedFile) As Boolean
    ' (Code omitted.)
End Function

Public Sub AddFile(ByVal file As SharedFile)
    ' (Code omitted.)
End Sub

End Class
```

The CheckForFile() method allows the application to verify that a file hasn't been downloaded before and isn't currently being downloaded. The code scans for the QueuedFiles and DownloadThreads collections to be sure.

```
Public Function CheckForFile(ByVal file As SharedFile) As Boolean

    ' Check the queued files.
    Dim Item As DisplayFile
    For Each Item In QueuedFiles
        If Item.File.Guid.ToString() = file.Guid.ToString() Then Return True
    Next

    ' Check the in-progress downloads.
    Dim DownloadThread As FileDownloadClient
    For Each DownloadThread In DownloadThreads
        If DownloadThread.File.Guid.ToString() = file.Guid.ToString() Then _
            Return True
    Next

    Return False

End Function
```

If this check succeeds, the AddFile() method is used to queue the file. Locking is used to ensure that no problem occurs if the FileDownloadClient is about to modify the QueuedFiles collection.

```
Public Sub AddFile(ByVal file As SharedFile)

    ' Add shared file.
    SyncLock QueuedFiles
        QueuedFiles.Add(New DisplayFile(file, ListView))
    End SyncLock

End Sub
```

The QueuedFile collection stores DisplayFile objects, not SharedFile objects. The DisplayFile object is a simple package that combines a SharedFile instance and a ListViewItemWrapper. The ListViewItemWrapper is used to update the status of the download on screen.

```
Public Class DisplayFile

    Private _ListViewItem As ListViewItemWrapper
    Private _File As SharedFile
```

```
Public ReadOnly Property File() As SharedFile
    Get
        Return _File
    End Get
End Property


Public ReadOnly Property ListViewItem() As ListViewItemWrapper
    Get
        Return _ListViewItem
    End Get
End Property


Public Sub New(ByVal file As SharedFile, ByVal linkedControl As ListView)

    _ListViewItem = New ListViewItemWrapper(linkedControl, file.FileName, _
        "Queued")
    _File = file

End Sub

End Class
```

As soon as the DisplayFile object is created, the underlying ListViewItem is created and added to the download list. That means that as soon as a download request is selected, it appears in the download status display, with the status "Queued." This differs from the approach used with file uploading, in which the ListViewItem is only created once the connection has been accepted.

The AllocateWork() method performs the real work for the FileDownloadQueue. It begins by scanning the collection for completed items and removing them for the collection. This is a key step, because the FileDownloadQueue relies on the Count property of the DownloadThreads collection to determine how many downloads are currently in progress. When scanning the collection, the code counts backward, which allows it to delete items without changing the index numbering for the remaining items.

```
Do
    ' Remove completed.
    Dim i As Integer
    For i = DownloadThreads.Count - 1 To 0 Step -1
        Dim DownloadThread As FileDownloadClient
        DownloadThread = CType(DownloadThreads(i), FileDownloadClient)
```

```
    If Not DownloadThread.Working Then
        SyncLock DownloadThreads
            DownloadThreads.Remove(DownloadThread)
        End SyncLock
    End If
Next
```

Next, new FileDownloadClient objects are created while threads are available.

```
Do While QueuedFiles.Count > 0 And _
DownloadThreads.Count < Global.Settings.MaxDownloadThreads

    ' Create a new FileDownloadClient.
    Dim DownloadThread As New FileDownloadClient(QueuedFiles(0))
    SyncLock DownloadThreads
        DownloadThreads.Add(DownloadThread)
    End SyncLock

    ' Remove the corresponding queued file.

    SyncLock QueuedFiles
        QueuedFiles.RemoveAt(0)
    End SyncLock

    ' Start the download (on a new thread).
    DownloadThread.StartDownload()

Loop
```

Finally, the thread doing the work allocation is put to sleep for a brief ten seconds, after which it continues through another iteration of the loop.

```
    Thread.Sleep(TimeSpan.FromSeconds(10))
Loop
```

The FileDownloadClient Class

The FileDownloadClient uses the same thread-wrapping design as the FileUpload class. The actual file transfer is performed by the Download() method. This method is launched asynchronously when the FileDownloadQueue calls the StartDownload() method, and canceled if the FileDownloadQueue calls Abort(). The current SharedFile and ListViewItem information is tracked using a private DisplayFile property.

Here's the basic structure:

```
Public Class FileDownloadClient

    ' The thread where the file download is performed.
    Private DownloadThread As System.Threading.Thread

    ' The current state.
    Private _Working As Boolean
    Public ReadOnly Property Working() As Boolean
        Get
            Return _Working
        End Get
    End Property

    ' The SharedFile and ListViewItem used for this download.
    Private DisplayFile As DisplayFile
    Public ReadOnly Property File() As SharedFile
        Get
            Return DisplayFile.File
        End Get
    End Property

    Public Sub New(ByVal file As DisplayFile)
        Me.DisplayFile = file
    End Sub

    ' The TCP/IP connection used to make the request.
    Private Client As TcpClient

    Public Sub StartDownload()
        If _Working Then
            Throw New ApplicationException("Already in progress.")
        Else
            _Working = True
            DownloadThread = New Threading.Thread(AddressOf Download)
            DownloadThread.Start()
        End If
    End Sub
```

```
Public Sub Abort()
    If _Working Then
        Client.Close()
        DownloadThread.Abort()
        _Working = False
    End If
End Sub

Private Sub Download()
    ' (Code omitted.)
End Sub
```

```
End Class
```

The Download() method code is lengthy, but straightforward. At first, the client attempts to connect with the remote peer by opening a TCP/IP connection to the indicated port and IP address. To simplify the code, no error handling is shown (although it is included with the online code).

```
DisplayFile.ListViewItem.ChangeStatus("Connecting...")

' Connect.
Dim Completed As Boolean = False

Do
    Client = New TcpClient()
    Dim Host As IPHostEntry = Dns.GetHostByAddress(DisplayFile.File.Peer.IP)
    Client.Connect(Host.AddressList(0), Val(DisplayFile.File.Peer.Port))
```

The next step is to define a new BinaryReader and BinaryWriter for the stream and check if the connection succeeded. If the connection doesn't succeed, the thread will sleep for ten seconds and the connection will be reattempted in a loop.

```
Dim r As New BinaryReader(Client.GetStream())
Dim w As New BinaryWriter(Client.GetStream())

Dim Response As String = r.ReadString()
If Response = Messages.Busy Then
    DisplayFile.ListViewItem.ChangeStatus("Busy - Will Retry")
    Client.Close()
```

```
    ElseIf Response = Messages.Ok Then
        DisplayFile.ListViewItem.ChangeStatus("Connected")

      ' (Download file here.)

    Else
        DisplayFile.ListViewItem.ChangeStatus("Error - Will Retry")
        Client.Close()

    End If

    If Not Completed Then Thread.Sleep(TimeSpan.FromSeconds(10))
Loop Until Completed

_Working = False
```

The actual file download is a multiple step affair. The first task is to request the file using its GUID.

```
' Request file.
w.Write(DisplayFile.File.Guid.ToString())
```

The server will then respond with the number of bytes for the file, or an error code if the file isn't found. Assuming no error is encountered, the FileSwapper will create a temporary file. Its name will be the GUID plus the extension *.tmp*.

```
Dim TotalBytes As Integer = r.ReadInt32()
If TotalBytes = Messages.FileNotFound Then
    DisplayFile.ListViewItem.ChangeStatus("File Not Found")

Else
    ' Write temporary file.
    Dim FullPath As String = Path.Combine(Global.Settings.SharePath, _
        File.Guid.ToString() & ".tmp")
    Dim Download As New FileInfo(FullPath)
```

The file transfer takes place 1KB at a time. The status for the in-progress download will be updated using the ListViewItem wrapper, no more than once per second.

```vbnet
Dim TotalBytesRead, BytesRead As Integer

Dim fs As FileStream = Download.Create()
Dim Buffer(1024) As Byte
Dim Percent As Single
Dim LastWrite As DateTime = DateTime.Now
Do
    ' Read a chunk of bytes.
    BytesRead = r.Read(Buffer, 0, Buffer.Length)
    fs.Write(Buffer, 0, BytesRead)
    TotalBytesRead += BytesRead

    ' Update the display once every second.
    If DateTime.Now.Subtract(LastWrite).TotalSeconds > 1 Then
        Percent = Math.Round((TotalBytesRead / TotalBytes) * 100, 0)
        LastWrite = DateTime.Now
        DisplayFile.ListViewItem.ChangeStatus( _
          Percent.ToString() & "% transferred")
    End If
Loop While BytesRead > 0
```

When the file transfer is complete, the file must be renamed. The new name will be the same as the file name on the remote peer. However, special care is needed to handle duplicate file names. Before attempting the rename, the code checks for a name collision and adds a number (1, 2, 3, 4, and so on) to the file name to ensure uniqueness.

```vbnet
fs.Close()

' Ensure that a unique name is chosen.
Dim FileNames() As String = Directory.GetFiles(Global.Settings.SharePath)
Dim FinalPath As String = Path.Combine(Global.Settings.SharePath, _
  File.FileName)

Dim i As Integer
Do While Array.IndexOf(FileNames, FinalPath) <> -1
    i += 1
    FinalPath = Path.Combine(Global.Settings.SharePath, _
      Path.GetFileNameWithoutExtension(File.FileName) & i.ToString() & _
        Path.GetExtension(File.FileName))
Loop

' Rename file.
System.IO.File.Move(FullPath, FinalPath)
```

```
        DisplayFile.ListViewItem.ChangeStatus("Completed")
End If

Client.Close()
Completed = True
```

Currently, the code doesn't add the newly downloaded file to the App.Shared Files collection, and it doesn't contact the discovery service to add it to the published catalog of files. However, you could easily add this code.

Figure 9-10 shows the upload status list with six entries. Two downloads are in progress while four are queued, because the maximum download thread count has been reached.

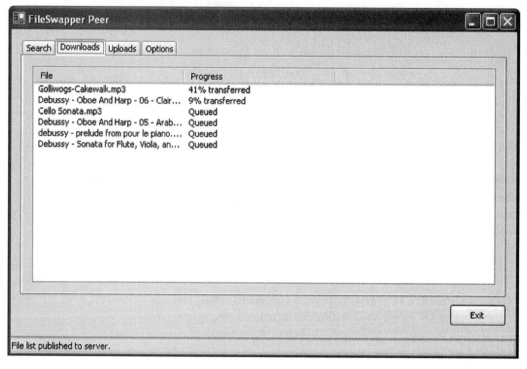

Figure 9-10. FileSwapper downloads

Possible Enhancements

FileSwapper contains the minimum amount of code needed to show a complete, well-designed framework for peer-to-peer request handling. It still lacks a number of niceties that you'd want to add in a production-level application. Some of these possible enhancements are listed here:

- Currently, new files that are downloaded to the shared directory are ignored. That means that any files you download will not be shared with other users unless you restart the application. To solve this problem, you could add a timer that periodically refreshes the catalog with the server, or you could use a FileSystemWatcher to monitor the directory. You might even want to add discovery-service methods to publish individual files and reduce the bandwidth and database effort required when single files are added.

- Currently, there's no ability for the user to cancel in-progress downloads. This would be easy to add, because each FileDownloadClient object stores the related ListViewItem. If a user selects a download to cancel from the ListView, you would simply have to look up the FileDownloadClient that references the corresponding ListViewItem and call its Abort() method.

- You could enhance the communication used between peers. For example, the uploading peer could send a status message before every chunk of data. Similarly, after every chunk of data, the downloading peer could send a single byte indicating whether it was ready to receive more data, about to cancel the download, or in some other state.

- You could improve the shutdown code by adding some sort of flag that can be set to instruct the download and upload threads to shut down, so that the application would not need to abort them forcefully. You might also want to poll for connection requests in the FileServer class using the TcpClient.Pending() method, and only call TcpClient.AcceptTcpClient() once a connection request has been received. This way, the thread will remain responsive and can be shut down more easily. Fortunately, .NET networking is very friendly—although these touches would improve the application, they aren't at all necessary.

- Currently, the error handling is quite rudimentary. You could add more sophisticated exception handlers to log problems, inform the user, and protect the application.

The Last Word

File-sharing applications are one of the best-known niches of peer-to-peer programming. In this chapter, you've learned that the greatest challenge with a peer-to-peer file sharer may not be networking, but using threads to handle the application's many responsibilities.

FileSwapper is only one example of a simple client, but it provides a solid, extensible framework that you can use when designing your own resource-sharing peer-to-peer applications. However, there are still a number of additional challenges to face, including firewalls and other network-connectivity issues (the bane of any peer-to-peer application), and security. We'll consider some of these issues in the following chapters.

CHAPTER 10

Using a Discovery Service with Remoting

CHAPTER 8 PRESENTED THE BASICS of discovery services and showed how you could use a discovery service to facilitate peer discovery and index peer content. To support this design, the registration database stored information about each peer and the TCP/IP endpoint it uses to listen for connections.

But what if you want to apply the same approach—using a stateless discovery web service—but allow your peers to interact using .NET Remoting? This simpler approach is less suitable for situations in which you need to stream large amounts of data over the wire (such as the file-sharer application), but it could be useful if you're building a distributed task processor or messaging application. Fortunately, the changes are easy to implement. You simply need to serialize Remoting's network pointer, the ObjRef.

In this chapter, we'll use this technique to develop a discovery web service that can support the Talk .NET application developed in Part Two. We'll use the decentralized version presented at the end of Chapter 4, because it allows peers to interact directly and only requires the server for peer discovery. Best of all, you'll see that you can implement these changes with minimal coding changes to the Talk .NET peer application—a fact that makes this the shortest chapter in this book!

The Registration Database

The first step is to design the back-end database. This database contains two tables (as shown in Figure 10-1):

- The Peers table stores a list of users, each of which has a unique e-mail address.

- The Sessions table stores a list of currently active users, with the information needed to connect to them.

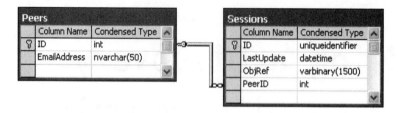

Figure 10-1. The Talk .NET registration database

Strictly speaking, you only require one table to store the list of currently connected peers. However, by creating two tables you gain the ability to define a list of allowed users, and validate them at the server before allowing them to join the peer community. In addition, you might want to add more tables to define "buddy lists"—groups of contacts that determine who a peer can see online and interact with.

The Sessions table doesn't directly store an IP address and port number—instead, it stores a serialized ObjRef, which is Remoting's network pointer. When serialized, the ObjRef typically takes about 1,008 bytes. The Sessions table provides space for up to 1,500 bytes to be safe, and the code verifies that this constraint is met when serializing the ObjRef.

Stored Procedures

The database includes six stored procedures, as described here:

- AddPeer creates a peer record for a newly registered user.

- CreateSession inserts a new session record when an existing user logs in.

- DeleteSession removes a session record.

- GetPeers retrieves a list of all the peers who are currently logged in. In a large system, this would be adapted so that it retrieved a list of logged-in users according to a contact list.

- GetPeerAndSessionInfo retrieves information about the peer, and the current contact information if the peer is logged in. This could be split into two stored procedures, but for simplicity's sake it's handled in one.

- RefreshSession updates the expiration date on the current session record. Peer sessions that haven't been updated within three minutes will be ignored (and optionally, can be removed).

The stored procedure code is similar to what you saw in Chapter 8. For example, AddPeer wraps a simple SQL Insert statement:

```
CREATE Procedure AddPeer
(
    @EmailAddress  nvarchar(50)
)
AS

INSERT INTO Peers ( EmailAddress ) VALUES ( @EmailAddress )
GO
```

The CreateSession stored procedure is more sophisticated. Before adding the session record, it removes any existing session records with the same e-mail address. It also performs a lookup to map the supplied peer e-mail address to the unique identity number the database uses in the Sessions table.

```
CREATE Procedure CreateSession
(
    @ID             uniqueidentifier,
    @EmailAddress   nvarchar(50),
    @ObjRef         varbinary(1500)
)
AS

DECLARE @PeerID int
SELECT @PeerID = ID FROM Peers WHERE EmailAddress = @EmailAddress

DELETE FROM Sessions WHERE PeerID=@PeerID

INSERT INTO Sessions (ID, PeerID, LastUpdate, ObjRef)
  VALUES (@ID, @PeerID, GETDATE(), @ObjRef)
GO
```

Note that the unique identifier is generated by the server rather than the database engine, and as such it doesn't need to be returned using a parameter.

The RefreshSession stored procedure simply updates the LastUpdate field.

```
CREATE Procedure RefreshSession
(
    @ID  uniqueidentifier
)
AS
```

```
UPDATE Sessions SET LastUpdate=GETDATE() WHERE [ID]=@ID
GO
```

The DeleteSession stored procedure removes the session based on its unique identifier.

```
CREATE Procedure DeleteSession
(
    @ID  uniqueidentifier
)
AS

DELETE FROM Sessions WHERE ID = @ID
GO
```

The GetPeers method returns the e-mail addresses for all the currently logged-on users by joining the Sessions and Peers tables. At the same time, any entry that hasn't been updated in more than three minutes is ignored.

```
CREATE PROCEDURE GetPeers AS

SELECT EmailAddress FROM Sessions INNER JOIN Peers ON Peers.ID = PeerID
   WHERE DATEDIFF(MINUTE, LastUpdate, GETDATE()) < 3
GO
```

Optionally, you could remove old sessions records, either by using a separate long-running application that periodically scans the database, or by adding the necessary code to a frequently invoked stored procedure such as CreateSession or DeleteSession. However, this additional step probably isn't necessary. The CreateSession stored procedure code already ensures that all of a user's old records are removed every time the user logs in.

Finally, the GetPeerAndSessionInfo stored procedure returns peer and session information. A left join is used to ensure that peer information is returned, even if the user isn't currently logged in and doesn't have a session record.

```
CREATE PROCEDURE GetPeerAndSessionInfo
(
    @EmailAddress  nvarchar(50)
)
AS
```

```
SELECT TOP 1 * FROM Peers Left JOIN Sessions ON PeerID = Peers.ID
  WHERE EmailAddress = @EmailAddress ORDER BY LastUpdate DESC
GO
```

If the system is working correctly, this will return only a single record. But just to be defensive, this stored procedure returns only the first record that was most recently updated by using the TOP 1 and ORDER BY clauses.

The Database Class

As in Chapter 8, a class named P2PDatabase is used to wrap the stored procedure code with the required ADO.NET commands. Information about a peer and its current session can be packaged into a PeerInfo object, as shown here:

```
Public Class PeerInfo

    Public ID As Integer
    Public EmailAddress As String
    Public PublicKeyXml As String
    Public ObjRef() As Byte

End Class
```

The P2PDatabase includes a method for each stored procedure. You won't see the full code here, but it's provided online with the Chapter 11 examples, and it's quite straightforward. However, there are two fine points worth identifying.

First of all, note how the CreateSession() method takes special care to validate that the ObjRef is less than the 1,500 bytes allocated for storage in the database. Because it's presumably impossible for an ObjRef to be larger, the code makes this check using a debug assertion. Alternatively, you might want to throw a custom error indicating the problem if the byte array is too large.

```
Public Function CreateSession(ByVal emailAddress As String, _
  ByVal objRef() As Byte) As Guid

    ' Define command and connection.
    Dim SessionID As Guid = Guid.NewGuid()

    Dim con As New SqlConnection(ConnectionString)
    Dim cmd As New SqlCommand("CreateSession", con)
    cmd.CommandType = CommandType.StoredProcedure
```

```
' Add parameters.
Dim param As SqlParameter
param = cmd.Parameters.Add("@ID", SqlDbType.UniqueIdentifier)
param.Value = SessionID
param = cmd.Parameters.Add("@EmailAddress", SqlDbType.NVarChar, 300)
param.Value = emailAddress

Debug.Assert(objRef.Length < 1500)

param = cmd.Parameters.Add("@ObjRef", SqlDbType.VarBinary, 1500)
param.Value = objRef

Try
    con.Open()
    cmd.ExecuteNonQuery()
Finally
    con.Close()
End Try

Return SessionID

End Function
```

The GetPeerInfo() method also requires special care. It calls the GetPeerAnd SessionInfo stored procedure, which may or may not return session information. To prevent a possible null reference exception, the code must check if session data is returned before trying to assign it to the properties of a PeerInfo object.

```
Public Function GetPeerInfo(ByVal email As String) As PeerInfo

    ' Define command and connection.
    Dim con As New SqlConnection(ConnectionString)
    Dim cmd As New SqlCommand("GetPeerAndSessionInfo", con)
    cmd.CommandType = CommandType.StoredProcedure

    ' Add parameters.
    Dim param As SqlParameter
    param = cmd.Parameters.Add("@EmailAddress", SqlDbType.VarChar, 50)
    param.Value = email
```

```
Dim Peer As New PeerInfo()
Try
    con.Open()
    Dim r As SqlDataReader = cmd.ExecuteReader()
    r.Read()
    Peer.EmailAddress = r("EmailAddress")
    Peer.ID = r("ID")
    If Not (r("ObjRef") Is DBNull.Value) Then
        Peer.ObjRef = r("ObjRef")
    End If
Finally
    con.Close()
End Try
Return Peer

End Function
```

The Discovery Service

The discovery service wraps the P2PDatabase component. As with the discovery service in Chapter 8, it catches all exceptions, logs them, and replaces them with a generic ApplicationException to ensure that no sensitive information will be returned to the client.

Peers interact with the discovery service as follows:

1. New users call RegisterNewUser() to create a new record in the Peers table.

2. Users call StartSession() to log in, supply their current connectivity information, and create a new record in the Sessions table.

3. Users call GetPeers() periodically to retrieve a list of other users. In turn, GetPeers() calls RefreshSession(), ensuring that the record for the requesting peer is kept current.

4. If a user wants to send a message, it calls GetPeer() to retrieve the connectivity information for a specific user. It can then contact the user directly.

5. When the user is finished and wants to leave the peer community, it calls EndSession() to remove the session record.

The full DiscoveryService code is shown here:

```
Public Class DiscoveryService
    Inherits System.Web.Services.WebService

    Private DB As New P2PDatabase()

    <WebMethod()> _
    Public Sub RegisterNewUser(ByVal emailAddress As String)

        Try
            DB.AddPeer(emailAddress)
        Catch err As Exception
            Trace.Write(err.ToString)
            Throw New ApplicationException("Could not register new user.")
        End Try

    End Sub

    <WebMethod()> _
    Public Function StartSession(ByVal emailAddress As String, _
      objRef() As Byte) As Guid

        Try
            Return DB.CreateSession(emailAddress, objRef)
        Catch err As Exception
            Trace.Write(err.ToString)
            Throw New ApplicationException("Could not create session.")
        End Try

    End Function

    <WebMethod()> _
    Public Sub RefreshSession(ByVal sessionID As Guid)

        Try
            DB.RefreshSession(sessionID)
        Catch err As Exception
            Trace.Write(err.ToString)
            Throw New ApplicationException("Could not refresh session.")
        End Try

    End Sub
```

```vb
<WebMethod()> _
Public Sub EndSession(ByVal sessionID As Guid)


    Try
        DB.DeleteSession(sessionID)
    Catch err As Exception
        Trace.Write(err.ToString)
        Throw New ApplicationException("Could not end session.")
    End Try

End Sub


<WebMethod()> _
Public Function GetPeerInfo(ByVal emailAddress As String, _
  ByVal sessionID As Guid) As PeerInfo


    Try
        Return DB.GetPeerInfo(emailAddress)
    Catch err As Exception
        Trace.Write(err.ToString)
        Throw New ApplicationException("Could not find peer.")
    End Try

End Function


<WebMethod()> _
Public Function GetPeers() As String()


    Try
        RefreshSession(sessionID)
        Return DB.GetPeers()
    Catch err As Exception
        Trace.Write(err.ToString)
        Throw New ApplicationException("Could not find peers.")
    End Try

End Function

End Class
```

The Talk .NET Peers

The final step is to modify the Talk .NET peer application to use the discovery service instead of the well-known Remoting server. Thanks to the well-encapsulated design of the Talk .NET client, you won't need to modify the main form code. Instead, almost all of the changes are confined to the remotable ClientProcess class.

The ClientProcess class is used to send and receive messages with .NET Remoting. In the revised version, it will also have the additional responsibility of interacting with the discovery web service. To support this design, we need to add two member variables, as shown here:

```
Public Class ClientProcess
    Inherits MarshalByRefObject
    Implements ITalkClient

    ' Holds a reference to the web-server proxy.
    Private DiscoveryService As New localhost.DiscoveryService()

    ' Tracks the GUID for the current session.
    Private SessionID As Guid

    ' (Other code omitted.)

End Class
```

The ClientProcess constructor accepts a Boolean parameter that indicates whether a new record needs to be created for this user. If the user hasn't registered before, the ClientProcess class calls the RegisterNewUser() web method.

```
Public Sub New(ByVal userEmailAddress As String, ByVal createUser As Boolean)

    Me.[Alias] = userEmailAddress
    If createUser Then
        DiscoveryService.RegisterNewUser(userEmailAddress)
    End If

End Sub
```

The Login() method registers ClientProcess to receive messages from other peers. It also retrieves the ObjRef for the current instance using the Remoting Services.Marshal() method, and submits it to the sever.

```
Public Sub Login()

    ' Configure the client channel for sending messages and receiving
    ' the server callback.
    RemotingConfiguration.Configure("TalkClient.exe.config")

    ' Retrieve the ObjRef for this class.
    Dim Obj As ObjRef = RemotingServices.Marshal(Me)

    ' Serialize the ObjRef to a memory stream.
    Dim ObjStream As New MemoryStream()
    Dim f As New BinaryFormatter()
    f.Serialize(ObjStream, Obj)

    ' Start a new session and record the session GUID.
    Me.SessionID = DiscoveryService.StartSession(ObjStream.ToArray())

End Sub
```

The GetUsers() method now calls the discovery web service to retrieve the list of peer e-mail addresses:

```
Public Function GetUsers() As ICollection
    Return DiscoveryService.GetPeers(Me.SessionID)
End Function
```

The SendMessage() method calls the discovery service to retrieve the appropriate ObjRef, deserializes it, converts it to a proxy, and then invokes the ITalkClient.ReceiveMessage() method.

```
Public Sub SendMessage(ByVal emailAddress As String, ByVal messageBody As
String)

    ' Retrieve the peer information.
    Dim PeerInfo As localhost.PeerInfo
    PeerInfo = DiscoveryService.GetPeerInfo(emailAddress)

    ' Deserialize the proxy.
    Dim ObjStream As New MemoryStream(PeerInfo.ObjRef)
    Dim f As New BinaryFormatter()
    Dim Obj As Object = f.Deserialize(ObjStream)
    Dim Peer As ITalkClient = CType(Obj, ITalkClient)
```

```
        ' Send the message to this peer.
        Try
            Peer.ReceiveMessage(messageBody, Me.Alias)
        Catch
            ' Ignore connectivity errors.
            ' Alternatively, you could raise an event or throw an error that the
main
            ' form could respond to and use to update the form display.
        End Try

    End Sub
```

The LogOut() method ends the session:

```
Public Sub LogOut()
    DiscoveryService.EndSession(Me.SessionID)
End Sub
```

Finally, the Login window is modified to include a check box that the user can select to create the account for the first time, as shown in Figure 10-2.

Figure 10-2. Logging in with a new or existing account

The startup code can retrieve the user's check box selection from the read-only CreateNew property:

```
Public ReadOnly Property CreateNew() As Boolean
    Get
        Return chkCreateNew.Checked
    End Get
End Property
```

This information is passed to the ClientProcess constructor, which then determines whether or not it needs to call the RegisterNewUser() web method.

```
Dim Client As New ClientProcess(frmLogin.UserName, frmLogin.CreateNew)
```

The new Talk .NET client is now fully functional. The next two sections describe some enhancements you can implement.

Adding Caching

Currently, the Talk .NET client contacts the discovery service every time it sends a message. You could improve upon this situation by increasing the amount of information the client keeps locally. For example, the client might keep a cache with peer-connectivity information in it. That way, if one user sends several messages to another, it will only need to contact the server once, when the first message is sent.

To add caching, you must first add a Hashtable collection to the ClientProcess class. This collection will store all the PeerInfo objects for recently contacted clients, indexed by the e-mail address.

```
' Contains all recently contacted clients.
Private RecentClients As New Hashtable()
```

Whenever a message is sent, the code will check the RecentClients collection. If it finds the corresponding user, it will use the stored ObjRef. Otherwise, it will retrieve the ObjRef from the server and add it to the hashtable.

```
Public Sub SendMessage(ByVal emailAddress As String, ByVal messageBody As
String)

    Dim PeerInfo As localhost.PeerInfo

    ' Check if the peer-connectivity information is cached.
    If RecentClients.Contains(emailAddress) Then
        PeerInfo = CType(RecentClients(emailAddress), localhost.PeerInfo)
    Else
        PeerInfo = DiscoveryService.GetPeerInfo(emailAddress, Me.SessionID)
        RecentClients.Add(PeerInfo.EmailAddress, PeerInfo)
    End If
```

```
' Deserialize the proxy.
Dim ObjStream As New MemoryStream(PeerInfo.ObjRef)
Dim f As New BinaryFormatter()
Dim Obj As Object = f.Deserialize(ObjStream)
Dim Peer As ITalkClient = CType(Obj, ITalkClient)

' Send the message to this peer.
Try
    Peer.ReceiveMessage(messageBody, Me.Alias)
Catch
    RecentClients.Remove(PeerInfo)
    ' Optionally, you might want to try retrieving new peer information
    ' and resending the message, if you used the connectivity information
    ' in the local cache.
End Try

End Sub
```

As implemented, this will retain ObjRef for the life of the application, or until a transmission error occurs. If you anticipate that connectivity information will change frequently, or that the Talk .NET client application will run for an extremely long period of time (for example, several days), you might want to take a few additional measures to help ensure that this information is valid. For example, you could use code in the GetUsers() method to check the currently logged-on users and remove an ObjRef as soon as a peer disappears from the network:

```
Public Function GetUsers() As ICollection

    Dim Peers() As String
    Peers = DiscoveryService.GetPeers()

    ' Identify any peers in the local cache that aren't online.
    Dim PeerSearch As New ArrayList()
    PeerSearch.AddRange(Peers)
    Dim PeersToDelete As New ArrayList()

    Dim Item As DictionaryItem
    Dim Peer As localhost.PeerInfo
    For Each Item In Me.RecentClients
        Peer = CType(Item.Value, localhost.PeerInfo)
```

```
    ' Check if this e-mail address is in the server list.
    If Not PeerSearch.Contains(Peer.EmailAddress) Then
        ' The e-mail address wasn't found. Mark this peer for deletion.
        PeersToDelete.Add(Peer)
    End If
Next


' Remove the peers that weren't found.
For Each Peer In PeersToDelete
    Me.RecentClients.Remove(Peer.EmailAddress)
Next

Return Peers

End Function
```

This code works in two steps because items cannot be removed from a collection while you're iterating through it, without causing an error.

Adding E-mail Validation

Currently, no validation is performed when a user registers with the server. This is simply intended as a convenience for testing purposes. Ideally, you would not create a new user account until you could confirm that the e-mail address is correct.

To validate an e-mail address, you can borrow a technique from the world of e-commerce. It works like this:

1. When the user makes a request, save the submitted information into a different table (for example, a NewUserRequests table). Create a new GUID to identify the request.

2. Next, send an e-mail to the user-supplied e-mail address (you can use the System.Web.Mail.SmtpServer class for this task). Here's the trick: This e-mail can include an HTTP GET link to a web-service method (or ASP.NET web page) that confirms the new user account. This link will submit the request GUID through the query string. For example, the link might take this form: *http://www.mysite.com/RegisterUser.asmx? requestGuid=382c74c3-721d-4f34-80e5-57657b6cbc27* (assuming "requestGuid" is the name of the web-method parameter).

3. When the user receives the message and clicks on the link, the confirmation method will run with the identifying GUID.

4. The confirmation method will first check that the response has been received within a reasonable amount of time (for example, three days). If so, it can then find the request record with the matching GUID, remove it from the database, and add the user information to the Users table.

The Last Word

This chapter demonstrated how to integrate a peer-to-peer community that uses Remoting with a discovery web service. Along the way, several changes were made to the overall system, including the addition of a list of registered users in the database. The next chapter builds on these changes to add security using the cryptography classes included with .NET. You'll learn how to validate peer identities and encrypt messages before they travel across the network.

Part Four

Advanced
Peer-to-Peer

CHAPTER 11

Security and Cryptography

WRITING SECURE CODE IS HARD. Even in traditional client-server applications, it's difficult to defend against the vast array of possible threats and attacks. Security considerations stretch across every area of programming, from design to deployment, and include everything from hiding sensitive information to restricting the abilities of different classes of users. Code that runs smoothly, requires user credentials, and uses encryption can still be filled with exploitable security holes. Most often, the professional developers who created it won't have any idea of the risk until these weaknesses are exploited.

In peer-to-peer programming, security considerations are multiplied. Communication is usually over the public Internet, but peers communicate with a wide array of different devices that are often anonymous, and there may not be any central authority for authenticating users. However, a little work can go a long way toward improving the security of any system. This chapter won't tell you how to make a bulletproof security infrastructure—for that you need highly complex protocols such as Kerberos and Secure Sockets Layer (SSL), which can't be easily applied to a peer-to-peer system. However, this chapter shows the security fundamentals that you need to prevent casual hacking, data tampering, and eavesdropping. In other words, if you apply the fundamentals in this chapter, you can change a wide-open application into one that requires significant effort to breach—and that's a worthwhile change.

Security and Peer-to-Peer

Part of the challenge of security is that it's an immense field that covers everything from the way users jot down passwords and lock server-room doors to advanced cryptography. This chapter focuses on two basic types of security issues:

- Authentication and authorization. How do you verify that a user is who he or she claims to be and how do you grant or restrict application privileges based on this identity?

- Encryption and cryptography. How can you ensure that sensitive data cannot be read by an eavesdropper or tampered with by an attacker?

This certainly isn't all there is to security in a peer-to-peer application. For example, you've already seen in Chapter 6 how you can use .NET code-access security to restrict the permissions you give to dynamically executed code. In addition, you might need to make decisions about how you enforce *non-repudiation*, which is how transactional systems ensure that user actions are nonreversible, even if compromised (generally using a combination of logging techniques). You also might want to create an incident response plan for dealing with security problems as well as an auditing system that logs user behavior and alerts users or administrators if a suspicious pattern of behavior emerges.

Security Challenges

The security discussion in this chapter takes the peer-to-peer perspective. The security issues with distributed applications are inherently more complex than in stand-alone applications, and the security considerations for peer-to-peer systems are some of the most complex of all. Unfortunately, the source of peer-to-peer flexibility—loosely defined networks and a lack of server control—can also be the source of endless security headaches.

Some of the challenges in secure peer-to-peer programming include the following:

- How can two peers validate each other's identity if they don't have access to a centralized user database or any authentication information?

- Once two peers validate each other's identity, how do they make trust decisions to determine what interactions are safe?

- As messages are sent over the network, how can a peer be certain that they aren't being tampered with?

- How can a peer hide sensitive data so a hacker can't sniff it out as it travels over the Internet?

- What happens if a malicious user tries to impersonate another user or computer? What happens if a hacker tries to capture the network packets you use for authentication and interaction, and use them later?

This chapter looks at all these considerations, but it won't directly deal with one of the most important details—trying to limit the damage of an attack by coding defensively. Secure programming isn't just about authentication and cryptography; it's also about making sensible coding choices and using basic validation and error-handling logic to close security holes. For example, a file-sharing application should check that it can't be tricked into returning or overwriting a system file. It should also include failsafes that allow it to stop writing a file if the hard drive is out of space or the size of the file seems grossly out of proportion. (For example, if you attempt to download a song and the end of the file still hasn't been reached after 100 MB.)

These common-sense measures can prevent serious security problems. For best results, review your code frequently with other programmers. Spend time in the design, testing, and review stage looking exclusively for security flaws. Take the perspective of a hacker trying to decide what features could be exploited to gain privileged access, steal data, or even just cripple the computer by wasting its CPU or hard-drive resources (a common and often overlooked tactic known as a *denial of service* attack). Unfortunately, you can't find the security problems in a piece of code until they are exploited—and it's far better for you to exploit them in the testing phase than for a hacker to discover them in a real-world environment.

Design Choices

In enterprise development, the best security choice is to rely on third-party security services whenever possible. For example, if you use integrated Windows authentication and SSL encryption, you gain a relatively well-protected system without needing to write a single line of code. Unfortunately, in peer-to-peer applications, your environment probably won't support these features. For example, Windows authentication won't work in its most secure forms between networks. SSL can't be accessed outside of the Internet Information Server (IIS), unless you want to deal with extremely complicated low-level Windows API code.

Fortunately, .NET provides a reasonable alternative: the rich set of classes in the System.Security.Cryptography namespace. These classes allow your code to manually perform various cryptography tasks such as encrypting and decrypting data, signing messages, and so on. However, these features come at a price. Typically, you'll find that the more cryptography code you write, the more tightly your solution becomes bound to a particular platform and implementation. You'll also need to manage a slew of additional details, such as keys, block sizes, .NET-to-binary data-type conversions, and so on. Lastly, although the System.Security.Cryptography namespace contains robust, professional-level classes, it's easy to use these classes incorrectly. In other words, by writing your own cryptography code you increase the chances of leaving security holes. That doesn't mean that it's better to avoid custom cryptography altogether, but it does mean that you should have your cryptography code reviewed by a security expert before a mission-critical application is deployed.

Understanding Cryptography

Before you see a full example with the System.Security.Cryptography classes, you need to understand the basics of three cryptography essentials: hash codes, encryption, and digital signatures.

Understanding Hash Codes

A hash algorithm takes a block of binary data and uses it to generate a fixed-side checksum. For example, the SHA-256 hash algorithm always creates a 256-bit (32-byte) hash for data, regardless of the size of the input data.

Hash codes serve a variety of purposes. One of the most common is to prevent data tampering. For example, consider a scenario in which you store important data on a disk file and record the hash of that data in a database. At a later point, you can open the file, recalculate the hash, and compare it with the value in the database. If the two hashes don't agree, the file has changed. If your program is the only application allowed to access that file, and if your program always records the hash value in the database after making changes, it's reasonable to assume that the file has been tampered with. You can use a similar technique to validate messages that are sent between computers.

Like any type of checksum, a hash algorithm works in one direction only. It's completely impossible to re-create the document from the hash because the hash doesn't include all the information that was in the document. However, cryptographic hash algorithms also have a key characteristic that distinguishes them from other types of checksums: They're collision resistant. Changing even a single byte in the source document has a fifty-fifty chance of independently changing each byte in the hash. It's extremely difficult for an attacker to look at a hash and create a new document that will generate the same hash. (The difficulty of this task is comparable to trying to break an encrypted message through brute force.) Thus, hashes play a key role in ensuring data integrity.

The System.Security.Cryptography namespace includes the following hash algorithms:

- MD5 (implemented by the MD5CryptoServiceProvider class) generates a 128-bit hash.

- SHA-1 (implemented by the SHA1CryptoServiceProvider class) generates a 160-bit hash.

- SHA-256 (implemented by the SHA256Managed class) generates a 256-bit hash.

- SHA-384 (implemented by the SHA384Managed class) generates a 384-bit hash.

- SHA-512 (implemented by the SHA512Managed class) generates a 512-bit hash.

As a rule of thumb, the larger the hash size, the more difficult it is to find another document that will generate a duplicate hash value.

> **NOTE** *Using hash codes isn't enough to protect messages exchanged between computers. The problem is that an attacker can tamper with a message and simply generate a new hash code that matches the altered message. To overcome this problem, you need to combine hashing with some form of encryption to create a keyed hash or digital signature. We'll look at digital signatures later in this chapter.*

Understanding Encryption

There are essentially two types of encryption: symmetric encryption and asymmetric encryption. In many peer-to-peer applications, you'll need to use both. Either way, the basic principle behind encryption is always the same: Encryption scrambles information so that it can only be understood by the recipient. A malicious third party might be able to intercept the message, using characteristics of the network that are beyond your control, but won't be able to decipher it.

Technically, any digitally encrypted message can be broken using a *brute force* attack, which is a process by which an attacker tries every possible sequence of bytes as a key until finally one combination works. In most cases, a brute-force attack is prohibitively expensive, which is to say that the value of the data is less than the cost (in time or computer hardware) of cracking it, or the data will no longer be valid by the time it's deciphered. Very few attacks use brute force. Usually, they rely on weak or compromised passwords or flaws in the application or platform that are much easier to exploit.

Symmetric encryption (also known as "secret-key" encryption) is the type of encryption that most people are familiar with. It depends on a shared, secret key that's used to encrypt and decrypt data. Technically, this secret key is a series of bytes that can be derived from a password or other information as needed. Symmetric encryption is far faster than asymmetric encryption but suffers from a significant limitation in distributed computing scenarios: Both parties need to know the secret key before the communication begins. There's no easy way to transmit the secret key information without compromising security.

The .NET Framework includes the following symmetric algorithms:

- DES (implemented by the DESCryptoServiceProvider class) uses a 64-bit key.

- TripleDES (implemented by the TripleDESCryptoServiceProvider class) uses a 128-bit or 192-bit key.

- RC2 (implemented by the RC2CryptoServiceProvider class) uses a 40- to 128-bit key.

- Rijndael (implemented by the RijndaelManaged class) uses a 128-bit, 192-bit, or 256-bit key.

The larger the key size, the harder it is for a brute-force attack to succeed. Generally, DES is supported for legacy uses only, because its 64-bit key size is considered dangerously weak. Rijndael is the recommended encryption algorithm.

Asymmetric encryption uses a pair of mathematically related keys that includes both a public and private key. The private key is carefully guarded, while the public key is made available to the entire world. The interesting thing about asymmetric encryption is that any data encrypted with one key can only be decrypted with the other matching key. This makes asymmetric encryption very versatile.

For example, consider two peers communicating on a network. Each peer has its own key pair.

1. Peer A encrypts a message using the public key that belongs to Peer B.

2. Peer A sends the message to Peer B.

3. Peer B decrypts the message using the corresponding private key. No other user can decrypt this message (not even Peer A, the one who created it) because no one else has the private key.

This demonstrates how asymmetric encryption can be used to protect information without needing to exchange a shared, secret key value. This makes it possible for any two parties on a network to exchange encrypted data, even if they have never met before. The process is diagrammed in Figure 11-1.

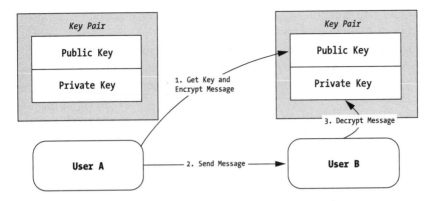

Figure 11-1. How user A can send an encrypted message to user B

Asymmetric encryption also underlies a special form of message validation. It works like this:

1. Peer A encrypts a message using its own private key.

2. Peer A sends the message to Peer B.

3. Peer B decrypts the message using the public key belonging to Peer A. Because this key is publicly available, any user can perform this step. However, because the message can only be encrypted using the private key, Peer B now knows beyond a doubt that the message originated from Peer A.

This shows you how message authentication works with asymmetric encryption. In practice, you don't need to encrypt the entire message—just a hash code, as described in the next section. Often, both validation and encryption will be combined in the same application to prevent message tampering and hide sensitive data. This is the approach taken in the peer-to-peer example shown later in this chapter.

.NET provides implementation for two asymmetric algorithms:

*   RSA (implemented by the RSACryptoServiceProvider class) allows key sizes from 364 to 16,384 bits (in 8-bit increments).

*   DSA (implemented by the DSACryptoServiceProvider class) allows key sizes from 364 to 512 bits (in 64-bit increments).

In most cases, you'll use RSA, because DSA can only be used for creating and verifying digital signatures, not for encrypting data. Note that asymmetric encryption allows for much larger key sizes. However, the key size can be misleading. It's estimated that a 1,024-bit RSA key (the default size) is roughly equivalent in strength to a 75-bit symmetric key.

Asymmetric encryption does have one significant shortcoming: It's slow, often hundreds of times slower than symmetric encryption. It also produces less compact ciphertext (encrypted data) than symmetric encryption. Thus, if you need to encode a large amount of information (for example in a file-sharing application), asymmetric encryption alone is probably not the approach you want. A better choice is to combine symmetric and asymmetric encryption. We'll discuss this topic a little later.

Understanding Digital Signatures

Digital signatures combine the concepts of hash codes and asymmetric encryption. Remember, hash codes are used to take a digital "fingerprint" of some data, and thereby prevent it from being altered. However, attackers can get around this defense if hash codes aren't stored in a secure location by regenerating and replacing the hash code. Digital signatures prevent this type of tampering using encryption.

To sign some data with a digital signature, a user creates a hash and then encrypts the hash using a private key. Any other user can validate the signature because the corresponding public key is freely available, but no other user can generate a new signature because they won't have the required private key. Thus, a digital signature is tamper-proof.

Of course, life isn't quite this simple. In order for this system to work, the recipient must already know the public key of the message author. Otherwise, the signature can't be validated. Unfortunately, you can't just transmit the public key, because then it could be read and replaced by the same attacker who will attempt to tamper with the message! The solution? Use a third party that can validate users and vouch for their public keys. On the Internet, this is often performed with digital certificates. Digital certificates contain a user's public and private keys and are signed by a third-party certificate authority (CA) such as VeriSign. When you establish an SSL connection with a website, your computer decides to trust the website's identity because it provides a certificate signed by a trusted CA.

In a peer-to-peer application, you could use certificates (in fact, Intel's Peer-to-Peer Accelerator Kit provides exactly this feature, as described in Chapter 13). However, .NET doesn't provide any classes either for working with certificates in a user's certificate store or validating that a certificate is signed by a trusted CA. In addition, the certificate itself cannot contain application-specific information, such as whether a user should be given supervisor or guest rights in a peer-to-peer application. To get around this limitation in this chapter, we'll use our discovery service to act as a central authority for user-identity validation. It will map public keys to application-specific permissions using the database.

NOTE *.NET does provide classes that allow you to read some basic certificate information from a certificate file. This rudimentary functionality is found in the System.Security.Cryptography.X509Certificates namespace. In addition, the downloadable Web Services Enhancements (WSE) provides some tools for reading information from installed certificates. In future versions of the .NET Framework, these features will be more closely integrated.*

Asserting Identity with Digital Signatures

To put these concepts into practice, we'll return to Talk .NET and the discovery service presented in the previous chapter. Using the discovery service, users query the server for a peer (by e-mail address), and receive an ObjRef that points to the peer. It shouldn't be possible for a malicious user to impersonate another user by logging in with the wrong e-mail address.

To prevent impersonation, you need to modify the Talk .NET server. The new server must take the following authentication steps:

- When a user creates a new account, the server tests the e-mail address and verifies that the user has access to that e-mail. It then stores a record for the user that includes public key information and the e-mail address. Duplicate e-mail addresses aren't allowed.

- When a user logs in for a session, the server validates the user's login request against the public key information stored in the database. The most secure way to perform this step is for the user to sign the login message using a digital signature. If the signatures can be verified with the public key information in the database, then the server can conclude that the user has access to the private key. The user is then authenticated, and a new session is started.

- When a user queries the discovery service for a reference to another user, they can now be sure that this reference corresponds to the originally registered user, unless the key has been stolen.

We'll walk through the .NET cryptography code needed for this operation—and consider some of its shortcomings—over the next few sections.

The Server Database

The discovery service developed in Chapter 10 stores a list of unique e-mail addresses, which serve as user IDs. In this example, we'll modify the database so that the Peers table also includes public key information, as shown in Figure 11-2.

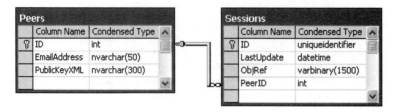

Figure 11-2. The revised Peers table

This information is stored as an XML string, because the .NET classes for asymmetric encryption provide a ToXmlString() method that can export public or private key information in a standardized format. You can then use this data to re-create the encryption object later. Here's a code snippet that demonstrates how it works:

```
' Create a new cryptographic object that encapsulates a new,
' dynamically generated key pair.
Dim Rsa As New RSACryptoServiceProvider()

' Retrieve the full key information as a string with XML data,
' using the True parameter.
Dim KeyPairInfo As String = Rsa.ToXmlString(True)

' Retrieve just the public key information as a string with XML data,
' using the False parameter.
Dim PublicKeyInfo As String = Rsa.ToXmlString(False)

' Create a new duplicate RSA object and load the full key data into it.
Dim RsaDuplicate As New RSACryptoServiceProvider()
RsaDuplicate.FromXmlString(KeyPairInfo)

' Create a duplicate RSA object with public key information only.
' This allows you to validate signatures and encrypt data, but you can't decrypt data.
Dim RsaPublicOnly As New RSACryptoServiceProvider()
RsaPublicOnly.FromXmlString(PublicKeyInfo)
```

Note that the database table only includes the *public* key information. This is enough for the server to validate signatures from the user. The server should never be given access to a user's private key, because that information must be carefully protected! The peer will store the full key pair on the local computer. In our example, this information is simply saved to the peer's hard drive, which means that an attacker could impersonate the user if the attacker can steal the key file. Other approaches might be to store this data in the registry, in a secure database, or even in a custom piece of hardware. The latter provides the best security, but it's obviously very unlikely in a peer-to-peer scenario.

Along with these changes, the database class, database stored procedure, and web service need to be modified so that they store the public key XML information in the database. These changes aren't shown here because they're all very trivial. As you'll see, the tricky part comes when you need to actually use the key.

The Client Login

When the client first loads, it presents the user with a choice of creating a new account or using an existing one, as shown in Figure 11-3. If the user chooses to create a new account, the key information is saved to disk. If the user chooses to use an existing account, the key information is retrieved from disk. Of course, the user should not be able to create an account if the matching key already exists, or allowed to use an existing account if the key information can't be found.

Figure 11-3. The Login window

The startup code is shown here. Note that the key information is stored in a file that uses the unique user ID, which is the e-mail address.

```
' Create the login window, which retrieves the user identifier.
Dim frmLogin As New Login()

' Create the cryptography object with the key pair.
Dim Rsa As New RSACryptoServiceProvider()

' Create the new remotable client object.
Dim Client As ClientProcess
```

```
' Only continue if the user successfully exits by clicking OK
' (not the Cancel or Exit button).
Do
    If Not frmLogin.ShowDialog() = DialogResult.OK Then End

    Try
        If frmLogin.CreateNew Then
            If File.Exists(frmLogin.UserName) Then
                MessageBox.Show("Cannot create new account. " & _
                    "Key file already exists for this user.")
            Else
                ' Generate a new key pair for this account.
                Rsa = New RSACryptoServiceProvider()

                Client = New ClientProcess(frmLogin.UserName, _
                    frmLogin.CreateNew, Rsa)

                ' Write the full key information to the hard drive.
                Dim fs As New FileStream(frmLogin.UserName, FileMode.Create)
                Dim w As New BinaryWriter(fs)
                w.Write(Rsa.ToXmlString(True))
                w.Flush()
                fs.Close()

                Exit Do
            End If
        Else

            If File.Exists(frmLogin.UserName) Then

                ' Retrieve the full key information from the hard drive
                ' and use it to set the Rsa object.
                Dim fs As New FileStream(frmLogin.UserName, FileMode.Open)
                Dim r As New BinaryReader(fs)
                Rsa.FromXmlString(r.ReadString())
                fs.Close()

                Client = New ClientProcess(frmLogin.UserName, _
                    frmLogin.CreateNew, Rsa)
                Exit Do
            Else
                MessageBox.Show("No key file exists for this user.")
            End If
```

```
        End If

    Catch Err As Exception
        MessageBox.Show(Err.Message)
    End Try

Loop

' (Create and show the client form as usual).
```

The SignedObject Class

In this example you only need to use digital signature authentication in the Login() web method. However, it would be a mistake to code this logic directly in the web method itself. In order to ensure that the logic that runs on the client is consistent with the logic that runs on the server, and in order to reuse the signing logic in other places if it becomes necessary, you should abstract this functionality in a dedicated class. This class should be placed in a separate component.

In this example, the dedicated class is called SignedObject. The SignedObject class allows you to attach a digital signature to any .NET object using serialization. Here's how the signing process works:

1. You define a serializable class that contains all the data you want to sign. For example, the StartSession() web method will use a serializable LoginInfo class that stores the e-mail address of the user attempting to log on.

2. You create and configure the serializable object in code. Then, you create the SignedObject class. The SignedObject class provides a constructor that takes any object, along with the key pair XML.

3. The SignedObject constructor serializes the supplied object to a byte array. It uses the key pair XML to create a new cryptography object and generate a signature.

4. Both the signature and the serialized object are stored in private member variables.

5. Because SignedObject is itself serializable, you can convert the entire package, signature and all, to a stream of bytes using .NET serialization. This is necessary for web methods, because they won't allow you to use SignedObject directly as a parameter type. Instead, you'll have to use the provided Serialize() method to convert it to a byte array, and submit that to the server.

In this example, the SignedObject will be used to sign instances of the LoginInfo class, which encapsulates the information required for a user to log in. The LoginInfo class is shown here:

```
<Serializable()> _
Public Class LoginInfo

    Public EmailAddress As String
    Public TimeStamp As DateTime
    Public ObjRef As Byte()


End Class
```

On the web-service side, these steps take place:

1. The server deserializes the byte array into the SignedObject, using the shared Deserialize() method.

2. Next, the server looks up the appropriate public key XML information, and submits it to the ValidateSignature() method. This method returns true if the newly generated computer signature matches the stored signature.

3. The GetObjectWithoutSignature() method can be used at any time to retrieve the inner object (in this case, the LoginInfo object). Remember, this doesn't mean the signature is valid, so before you call this method make sure to validate the signature. (Another approach would be to perform the signature validation in the GetObjectWithoutSignature() method, and throw an exception if the signatures don't match.)

Figure 11-4 shows the end-to-end process on the client and server.

The full SignedObject code is shown in the code listing that follows. Notice that data is serialized between .NET data types and binary data using the BinaryFormatter class. To create a signature with the RsaCryptoServiceProvider class, you use the SignData() method. To validate the signature, you use the VerifyData() method.

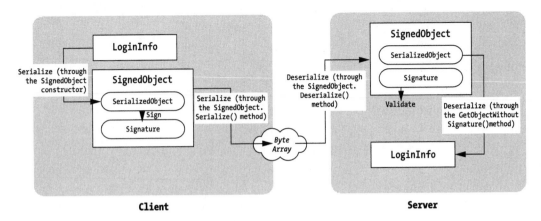

Figure 11-4. Using SignedObject to sign a LoginInfo

```vb
Imports System.Security.Cryptography
Imports System.IO
Imports System.Runtime.Serialization.Formatters.Binary

<Serializable()> _
Public Class SignedObject

    ' Stores the signed object.
    Private SerializedObject As New MemoryStream()

    ' Stores the object's signature.
    Private Signature() As Byte

    Public Sub New(ByVal objectToSign As Object, ByVal keyPairXml As String)

        ' Serialize a copy of objectToSign in memory.
        Dim f As New BinaryFormatter()
        f.Serialize(Me.SerializedObject, objectToSign)

        ' Add the signature.
        Me.SerializedObject.Position = 0
        Dim Rsa As New RSACryptoServiceProvider()
        Rsa.FromXmlString(keyPairXml)
        Me.Signature = Rsa.SignData(Me.SerializedObject, HashAlgorithm.Create())

    End Sub
```

```vbnet
Public Shared Function Deserialize(ByVal signedObjectBytes() As Byte) _
  As SignedObject

    ' Deserialize the SignedObject.
    Dim ObjectStream As New MemoryStream()
    ObjectStream.Write(signedObjectBytes, 0, signedObjectBytes.Length)
    ObjectStream.Position = 0
    Dim f As New BinaryFormatter()
    Return CType(f.Deserialize(ObjectStream), SignedObject)

End Function


Public Function Serialize() As Byte()

    ' Serialize the whole package, signature and all.
    Dim f As New BinaryFormatter()
    Dim ObjectStream As New MemoryStream()
    f.Serialize(ObjectStream, Me)
    Return ObjectStream.ToArray()

End Function


Public Function ValidateSignature(ByVal publicKeyXml) As Boolean

    ' Calculate a new signature using the supplied public key, and
    ' indicate whether it matches the stored signature.
    Dim Rsa As New RSACryptoServiceProvider()
    Rsa.FromXmlString(publicKeyXml)
    Return Rsa.VerifyData(Me.SerializedObject.ToArray(), _
      HashAlgorithm.Create(), Me.Signature)

End Function


Public Function GetObjectWithoutSignature() As Object

    ' Deserialize the inner (packaged) object.
    Dim f As New BinaryFormatter()
    Me.SerializedObject.Position = 0
    Return f.Deserialize(Me.SerializedObject)

End Function


End Class
```

The code in this class may appear complex, but it's vastly simpler to work with than it would be if you didn't use .NET serialization. In that case, you would have to manually calculate hash sizes, copy the hash to the end of the message bytes, and so on. Even worse, if you made a minor mistake such as miscalculating a byte offset, an error would occur.

The Login Process on the Client Side

The ClientProcess.Login() method requires some minor changes to work with the cryptographic components. The modified lines are emphasized.

```
Public Sub Login()

    ' Configure the client channel for sending messages and receiving
    ' the server callback.
    RemotingConfiguration.Configure("TalkClient.exe.config")

    ' Retrieve the ObjRef for this class.
    Dim Obj As ObjRef = RemotingServices.Marshal(Me)

    ' Serialize the ObjRef to a memory stream.
    Dim ObjStream As New MemoryStream()
    Dim f As New BinaryFormatter()
    f.Serialize(ObjStream, Obj)

    ' Define the login information.
    Dim Login As New LoginInfo()
    Login.EmailAddress = Me.Alias
    Login.ObjRef = ObjStream.ToArray()
    Login.TimeStamp = DiscoveryService.GetServerDateTime()

    ' Sign the login information.
    Dim Package As New SignedObject(Login, Me.Rsa.ToXmlString(True))

    ' Start a new session by submitting the signed object,
    ' and then record the session GUID.
    Me.SessionID = DiscoveryService.StartSession(Package.Serialize())

End Sub
```

The Login Process on the Web-Server Side

One detail we haven't addressed is the use of a timestamp. This prevents a type of exploit known as a *replay attack*, whereby a malicious user records network traffic and then "replays" it (copies it back into the network stream) to become authenticated later on. It's doubtful that a replay attack would succeed with this application, because the ObjRef would no longer be valid. Still, using a time-stamp tightens security. The server can check the time, and if it's set in the future or more than two minutes in the past, the server will reject the request. Of course, in order for this to work in systems in which clients could have different regional time settings (or just incorrect times), the client must retrieve the server time using the GetServerDateTime() web method.

```
<WebMethod()> _
Public Function GetServerDateTime() As DateTime
    Return DateTime.Now
End Function
```

The StartSession method that deserializes the package, validates the time information, retrieves the public key that matches the user e-mail address from the database, and uses it to validate the signature. Assuming all these checks pass, it stores the ObjRef in the database.

```
<WebMethod()> _
Public Function StartSession(ByVal signedLoginInfo As Byte()) As Guid

    Try
        Dim Package As SignedObject = SignedObject.Deserialize(signedLoginInfo)
        Dim Login As LoginInfo = CType(Package.GetObjectWithoutSignature, _
          LoginInfo)

        ' Check date.
        If DateTime.Now.Subtract(Login.TimeStamp).TotalMinutes > 2 Or _
          DateTime.Now.Subtract(Login.TimeStamp).TotalMinutes < 0 Then
            Throw New ApplicationException("Invalid request message.")
        End If

        ' Verify the signature.
        Dim Peer As PeerInfo = DB.GetPeerInfo(Login.EmailAddress)
        If Not Package.ValidateSignature(Peer.PublicKeyXml) Then
            Throw New ApplicationException("Invalid request message.")
        End If
```

```
      Return DB.CreateSession(Peer.EmailAddress, Login.ObjRef)
   Catch err As Exception
      Trace.Write(err.ToString)
      Throw New ApplicationException("Could not create session.")
   End Try

End Function
```

One side effect of using custom cryptography is the fact that the web service becomes much less generic. The design we've introduced forces clients not only to use the SignedObject class, but to know *when* to use it. Data is simply supplied as a byte array, so problems could occur if the client serializes the wrong type of object (or uses a different version of the cryptographic component from the one the server is using). These details must be tightly controlled, or they will quickly become a source of new headaches. Unfortunately, this is a necessary trade-off.

> **TIP** *You may want to place the LoginInfo class into a separate assembly, and never update that assembly in order to prevent any versioning problems with serialization. Alternatively, you can write custom serialization code, which is beyond the scope of this book.*

Weaknesses in This Approach

The key limitation in this design is the server, which is trusted implicitly. What happens if a malicious user is able to perform some type of IP spoofing, or intercept communication before it reaches the server? This type of attack generally requires some type of privileged network access (and thus is less common than some other attacks), but it's a significant risk in a large-scale application. The attacker then has the ability to impersonate the server and return a validated ObjRef that actually points to the wrong user.

There's no easy way around the challenge of validating the server identity. One option is for the server to sign all its response using the SignedObject class. The peer will then retrieve the response and validate the digital signature before attempting to use the ObjRef. In order for this to work, each client would need to be deployed with the information about the server's public key (perhaps stored in a configuration file). Otherwise, they would have no way to validate the signature.

Another problem is that the identity validation currently works only in one direction. In other words, a peer can validate the identity of another peer before contacting it. However, when a peer is contacted, the peer has no way to validate the user that's initiating the contact. In order to remedy this problem, the peers would need to exchange digitally signed messages. Any peer could then retrieve the public key XML for another peer from the server, and then use it to authenticate incoming messages. To ensure optimum performance, the peer XML information could be cached in memory in a local hashtable, so that the peer doesn't need to repeatedly contact the remote web service to request the same key information. (This pattern is shown in the previous chapter with the RecentClients collection.)

You should also remember that the use of signatures simply helps to ensure that a user identity remains consistent between the time it's created and the time the user starts a session. It doesn't necessarily indicate anything about the trustworthiness of the user—you need to perform those verifications before you register the user in the database. And no matter what approach you use, you're still at the mercy of a properly authenticated user who behaves improperly.

Trust Decisions

In the messaging example, the service is used to return a single piece of information: an object reference that can be used for a Remoting interaction. However, there's no reason why the server can't store additional information. For example, it might provide personal contact information for the user, or assign the user a specific set of permissions at a custom security level using a custom database. It's up to your application to retrieve and interpret this information, but the overall design is still the same.

Hiding Information with Encryption

In the previous example, cryptography is used to assist in user authentication. However, no steps are taken to hide data as it flows over the wire. Malicious users can eavesdrop and discover valuable information such as the ObjRef (where a client can be reached), or the e-mails of users that are currently online, and so on. The same problem occurs with communication between peers. Currently, messages flow over the network as plain text, which is visible to any user in the right place with a network sniffer.

You can solve this problem by adding a new class to the cryptography component, which you can use on both the client and web-server end. This is the EncryptedObject class.

The EncryptedObject Class

In adding an encryption solution, you can use the same approach we used for signing data. In this case, you'll need a dedicated class, which we'll name EncryptedObject. The methods exposed by this class are quite similar to those provided by the SignedObject class, but the code involved is somewhat more complicated. This is because when you use asymmetric encryption you must encrypt data one block at a time. If you need to encrypt data that's larger than one block, you must divide it into multiple blocks, encrypt each one individually, and piece the encrypted blocks back together.

Here's an overview of how you would use the EncryptedObject:

1. First, create and configure a serializable object.

2. Create the EncryptedObject class. The EncryptedObject class provides a constructor that takes any object, along with the public key XML (which should be the public key of the recipient). This constructor serializes the object, encrypts it, and stores it in an internal member variable.

3. You can then convert the encrypted object into a byte array through .NET serialization using the Serialize() method. This is the data you'd send to the other peer.

4. The recipient deserializes the byte array into an EncryptedObject, using the shared Deserialize() method.

5. The recipient calls the DecryptContainedObject() method with its private key to retrieve the original object.

The EncryptedObject code is shown here. The Serialize() and Deserialize() methods are omitted, because they're identical to those used in the SignedObject class.

```
<Serializable()> _
Public Class EncryptedObject

    Private SerializedObject As New MemoryStream()

    Public Sub New(ByVal objectToEncrypt As Object, ByVal publicKeyXml As String)

        ' Serialize a copy of objectToEncrypt in memory.
        Dim f As New BinaryFormatter()
        Dim ObjectStream As New MemoryStream()
        f.Serialize(ObjectStream, objectToEncrypt)
        ObjectStream.Position = 0

        Dim Rsa As New RSACryptoServiceProvider()
        Rsa.FromXmlString(publicKeyXml)
```

```
    ' The block size depends on the key size.
    Dim BlockSize As Integer
    If Rsa.KeySize = 1024 Then
        BlockSize = 16
    Else
        BlockSize = 5
    End If

    ' Move through the data one block at a time.
    Dim RawBlock(), EncryptedBlock() As Byte
    Dim i As Integer
    Dim Bytes As Integer = ObjectStream.Length
    For i = 0 To Bytes Step BlockSize

        If Bytes - i > BlockSize Then
            ReDim RawBlock(BlockSize - 1)
        Else
            ReDim RawBlock(Bytes - i - 1)
        End If

        ' Copy a block of data.
        ObjectStream.Read(RawBlock, 0, RawBlock.Length)

        ' Encrypt the block of data.
        EncryptedBlock = Rsa.Encrypt(RawBlock, False)

        ' Write the block of data.
        Me.SerializedObject.Write(EncryptedBlock, 0, EncryptedBlock.Length)
    Next

End Sub

' (Serialize and Deserialize methods omitted.)

Public Function DecryptContainedObject(ByVal keyPairXml As String) As Object

    Dim Rsa As New RSACryptoServiceProvider()
    Rsa.FromXmlString(keyPairXml)

    ' Create the memory stream where the decrypted data
    ' will be stored.
    Dim ObjectStream As New MemoryStream()
```

```
'Dim ObjectBytes() As Byte = Me.SerializedObject.ToArray()
Me.SerializedObject.Position = 0
' Determine the block size for decrypting.
Dim keySize As Integer = Rsa.KeySize / 8

' Move through the data one block at a time.
Dim DecryptedBlock(), RawBlock() As Byte
Dim i As Integer
Dim Bytes As Integer = Me.SerializedObject.Length
For i = 0 To bytes - 1 Step keySize

    If ((Bytes - i) > keySize) Then
        ReDim RawBlock(keySize - 1)
    Else
        ReDim RawBlock(Bytes - i - 1)
    End If

    ' Copy a block of data.
    Me.SerializedObject.Read(RawBlock, 0, RawBlock.Length)

    ' Decrypt a block of data.
    DecryptedBlock = Rsa.Decrypt(RawBlock, False)

    ' Write the decrypted data to the in-memory stream.
    ObjectStream.Write(DecryptedBlock, 0, DecryptedBlock.Length)
Next

ObjectStream.Position = 0
Dim f As New BinaryFormatter()
Return f.Deserialize(ObjectStream)

End Function

End Class
```

Sending and Receiving Encrypted Messages

Now, you only need to make minor changes to the ClientProcess class in order
to use encryption with the EncryptedObject class. First, you need to define
a Message class that will contain the information that's being sent:

```
<Serializable()> _
Public Class Message

    Public SenderAlias As String
    Public MessageBody As String

    Public Sub New(ByVal sender As String, ByVal body As String)
        Me.SenderAlias = sender
        Me.MessageBody = body
    End Sub

End Class
```

You also need to modify the ITalkClient interface:

```
Public Interface ITalkClient

    ' The server calls this to forward a message to the appropriate client.
    Sub ReceiveMessage(ByVal encryptedMessage As EncryptedObject)

End Interface
```

When sending a message, you need to construct a Message object and encrypt it. You don't need to use the Serialize() method to convert it to a byte stream because the .NET Remoting infrastructure can automatically convert serializable types for you. The full code is shown here, with the modified lines highlighted in bold. Note that the public XML information is retrieved from the web service as needed for the peer.

```
Public Sub SendMessage(ByVal emailAddress As String, ByVal messageBody As String)

    Dim PeerInfo As localhost.PeerInfo

    ' Check if the peer-connectivity information is cached.
    If RecentClients.Contains(emailAddress) Then
        PeerInfo = CType(RecentClients(emailAddress), localhost.PeerInfo)
    Else
        PeerInfo = DiscoveryService.GetPeerInfo(emailAddress)
        RecentClients.Add(PeerInfo.EmailAddress, PeerInfo)
    End If

    Dim ObjStream As New MemoryStream(PeerInfo.ObjRef)
    Dim f As New BinaryFormatter()
    Dim Obj As Object = f.Deserialize(ObjStream)
```

```
    Dim Peer As ITalkClient = CType(Obj, ITalkClient)

    Dim Message As New Message(Me.Alias, messageBody)
    Dim Package As New EncryptedObject(Message, PeerInfo.PublicKeyXml)

    Try
        Peer.ReceiveMessage(Package)
    Catch
        ' Ignore connectivity errors.
    End Try

End Sub
```

When receiving a message, the peer simply decrypts the contents using its private key.

```
Private Sub ReceiveMessage(ByVal encryptedMessage As EncryptedObject) _
  Implements ITalkClient.ReceiveMessage

    Dim Message As Message
    Message = CType(encryptedMessage.DecryptContainedObject( _
      Me.Rsa.ToXmlString(True)), Message)
    RaiseEvent MessageReceived(Me, _
      New MessageReceivedEventArgs(Message.MessageBody, Message.SenderAlias))

End Sub
```

The same technique can be applied to protect any data. For example, you could (and probably should) use it to encrypt messages exchanged between the client and discovery service.

Chaining Encryption and Signing

The designs of the EncryptedObject and SignedObject classes lend themselves particularly well to being used together. For example, you can create a signed, encrypted message by wrapping a Message object in an EncryptedObject, and then wrapping the EncryptedObject in a SignedObject. (You could also do it the other way around, but the encrypt-and-sign approach is convenient because it allows you to validate the signature before you perform the decryption.) Figure 11-5 diagrams this process.

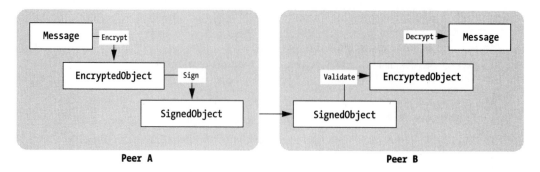

Figure 11-5. Encrypting and signing a message

Here's the code you would use to encrypt and sign the message:

```
Dim Message As New Message(Me.Alias, messageBody)

' Encrypt the message using the recipient's public key.
Dim EncryptedPackage As New EncryptedObject(Message, PeerInfo.PublicKeyXml)

' Sign the message with the sender's private key.
Dim SignedPackage As New SignedObject(Message, Me.Rsa.ToXmlString(True))

Try
    Peer.ReceiveMessage(SignedPackage)
Catch
    ' Ignore connectivity errors.
End Try
```

The recipient would then validate the signature, deserialize the encrypted object, and then decrypt it:

```
' Verify the signature.
If Not encryptedPackage.ValidateSignature(PeerInfo.PublicKeyXml) Then
    ' Ignore this message.
Else
    Dim EncryptedMessage As EncryptedObject
    EncryptedMessage = CType(encryptedPackage.GetObjectWithoutSignature, _
        EncryptedObject)

    ' Decrypt the message.
    Dim Message As Message
    Message = CType(EncryptedMessage.DecryptContainedObject( _
        Me.Rsa.ToXmlString(True)), Message)
```

```
RaiseEvent MessageReceived(Me, _
    New MessageReceivedEventArgs(Message.MessageBody, Message.SenderAlias))


End If
```

Using Session Keys

There's one other enhancement that you might want to make to this example. As described earlier, asymmetric encryption is much slower than symmetric encryption. In the simple message-passing example this won't make much of a difference, but if you need to exchange larger amounts of data it becomes much more important.

In this case, the solution is to use symmetric encryption. However, because both peers won't share a symmetric key, you'll have to create one dynamically and then encrypt it asymmetrically. The recipient will use its private key to decrypt the symmetric key, and then use the symmetric key to decrypt the remainder of the message.

This pattern is shown, in abbreviated form, with the following LargeEncryptedObject class. It includes the code used to encrypt the serializable object, but leaves out the asymmetric encryption logic used to encrypt the dynamic symmetric key for brevity. The code used for symmetric encryption is much shorter, because it can use a special object called the CryptoStream. The CryptoStream manages blockwise encryption automatically and can be used to wrap any other .NET stream object. For example, you can use a CryptoStream to perform automatic encryption before data is sent to a FileStream, or perform automatic decryption as it is read to memory. In the case of the LargeEncryptedObject, the CryptoStream wraps another memory stream.

```
<Serializable()> _
Public Class LargeEncryptedObject

    Private SerializedObject As New MemoryStream()
    Private EncryptedDynamicKey() As Byte

    Public Sub New(ByVal objectToEncrypt As Object, ByVal publicKeyXml As String)

        ' Generate the new symmetric key.
        ' In this example, we'll use the Rijndael algorithm.
        Dim Rijn As New RijndaelManaged()
```

```
' Encrypt the RijndaelManaged.Key and RijndaelManaged.IV properties.
' Store the data in the EncryptedDynamicKey member variable.
' (Asymmetric encryption code omitted.)

' Write the data to a stream that encrypts automatically.
Dim cs As New CryptoStream(Me.SerializedObject,_
  Rijn.CreateEncryptor(), CryptoStreamMode.Write)

' Serialize and encrypt the object in one step using the CryptoStream.
Dim f As New BinaryFormatter()
f.Serialize(cs, objectToEncrypt)

' Write the final block.
cs.FlushFinalBlock()

End Sub

Public Function DecryptContainedObject(ByVal keyPairXml As String) As Object

' Generate the new symmetric key.
Dim Rijn As New RijndaelManaged()

' Decrypt the EncryptedDynamic key member variable, and use it to set
' the RijndaelManaged.Key and RijndaelManaged.IV properties.
' (Asymmetric decryption code omitted.)

' Write the data to a stream that decrypts automatically.
Dim ms As New MemoryStream()
Dim cs As New CryptoStream(ms, Rijn.CreateDecryptor(), _
  CryptoStreamMode.Write)

' Decrypt the object 1 KB at a time.
Dim i, BytesRead As Integer
Dim Bytes(1023) As Byte
For i = 0 To Me.SerializedObject.Length
    BytesRead = Me.SerializedObject.Read(Bytes, 0, Bytes.Length)
    cs.Write(Bytes, 0, BytesRead)
Next

' Write the final block.
cs.FlushFinalBlock()
```

```
' Now deserialize the decrypted memory stream.
ms.Position = 0
Dim f As New BinaryFormatter()
Return f.Deserialize(ms)

End Function

' (Serialize and Deserialize methods omitted.)

End Class
```

A full description of the .NET cryptography classes and the CryptoStream is beyond the scope of this book.

The Last Word

This chapter examined two core security topics. First, we considered how you can use a third party to provide authentication services to a peer-to-peer application. Second, we looked at how you can implement encryption between peers to protect sensitive data. Both of these techniques require .NET cryptography classes and some custom code, and they won't ever be as foolproof as a standard system such as SSL or Kerberos. However, they can add a valuable layer of protection in environments where these protocols aren't supported. Understanding how to implement this type of security also makes you better prepared to evaluate the security that's implemented in third-party platforms such as the Intel Peer-to-Peer Accelerator Kit and Groove.

Security is an enormous topic, and there are countless books dedicated exclusively to cryptography and .NET security. Security isn't just about cryptography, and using cryptography doesn't ensure that your data is safe! Always evaluate your peer-to-peer applications from an attacker-centric point of view when testing it. And remember, a small amount of validation code can often dramatically reduce the damage of a successful attack.

CHAPTER 12

Working with Messenger and Groove

ALL OF THE PEER-TO-PEER APPLICATIONS developed so far in this book have been designed from the ground up, using nothing but built-in .NET technologies. You need to code the business logic, decide how the interaction of distributed nodes will take place, and create the network and directory or lookup services. Now, in the last two chapters, we'll consider some new options.

In this chapter, we'll look at how you can create a peer-to-peer application by using an existing peer-to-peer network. You'll learn how you can create your own application that piggybacks on the popular Windows Messenger network or uses the Groove platform. Both of these choices are best suited for specialized applications over which you don't need complete control. They also present some interesting choices. For example, you might want to build a collaborative tool that you can run with a Groove tool or use the Windows Messenger as a background to send messages that coordinate multiple workers as they process a distributed task such as the one shown in Chapter 6. We'll also briefly consider some other peer-to-peer development platforms.

Using Windows Messenger

Windows Messenger is a popular protocol for instant messaging between peers. It uses a centralized peer-to-peer model. All messages are sent through the server using peer-to-server connections, except for file transfer and voice chat.

There are three types of servers involved in the Messenger system:

- Dispatch server. This is the initial point of connection. It refers users to the appropriate notification server. The dispatch server can be found at *messenger.hotmail.com* on port 1863.

- Notification server. This is where the sessions are maintained while users are interacting with the system.

- Switchboard server. This server acts as a gateway between users for chat. A new switchboard session is opened for every chat window in Messenger. All messages are routed through the switchboard, including file transfer and voice chat invitations.

The actual MSN Messenger protocol is fairly simple. It consists of predefined ASCII messages that are exchanged over a TCP connection. The latest version of this protocol (MSNP7) is described unofficially by Mike Mintz at http://www.hypothetic.org/docs/msn. Using the information provided here, in conjunction with the standard .NET TCP classes, you could connect to a Messenger server, retrieve contacts, send messages, and so on.

Writing this type of application wouldn't be too difficult, but it would involve some detailed study of the Messenger protocol. A much easier option is to use the MSNP Helper API for .NET, an open-source .NET component that allows you to interact with the Windows Messenger network almost effortlessly. You can download the MSNP Helper API and documentation and read any recent news at its SourceForge.net home page, http://msnphelper.sourceforge.net. Documentation is in the form of an HTML Help class library reference, and the component is included in a single assembly named *msnp.dll,* which you can reference in your projects.

> **NOTE** *The MSNP Helper API for .NET doesn't use the MSNP7 protocol. Instead, it uses the somewhat older MSNP2 protocol, which is the only protocol to have been released officially. Presumably, the officially undocumented MSNP7 protocol could change without warning. Neither protocol has any official support.*

So why would you want to create a custom program that uses the Messenger network? One reason might just be to access or add features that wouldn't otherwise be available, such as the ability to send large messages, encrypt messages before they reach the server, or log the status of users over a long period of time. Or, you might want to create another type of application that isn't primarily concerned with sending and receiving messages. Some possibilities include the following:

- A long-running service that monitors when a user appears or leaves and launches other tasks accordingly.

- An automated tool that sends certain types of messages to specified users at specified times.

- Some type of task processor that routes business-specific commands through Messenger. In this case, you would probably define the commands using string constants (much as in Chapter 9).

Microsoft doesn't officially support using the Messenger network in this way. However, it hasn't acted to discourage individual developers from "reasonable" use that doesn't abuse the system.

Creating a Windows Messenger Client

To learn how to use the MSNP component, it helps to create a simple Messenger client that emulates some of the standard features found in the Windows Messenger application. As a prerequisite, you should understand how a basic Messenger interaction works, as described here:

1. You sign in to Messenger with a valid user name and get authenticated.

2. If desired, you retrieve your list of contacts and their statuses.

3. You start a *session* with one of your Messenger contacts. A session can be thought of as a separate chat window in the Messenger application. Before you can send messages to any user, either you (or the recipient) must start a session by opening a chat window. You can also create multiple sessions at once (although our simple example won't use this feature). Whenever a session is established, the contact list is updated.

4. You send and receive messages through the server switchboard.

5. At some later point, you end the session and sign out.

Figure 12-1 shows the client we'll create to demonstrate the MSNP component. It allows a user to log in, see other contacts, start a session, and send messages.

To create this client, start by creating a new Windows project. Add the reference to the *msnp.dll* and import the MSNP namespace if desired.

In order to send and receive messages with the MSNP component, you must create a class that implements the ISessionHandler interface. As part of this interface, you'll need to implement methods such as MessageReceived() and ErrorReceived(). These methods will be triggered by the MSNP component in response to messages received from the Messenger network. (A more typical way to implement this type of design is to use events. However, this approach is equivalent.)

The ISessionHandler interface allows you to receive messages. To send messages, you must create an instance of the MSNPHelper class. The MSNPHelper class allows you to retrieve contacts, sign in and sign out, and create sessions. Every session is handled by a separate instance of the Session class. You use the Session class to send messages. Figure 12-2 diagrams this interaction.

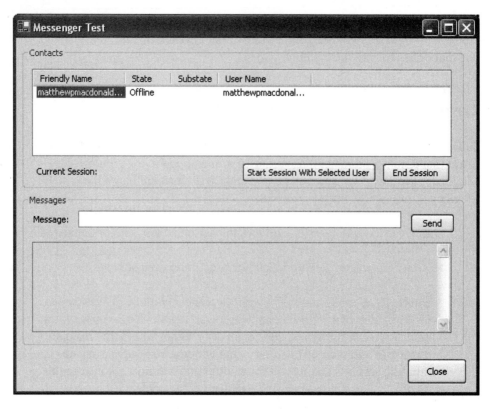

Figure 12-1. The custom Messenger client

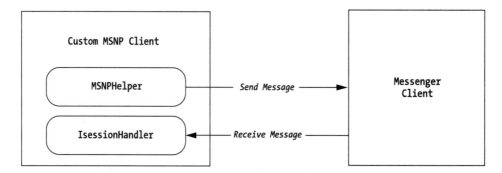

Figure 12-2. Interacting with Messenger through the MSNP component

In our simple example, the ISessionHandler interface is implemented directly by the form:

```
Public Class MessengerForm
    Inherits System.Windows.Forms.Form
    Implements MSNP.ISessionHandler
```

The form also uses some form-level variables to track the current
MSNPHelper and Session objects:

```
' The helper used to sign in and out and retrieve contacts.
Private Helper As MSNP.MSNPHelper

' These variables track the current session as well as the related user.
Private CurrentSessionUser As String
Private CurrentSession As MSNP.Session
```

When the form loads, it signs in to a new Messenger session. The user e-mail
address and password are hard-coded to facilitate testing, but you could easily
add a login window. The IP address is retrieved for the dispatch server using the
System.Net.Dns class.

```
Private Sub MessengerForm_Load(ByVal sender As System.Object, _
  ByVal e As System.EventArgs) Handles MyBase.Load

    ' Retrieve the IP address for the messenger server.
    Dim IP As String
    IP = System.Net.Dns.GetHostByName( _
      "messenger.hotmail.com").AddressList(0).ToString()

    ' For simplicity's sake, a test user is hard-coded.
    ' Note that that communication is always performed on port 1863.
    Helper = New MSNP.MSNPHelper(IP, 1863, "mymsgtest@hotmail.com", _
      "letmein", Me)

    ' SignIn with the supplied information.
    ' This method blocks until the sign operation is complete.
    ' An invalid user or password may simply stall the application without
    ' generating an error, so you may want to execute this method asynchronously.
    Helper.Signin()

    Me.RefreshContactList()

End Sub
```

> **NOTE** *Although the MSNPHelper requires that you supply the password in
> clear text, this password is never transmitted over the network. Instead, the
> password is hashed using the MD5 hashing algorithm and a value supplied by
> the server. For more information, refer to the detailed description of the under-
> lying protocol at* http://www.hypothetic.org/docs/msn/connecting.php.

When you create the MSNPHelper you supply the login information, the IP address and port to use, and an ISessionHandler object. In this example, the current form implements the ISessionHandler, so we pass that as a reference.

The next step is to call the form-level RefreshContactList() subroutine, which retrieves contact information and uses it to fill a ListView control:

```
Private Sub RefreshContactList()

    ' Fill the contact list.
    Dim Item As ListViewItem
    Dim Peer As MSNP.Contact
    For Each Peer In Me.Helper.FLContacts
        Item = lstContacts.Items.Add(Peer.FriendlyName)
        Item.SubItems.Add(Peer.State.ToString())
        Item.SubItems.Add(Peer.Substate.ToString())
        Item.SubItems.Add(Peer.UserName)
    Next

End Sub
```

This method is also called by the ISessionHandler UserJoined() and UserDeparted() methods. However, in this case the method won't execute on the main application thread, so the call must be marshaled using the Control.Invoke() method.

```
Public Sub UserDeparted(ByVal session As MSNP.Session, _
  ByVal userHandle As String) Implements MSNP.ISessionHandler.UserDeparted

    ' Refresh the contact list.
    Dim Invoker As New MethodInvoker(AddressOf Me.RefreshContactList)
    Me.Invoke(Invoker)

End Sub

Public Sub UserJoined(ByVal session As MSNP.Session, _
  ByVal userHandle As String, ByVal userFriendlyName As String) _
  Implements MSNP.ISessionHandler.UserJoined

    ' Refresh the contact list.
    Dim Invoker As New MethodInvoker(AddressOf Me.RefreshContactList)
    Me.Invoke(Invoker)

End Sub
```

Note that if the user's friendly name is different from his or her e-mail address, multiple entries may appear for the user in the contact list (you may have also noticed this phenomenon if you use the Microsoft Outlook Express Hotmail integration). You can use additional code to ignore entries with duplicate UserName values.

Nothing else happens until a user starts a session, or a session is started when another user sends a message. The user can start a session by selecting a user in the contact list and clicking the Create Session button. The button event handler uses the MSNPHelper.RequestSession() method, which returns immediately. The MSNP component will continue trying to establish the session for a maximum of about 30 seconds.

```
Private Sub cmdStartSession_Click(ByVal sender As System.Object, _
   ByVal e As System.EventArgs) Handles cmdStartSession.Click

   If Not Me.CurrentSession Is Nothing Then
       MessageBox.Show("There is already a current session.")
       Return

   Else
       If lstContacts.SelectedIndices.Count = 0 Then
           MessageBox.Show("No user is selected.")
            Return

       Else
           Dim Contact As String
           Contact = lstContacts.Items( _
              lstContacts.SelectedIndices(0)).SubItems(3).Text
           Helper.RequestSession(Contact, Guid.NewGuid())

       End If
   End If


End Sub
```

Note that every session requires an identifier that's generated by the client and is unique within the application. Our custom client simply creates a new GUID.

If the session is successfully established, the ISessionHandler.Session Started() method will be triggered. In our example, the method handler simply updates the form with the retrieved session ID and stores the session object in a member variable for use when sending messages later on. In addition, the ISessionHandler.SessionEnded() method removes these details.

```
Public Sub SessionStarted(ByVal session As MSNP.Session) _
   Implements MSNP.ISessionHandler.SessionStarted

    Dim Updater As New UpdateControlText(lblSession)
    Updater.ReplaceText(session.SessionIdentifier.ToString())
    Me.CurrentSession = session

End Sub

Public Sub SessionEnded(ByVal session As MSNP.Session) _
   Implements MSNP.ISessionHandler.SessionEnded

    ' Don't try to update the form if it's in the process of closing.
    If Not IsClosing Then
        Dim Updater As New UpdateControlText(lblSession)
        Updater.ReplaceText("")
    End If
    Me.CurrentSession = Nothing

End Sub
```

This code uses the UpdateControlText class, which can update the Text property of any control on the correct thread. This useful class is shown here:

```
Public Class UpdateControlText

    Private NewText As String
    Private ControlToUpdate As Control

    Public Sub New(ByVal controlToUpdate As Control)
        Me.ControlToUpdate = controlToUpdate
    End Sub

    Public Sub AddText(ByVal newText As String)
        SyncLock Me
            Me.NewText = newText
            Dim Invoker As New MethodInvoker(AddressOf AddText)
            Me.ControlToUpdate.Invoke(Invoker)
        End SyncLock
    End Sub

    ' This method executes on the user-interface thread.
    Private Sub AddText()
        Me.ControlToUpdate.Text &= NewText
    End Sub
```

```
Public Sub ReplaceText(ByVal newText As String)
    SyncLock Me
        Me.NewText = newText
        Dim Invoker As New MethodInvoker(AddressOf ReplaceText)
        Me.ControlToUpdate.Invoke(Invoker)
    End SyncLock
End Sub


' This method executes on the user-interface thread.
Private Sub ReplaceText()
    Me.ControlToUpdate.Text = NewText
End Sub
```

```
End Class
```

Now that a session is established, the client can send messages by clicking the Send button. The button event handler checks that there's a current session and uses the Session.SendMessage() method.

```
Private Sub cmdSend_Click(ByVal sender As System.Object, _
  ByVal e As System.EventArgs) Handles cmdSend.Click

    If Me.CurrentSession Is Nothing Then
        MessageBox.Show("There is no current session.")
        Return
    Else
        Me.CurrentSession.SendMessage(txtSend.Text)
        Dim NewText As String
        NewText = "SENT: " & txtSend.Text
        NewText &= Environment.NewLine & Environment.NewLine
        txtMessages.Text &= NewText
    End If

End Sub
```

Messages are received through the ISessionHandler.MessageReceived() method. Blank messages are ignored, because they're used to indicate that the user has started typing, thereby allowing you to display the "User is typing a message" status message in your application.

```
Public Sub MessageReceived(ByVal session As MSNP.Session, _
  ByVal message As MSNP.MimeMessage) _
  Implements MSNP.ISessionHandler.MessageReceived
```

```
' Add text.
If message.Body <> "" Then
    Dim Updater As New UpdateControlText(txtMessages)
    Dim NewText As String
    NewText = "FROM: " & message.SenderFriendlyName
    NewText &= Environment.NewLine
    NewText &= "RECEIVED: " & message.Body
    NewText &= Environment.NewLine & Environment.NewLine
    Updater.AddText(NewText)
End If
End Sub
```

Finally, when the form closes, it signs the user out of Windows Messenger.

```
Private Sub MessengerForm_Closed(ByVal sender As Object, _
  ByVal e As System.EventArgs) Handles MyBase.Closed

    If Not Me.CurrentSession Is Nothing Then
        Me.CurrentSession.EndSession()
    End If
    Helper.Signout()

End Sub
```

Figure 12-3 shows the interaction of two Windows Messenger peers, one of which uses the custom client.

Figure 12-3. Interaction with the custom Messenger

Understanding the Groove Platform

Groove is a remarkable platform for building collaborative peer-to-peer applications. It's the invention of Lotus Notes creator Ray Ozzie, it's partly owned by Microsoft, and it can integrate with COM and .NET applications.

The core concept behind Groove is *shared spaces,* where multiple users work on a single task. Examples of shared spaces include a chat window, or a shared whiteboard or calendar. Each user interacts with the shared space on his or her local computer, and changes are seamlessly applied to all other users in the shared space. The basic Groove Workspace includes tools that allow users to jointly edit Word documents, view PowerPoint slides, surf Internet pages, share files, chat, and more.

All of these tools run inside the Groove *transceiver.* It's through the Groove transceiver that you log in, see who else is online, create a new shared space, and invite users to join you in a shared space. A shared space (see Figure 12-4) can include a single Groove tool (like chat) or it can combine more than one Groove tool (for example, if you want to create a synchronized discussion, calendar, and document review session). The important point to remember is that it's the Groove infrastructure that synchronizes changes with all the subscribed users.

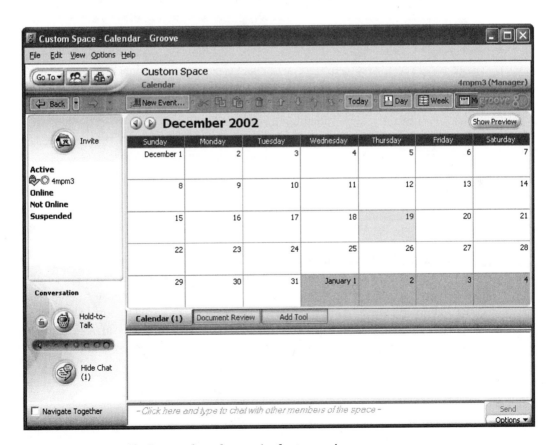

Figure 12-4. A sample Groove shared space in the transceiver

The Groove infrastructure also adds the following benefits that aren't as easy to incorporate into your custom peer-to-peer applications:

- Security. Groove uses encryption to protect data on the wire, digital finger-prints (essentially a GUID) to uniquely track users, and digital signatures to verify that messages aren't tampered with and users aren't impersonated.

- Firewall traversal. Groove uses its own proprietary central server compo-nents that solve firewall and network address translation (NAT) problems. (Incidentally, you can host your own Groove Enterprise server for a signifi-cant fee.)

- Offline support. Groove synchronization can automatically update clients when they come online, thereby allowing your application to work even in the face of variable network connectivity.

But Groove isn't just a collection of typical peer-to-peer collaborative tools. It's also a framework that allows you to create your own tools and add them to shared spaces. In this case, the goal is to make creating a Groove tool nearly as easy as creating a stand-alone Windows application, so that the developer doesn't need to worry about security, synchronization, networking, and so on. Groove even provides a Visual Studio .NET add-in that makes this process relatively easy. You'll still need to learn the Groove toolset object model and its deployment and configuration system (particularly if you want to develop more advanced tools), but you won't need to overcome the same challenges as you would if you were writing a collaborative application from scratch.

Groove provides a .NET developer hub at http://www.groove.net/developers/ dotnet. Using this link, you can download the Groove 2.1 Workspace, the Groove toolkit for Visual Studio .NET, and a more generic Groove development kit with samples. You can also read whitepapers and other documentation about develop-ing with Groove. Groove Networks was one of the first organi-zations to become a Visual Studio .NET Integration Partner (VSIP), and both Groove and Microsoft are committed to collaborating in the future and extending their tools together into the world of collaborative peer-to-peer.

From a business point of view, the only downside to using Groove is that it isn't free. You can use the scaled-down trial version to test your custom tools, but you need to purchase the full version to access advanced features and use automated deployment. You can find information about purchasing Groove at http://www.groove.net/products/workspace/starterkit-smb.

Creating a Simple Groove Application

Once you've installed the Groove toolkit for Visual Studio .NET, you'll be able to directly create a Groove project. Simply select Groove Tool Projects ➤ Groove Tool in VB .NET from the Create Project window (see Figure 12-5).

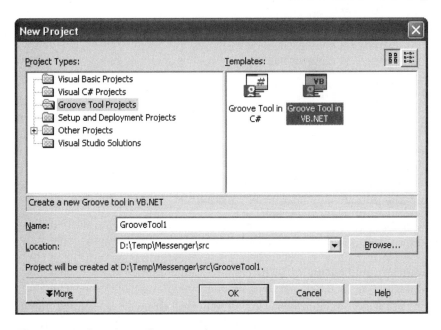

Figure 12-5. Creating a Groove project

Groove projects resemble user controls. They have a Windows design surface, but no form border (because they're hosted in the transceiver). You can code any valid VB .NET code in a Groove project, including code that interacts with a web service, reads from a database, launches new threads, opens new windows, and so on.

Figure 12-6 shows the contents of a simple Groove project and its assembly references.

NOTE *Behind the scenes, the Groove toolkit makes heavy use of .NET-to-COM interoperability. It uses runtime callable wrappers (RCW) to make its COM library of components available to your .NET applications, and COM callable wrappers (CCW) to wrap your .NET Groove tools so they can be hosted in the unmanaged Groove transceiver. You won't need to deal with this layer of interoperability directly.*

Figure 12-6. The contents of a Groove project

The Groove Designer Code

If you look at the auto-generated code for the default Groove user control, you'll see three collapsed regions with Groove code. The first ("Groove member variables") defines two form-level variables:

```
Private WithEvents propertyList As GroovePropertyList
Private WithEvents recordSetEngine As GrooveRecordSetEngine
```

The propertyList variable is used to access a small amount of tool-specific information (such as the tool name and assembly). The recordSetEngine variable is used to access data that will be synchronized across all users in the shared space.

Both the property list and record set rely on Groove's *persistence engines*. Groove provides four persistence engines:

- PropertyListEngine. This models data as a series of name and value pairs. You can store any basic type of data (numeric, string, and so on). Property lists are used extensively by Groove to provide information about the environment.

- RecordSetEngine. This models a set of records. Each record is divided into multiple fields that can use basic data types such as strings and numbers as well as XML elements. A record set can include many different types of records. This is the most commonly used Groove persistence engine for storing data in a custom tool.

- HierarchicalRecordSetEngine. This is similar to the RecordSetEngine, except that it allows you to organize different record sets into a tree-like hierarchy.

- DocumentShareEngine. This engine allows you to share files in a distributed space.

In this example, we'll use the RecordSetEngine to manage shared data. To change data, the application opens a RecordSetEngine transaction and makes the desired changes. The RecordSetEngine then replicates the changes over all the peers in the shared space, using encryption. The change then appears in each local copy of the tool as a RecordSetEngine event. The tool responds to this event and updates the local display accordingly. Figure 12-7 diagrams this arrangement.

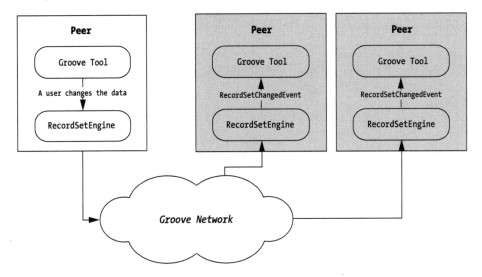

Figure 12-7. Synchronization in a Groove shared space

Continuing our exploration of the designer code, you'll find a collapsed region named "IGrooveComponent default implementation." It includes a basic implementation of the IGrooveComponent interface, including an Initialize() subroutine that retrieves the property list and some basic information from the Groove environment:

```
' Common Groove property names.
Private Const CommonPropertyName = "Name"
Private Const CommonPropertyBindableURL = "_BindableURL"
Private Const CommonPropertyCanonicalURL = "_CanonicalURL"
Private Const RecordSetEngineConnection = 0
```

```
' Cached Groove property values.
Private componentName As String
Private componentBindableURL As String
Private componentCanonicalURL As String

Public Sub Initialize(ByVal propertyListInterop _
   As Groove.Interop.Components.IGroovePropertyList) _
   Implements Groove.Interop.Components.IGrooveComponent.Initialize

      ' Create the property list wrapper object.
      propertyList = new GroovePropertyList(propertyListInterop)

      componentBindableURL = _
         propertyList.OpenPropertyAsString(CommonPropertyBindableURL)
      componentCanonicalURL = _
         propertyList.OpenPropertyAsString(CommonPropertyCanonicalURL)

      ' This is a GUID that uniquely identifies the tool.
      componentName = propertyList.OpenPropertyAsString(CommonPropertyName)

End Sub
```

This information is made available through several property procedures that also implement the IGrooveComponent interface:

```
Public ReadOnly Property BindableURL() As String _
   Implements Groove.Interop.Components.IGrooveComponent.BindableURL
      Get
            Return componentBindableURL
      End Get
End Property

Public ReadOnly Property CanonicalURL() As String _
   Implements Groove.Interop.Components.IGrooveComponent.CanonicalURL
      Get
            Return componentCanonicalURL
      End Get
End Property

Public Function OpenName() As String _
   Implements Groove.Interop.Components.IGrooveComponent.OpenName
      Return componentName
End Function
```

Finally, the component includes code to create a new RecordSetEngine instance, and disposes of it when the application ends. This manual dispose step is used because the RecordSetEngine is actually a wrapper for a COM component, and therefore it holds unmanaged resources.

```
Public Sub ConnectToComponent(ByVal componentInterop As _
    Groove.Interop.Components.IGrooveComponent, ByVal connectionID As Integer) _
    Implements Groove.Interop.Components.IGrooveComponent.ConnectToComponent

        Select Case connectionID
            Case RecordSetEngineConnection
                ' Create the recordSetEngine wrapper object.
                Dim recordSetEngineInterop As _
                    Groove.Interop.CollectionComponents.IGrooveRecordSetEngine
                recordSetEngineInterop = componentInterop
                recordSetEngine = New GrooveRecordSetEngine(recordSetEngineInterop)
        End Select

End Sub


Public Sub UnconnectFromComponents() _
    Implements Groove.Interop.Components.IGrooveComponent.UnconnectFromComponents
        recordSetEngine.Dispose()
End Sub


Public Sub Terminate() _
    Implements Groove.Interop.Components.IGrooveComponent.Terminate
        propertyList.Dispose()
End Sub
```

The third and final designer region is used to hold a default implementation of the RecordSetChanged event handler:

```
Private Sub OnRecordSetChanged(ByVal sender As GrooveRecordSetEngine, _
    ByVal e As GrooveRecordSetListenerEventArgs) _
    Handles recordSetEngine.RecordSetChangedEvent

        ' (By default, no code is included.)

End Sub
```

The Groove Application Logic

The next step is to use this basic framework to add some application-specific logic. At a minimum, a Groove tool allows the user to create and manage some information and responds when this information is changed by updating the display accordingly.

Our simple example is a collaborative party planner. It displays a list of food items that are being brought to the party by various individuals. Any individual in the shared space can add or remove items from this list. The interface (shown in Figure 12-8) includes a ListView and two buttons, one for removing items and one for adding them.

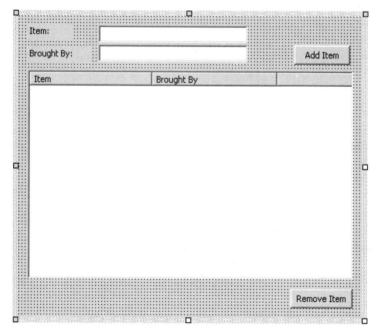

Figure 12-8. A custom Groove tool with a shared list

> **TIP** *Remember to anchor your controls to the sides of the user control container so they can adapt to fit the space allocated to them in the Groove transceiver. You can also improve your interfaces with docking and splitter bars and other niceties.*

When a user clicks the Add button, the item information is read from the text boxes, added to a new Groove record, and then inserted into the Groove record set.

```
Private Sub cmdAdd_Click(ByVal sender As System.Object, _
    ByVal e As System.EventArgs) Handles cmdAdd.Click

    ' Verify the item information is present.
    If txtItem.Text = "" Or txtBroughtBy.Text = "" Then
        MessageBox.Show("Enter your name and the item name.")
        Return
    End If

    ' Create a new record to add to the Groove record set.
    Dim Record As New GrooveRecord()

    Try
        ' Set the new field values.
        Record.SetField("Item", txtItem.Text)
        Record.SetField("BroughtBy", txtBroughtBy.Text)

        ' Add the record.
        Me.recordSetEngine.AddRecord(Record)

    Finally
        ' Explicitly release the unmanaged resources held by the record.
        Record.Dispose()
    End Try

End Sub
```

Note that this code does not actually modify the ListView control—it only changes the Groove record set. The local peer must respond, like all peers in the shared space, to the RecordSetChanged event in order to update the ListView. At this point, the peer reads the information from the record (along with the record ID that's assigned by Groove to uniquely identify this record) and inserts a new ListViewItem. Individual values are read using Record.OpenFieldAsString() method.

```
Private Sub OnRecordSetChanged(ByVal sender As GrooveRecordSetEngine, _
    ByVal e As GrooveRecordSetListenerEventArgs) _
    Handles recordSetEngine.RecordSetChangedEvent

    Dim RecordID As Double
    Dim Record As IGrooveRecord
```

```
' The ToolHelper is used to start a new transaction.
' This prevents the data from changing while the display is being updated.
Dim ToolHelper As New GrooveToolHelper(Me.propertyList)
ToolHelper.StartTelespaceTransaction(True)

Try
    ' Determine the type of change.
    Select Case e.RecordSetChangeType

        Case GrooveRecordSetChangeType.GrooveRecordSetChangeType_Added

            ' The record set contains one or more items to be added.
            Do While e.RecordIDEnum.HasMore()
                RecordID = e.RecordIDEnum.OpenNext()
                If recordSetEngine.HasRecord(RecordID) Then

                    Record = recordSetEngine.OpenRecord(RecordID)
                    Dim Item As New ListViewItem( _
                      Record.OpenFieldAsString("Item"))
                    Item.SubItems.Add(Record.OpenFieldAsString( _
                      "BroughtBy"))
                    lstItems.Items.Add(Item)

                    ' Store the unique record ID.
                    item.Tag = RecordID

                    ' Explicitly release the record.
                    Record.Dispose()
                End If
            Loop

        ' (The code for other types of changes is omitted.)

Catch Err As Exception
    ' Abort transaction.
    ToolHelper.AbortTelespaceTransaction()
    MessageBox.Show(Err.Message)

End Try

End Sub
```

The Remove button uses similar logic. It verifies that an item is selected, starts a transaction, and removes it from the record set.

```
Private Sub cmdRemove_Click(ByVal sender As System.Object, _
    ByVal e As System.EventArgs) Handles cmdRemove.Click

    If lstItems.FocusedItem Is Nothing Then
        MessageBox.Show("No item selected.")

    Else
        ' Get the unique record ID.
        Dim RecordID As Double = CType(lstItems.FocusedItem.Tag, Double)

        ' Open a transaction on the telespace to prevent data from
        ' changing out from under us.
        Dim ToolHelper As New GrooveToolHelper(Me.propertyList)
        ToolHelper.StartTelespaceTransaction(False)

        Try
            ' Remove the record.
            Me.recordSetEngine.RemoveRecord(RecordID)
            ToolHelper.CommitTelespaceTransaction()

        Catch Err As Exception
            ToolHelper.AbortTelespaceTransaction()
            MessageBox.Show(Err.Message)

        End Try
    End If

End Sub
```

Once again, the code reacts to the RecordSetChanged event and uses this opportunity to update the ListView. This time, the code loops through the ListView items until it finds one that matches the unique record ID.

```
Case GrooveRecordSetChangeType.GrooveRecordSetChangeType_Removed

    ' RecordSet contains one or more items to be removed.
    Do While e.RecordIDEnum.HasMore()
        RecordID = e.RecordIDEnum.OpenNext()

        ' Check the ListView for this item.
        Dim Item As ListViewItem
        For Each Item In lstItems.Items
            If CType(Item.Tag, Double) = RecordID Then
                lstItems.Items.Remove(item)
```

```
                End If
        Next
Loop
```

This is all the custom code you need to add. The next step is to test the custom Groove tool in the transceiver.

Debugging a Groove Application

The Groove toolkit allows you to debug your Groove application inside Visual Studio .NET. When you run your Groove project, a special instance of the transceiver will appear with your tool loaded in a new shared space. You can interact with the tool and even set breakpoints or use variable watches in your code. When you close the transceiver, the debugging session will end and you can continue to edit your code.

Figure 12-9 shows the party planner running in Groove.

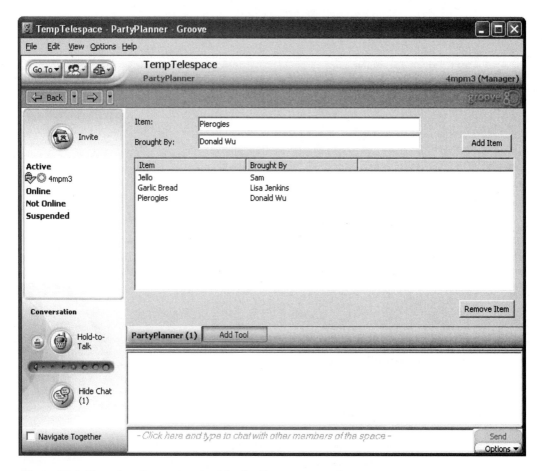

Figure 12-9. Running the custom tool in the Groove transceiver

NOTE *In order to debug your tool, Groove cannot already be running. If it is, shut it down before starting your project.*

Even in a single user environment, you can test all of your code. That's because all peers respond to changes in the exact same way, including the peer that originates the change. For example, in the party planner example, the ListView control isn't updated until the Groove infrastructure notifies the application that the record set has been altered. This is the same process that will happen with any other users working in the same shared space.

For a more detailed multiuser test, you'll need to compile your project, create the Groove XML files that describe it, sign it, and then inject it into the Groove Workspace. This is outside the scope of this book, although it's well-explained in the Groove toolkit documentation.

Enhancing the Groove Application

The current party application treats all peers equivalently. However, in a real peer-to-peer application you almost always want some ability to track user identities and possibly assign different sets of abilities to different types of users. This type of design is possible with Groove's rich class library—provided you know where to work.

The first step is to import some additional Groove assemblies that you'll need to use to add the identity features. These include Groove.Interop.Account Services, Groove.Interop.IdentityServices, and Groove.Interop.ContactServices, as shown in Figure 12-10. All of these assemblies can be added directly from the global assembly cache.

Using the property list information provided in the Groove environment, you can retrieve two types of information:

- Identity information for the user who created the shared space. This user might be given some sort of administrator-like privileges.

- Identity information about the current user. This can be used to log changes accurately and even restrict what operations a user is allowed to perform.

Groove provides several identity-related interfaces, as shown in Figure 12-11. One of the most import is IGrooveIdentity, which allows you to uniquely identify users. Other important interfaces include IGrooveVCard and IGrooveIdentification. IGrooveVCard returns information about the user-specific VCard, which is the Groove equivalent of a digital certificate. The IGrooveIdentification returns a specific subset of VCard information such as the user name, organization, and so on.

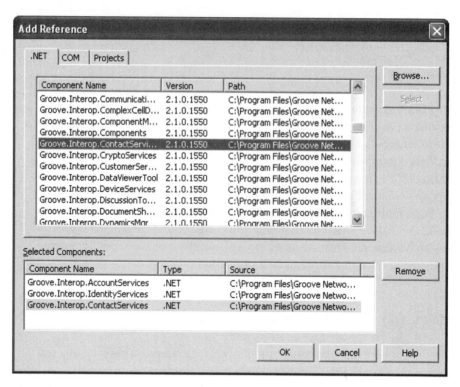

Figure 12-10. Groove assemblies for identity management

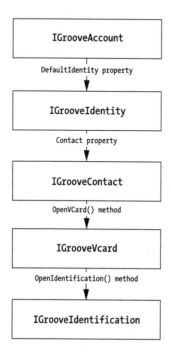

Figure 12-11. Groove identity interfaces

Here's how you might retrieve identity information when the shared space is first initialized. In this case, the code retrieves the unique URL identifier for both users and stores them in form-level variables. It also presets the txtBoughtBy text box with the user's name and displays the shared space owner information.

```
' Track unique identifiers that indicate who created the
' shared space and who is currently using it.
Private UserUrl As String
Private CreatorUrl As String


Private Sub GrooveUserControl_Load(ByVal sender As System.Object, _
   ByVal e As System.EventArgs) Handles MyBase.Load

   ' Define some basic Groove identity interfaces.
   Dim Account As Groove.Interop.AccountServices.IGrooveAccount
   Dim Identity As Groove.Interop.IdentityServices.IGrooveIdentity
   Dim Contact As Groove.Interop.ContactServices.IGrooveContact
   Dim VCard As Groove.Interop.ContactServices.IGrooveVCard
   Dim Identification As Groove.Interop.ContactServices.IGrooveIdentification

   ' Retrieve the identity information for the shared space creator.
   Account = CType(Me.propertyList.OpenProperty("_Account"), _
      Groove.Interop.AccountServices.IGrooveAccount)
   Identity = Account.DefaultIdentity
   Me.CreatorUrl = Identity.URL
   Contact = Identity.Contact
   VCard = Contact.OpenVCard()
   Identification = VCard.OpenIdentification()

   ' Display this identity in the window.
   lblCreator.Text = "Space hosted by: " & Identification.OpenFullName()

   ' Retrieve the identify information for the current user.
   Identity = CType(Me.propertyList.OpenProperty("_CurrentIdentity"), _
      Groove.Interop.IdentityServices.IGrooveIdentity)
   Me.UserUrl = Identity.URL
   Contact = Identity.Contact
   VCard = Contact.OpenVCard()
   Identification = VCard.OpenIdentification()

   ' Pre-fill in the txtBroughtBy textbox.
   txtBroughtBy.Text = Identification.OpenFullName()


End Sub
```

Now you can add some useful identity integrity features. First of all, you can make the txtBroughtBy textbox read-only, and you can add the user URL information to the record set and ListView. This way, you'll be assured that the user offering to bring a party item is who he or she claims to be.

Here's the updated code for adding new entries:

```
' Set the new field values.
Record.SetField("Item", txtItem.Text)
Record.SetField("BroughtBy", txtBroughtBy.Text)
Record.SetField("UserURL", Me.UserUrl)
```

And here's the code that responds to the change and inserts the new ListViewItem:

```
Record = recordSetEngine.OpenRecord(RecordID)

Dim Item As New ListViewItem(Record.OpenFieldAsString("Item"))
Item.SubItems.Add(Record.OpenFieldAsString("BroughtBy"))
Item.SubItems.Add(Record.OpenFieldAsString("UserURL"))
lstItems.Items.Add(Item)

' Store the unique record ID.
item.Tag = RecordID
```

Next, you can tweak the code for removing items so that items can't be removed unless the removing user is the user who added the item originally.

```
Private Sub cmdRemove_Click(ByVal sender As System.Object, _
  ByVal e As System.EventArgs) Handles cmdRemove.Click

    If lstItems.FocusedItem Is Nothing Then
        MessageBox.Show("No item selected.")
    ElseIf lstItems.FocusedItem.SubItems(2).Text <> Me.UserUrl Then
        MessageBox.Show("You did not add this item.")
    Else
        ' (Code omitted.)
    End If
End Sub
```

Figure 12-12 shows the revamped Groove tool in action.

This only scratches the surface of some of Groove's more advanced features. For more information, refer to the Groove developer documentation. Keep in mind, however, that the Groove toolkit for Visual Studio .NET is still considered to be a preview of new Groove technology. It will likely change as the COM interoperability code is replaced with native .NET solutions.

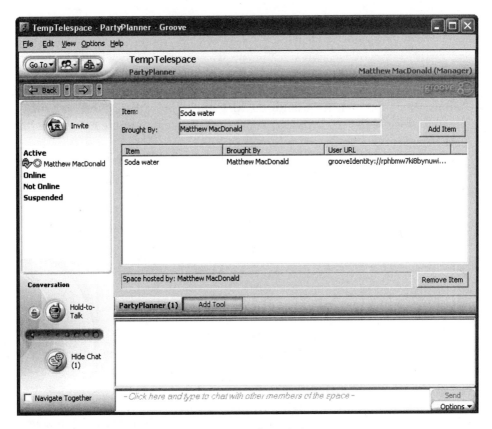

Figure 12-12. A Groove tool that recognizes identities

Other Peer-to-Peer Platforms

In the future, most programmers who want to write peer-to-peer applications will use a third-party platform rather than creating the infrastructure from scratch. The two platforms shown in this chapter are useful choices, but they won't meet the needs of all developers. Windows Messenger is primarily suited for small-scale implementations, particularly when adding peer-to-peer messaging to an existing application. Groove is a more comprehensive platform that's well suited to creating all types of collaborative applications. In this section, we'll consider two other choices.

Gnutella

Windows Messenger isn't the only instant-messaging platform—AOL provides a similar product, as does the pioneer, ICQ. It's possible to use these protocols, and there are some open-source projects dedicated to the task, but there are currently no .NET components that make it easy. Thus, if you want to use these other platforms, you need to study the platform and write a significant amount of custom code with .NET's networking classes.

The same is true of Gnutella, the fully decentralized protocol used for file sharing. There is a decentralized set of Java classes (known as JTella and available at http://jtella.sourceforge.net) that provides this functionality for Java applications, but there is currently no .NET equivalent, although there are several in-progress projects on SourceForge.net and at least one attempt to port the JTella logic to C#.

In addition, for the truly ambitious, information about the Gnutella protocol can be found at http://rfc-gnutella.sourceforge.net and various other locations on the Internet. There is currently one Gnutella client totally implemented on the .NET platform using C# code. It's Swapper.NET by Jason Thomas, which is available for download (in compiled form only) at http://www.revolutionarystuff.com/swapper.

DirectPlay

Microsoft's DirectX includes DirectPlay, a technology that's designed with peer-to-peer game play in mind. DirectPlay can be used in a server-based or pure peer-to-peer environment. Either way, it plays the same role: completely managing network communication and data exchange. Generally, a developer will use DirectPlay to keep multiple peers synchronized in a multiplayer game, although the technology is impressive enough that it could conceivably be incorporated into a variety of different application types.

Some of the features that DirectPlay offers include group management (registration and deregistration of users), bandwidth management that allows large amounts of data to be exchanged without introducing problems, and connection statistics. DirectPlay also includes a variety of message services, such as guaranteed delivery and guaranteed sequencing, both of which are optional. DirectPlay even includes a related API named DirectPlay voice, which is fine-tuned for real-time voice communication between players.

To learn about DirectPlay, you can download the full DirectX 9.0 SDK for .NET from http://msdn.microsoft.com/library/default.asp?url=/downloads/list/directx.asp. You can also refer to *.NET Game Programming with DirectX 9.0* (Apress 2003), which includes a full chapter on the subject.

Windows Peer-to-Peer Networking

It may be that the infrastructure for peer-to-peer systems won't be built-in to the next generation of programming toolkits, but rather into the next generation of Windows. Microsoft has recently released a peer-to-peer upgrade for Windows XP that adds decentralized peer connectivity features, and a peer-to-peer SDK with examples (currently all in unmanaged code). To download the update and the SDK, visit `http://msdn.microsoft.com/library/default.asp?url=/downloads/list/winxppeer.asp`.

However, there's one huge limitation: These technologies rely in large part on the next generation of Internet addressing technology, IPv6. Even though there are facilities to "work through" NATs based on IPv4, the solution is far from complete, and it will be some time before it matures into a practical platform for building applications. But you can get a head start on this emerging field by referring to Microsoft's peer-to-peer networking home page, `http://www.microsoft.com/windowsxp/p2p`.

The Last Word

This chapter looked at the shortcuts you can use to create certain types of peer-to-peer applications by working with existing peer-to-peer networks. The first choice, using Windows Messenger, provides a reliable communication infrastructure that could support your own custom business processes and clients. The second option, using Groove, allows you to develop a rich set of collaborative tools with a full-featured toolset, although it requires a user license.

In the next chapter, we'll consider a free peer-to-peer framework that extends the Remoting infrastructure included with .NET: the Intel Peer-to-Peer Accelerator Kit.

CHAPTER 13

The Intel Peer-to-Peer Accelerator Kit

OVER THE LAST TWELVE CHAPTERS we've considered a variety of peer-to-peer applications implemented on technologies such as Remoting, web services, and the .NET networking classes. Some used central coordinators while others relied on a simple discovery service. All of them required a substantial amount of custom programming, and they'll experience significant problems when faced with issues such as network address translation (NAT) and firewalls.

What if there was a way to avoid the work of infrastructure programming and only worry about coding application-specific logic? As shown in the last chapter, you can create collaborative applications that piggyback on Windows Messenger and Groove, but the former is limited in scope while the latter forces you to buy a specific product. An ideal solution would be a generic peer-to-peer programming platform, on top of which developers could create a wide variety of distributed applications.

If you're hoping that this chapter will present that ideal peer-to-peer platform, then you'll be at least somewhat disappointed. Intel's Peer-to-Peer Accelerator Kit is only a beginning, and it's still too early to determine whether this software will fall by the wayside or mature into a powerful, widely accepted platform. In the meantime, you have to choose between coding peer-to-peer applications the hard way or investing some time in learning an ambitious new component with an uncertain future.

This chapter introduces the Intel Peer-to-Peer Accelerator Kit and discusses its architecture. You'll learn how to modify the Talk .NET messaging application to use the toolkit and analyze the basic samples that Intel includes to see how they resemble, and differ from, the projects developed in this book.

> **NOTE** *As this book goes to print, the Intel Peer-to-Peer Accelerator Kit is no longer available from the Microsoft-supported GotDotNet website (http://www.gotdotnet.com). Whether this represents the end of the Intel Peer-to-Peer Accelerator Kit or the start of another toolkit is still uncertain. However, no matter what its ultimate fate will be, you can still use version 1.0 of the Peer-to-Peer Accelerator Kit to create peer-to-peer applications, and you can study the toolkit to learn more about peer-to-peer programming in general. You can even use the Intel Peer-to-Peer Accelerator Kit source code (provided in C#) when crafting your own peer-to-peer applications.*

About the Intel Peer-to-Peer Accelerator Kit

The goal of the Intel Peer-to-Peer Accelerator Kit is to promote the adoption of peer-to-peer designs by providing a set of easy-to-use peer-to-peer enhancements for .NET applications. These enhancements are built on top of the .NET Framework. They include

- A set of messaging enhancements that use SOAP and HTTP to transport data on a network. The messaging enhancements are designed to increase reliability, availability, and security in a peer-to-peer application.

- Extensions to .NET that allow you to use the messaging enhancements with Remoting and other network classes.

- A peer-to-peer daemon (a long-running Windows service) that runs on each peer and facilitates the messaging enhancements features. If you develop multiple peer-to-peer applications with the Intel toolkit, they'll all share the same local service.

- Use of a web service for peer discovery. The operation of the web service is completely transparent; you simply host it and configure the clients to be able to locate the server. They'll form peer lookups as required.

- An application-level FileCopy API that you can use to transfer files between peers.

Out of this feature set, the last point (the FileCopy API) is probably the least impressive. Although it saves some custom coding work if you need to create a file sharing application, it roughly parallels the type of file transfer approach you would be able to create on your own without too much effort (as described in Chapter 9). The messaging enhancements contain the most useful functionality in the Peer-to-Peer Accelerator Kit, including enhancements that allow you to use Secure Sockets Layer (SSL) automatically, and cross firewall boundaries.

Currently, there are no other .NET products that compete with Intel's Peer-to-Peer Accelerator Kit. Other peer-to-peer platforms exist (notably JXTA, which is usually applied to Java development), but none have a .NET-specific implementation at the time of this writing. For more information about JXTA and to see how its architecture compares to Intel's toolkit, you may want to consider Brendon Wilson's excellent website, which provides a complete JXTA book from New Riders in PDF format. This material is ideal for getting acquainted with a different platform—check it out at http://www.brendonwilson.com/projects/jxta.

The Messaging Enhancements

The messaging enhancements are the most compelling part of the Intel Peer-to-Peer Accelerator Kit. They include the following:

- Store-and-forward. If this is enabled and you attempt to send a one-way message to a peer that appears to be offline, the message will be cached locally and delivery will be attempted later.

- Tunnel and relay. This feature allows two peers to communicate over a firewall by sending messages through a relay service.

- SSL. As you saw in Chapter 11, it's not possible to use SSL certificate authentication and encryption directly from a peer-to-peer application. Intel's Peer-to-Peer Accelerator Kit solves this problem (with the use of some intensive C++ plumbing).

The messaging enhancements are designed so that they can be easily enhanced in the future. For example, Intel documentation references different methods of firewall traversal such as UPnP NAT and the SOCKS Protocol, which would allow for more flexible handling of peer connectivity. Unfortunately, these solutions aren't implemented in the current (version 1.0) release.

The Intel Peer-to-Peer Daemon

The core piece of technology in the Intel Peer-to-Peer Accelerator Kit is a special Windows service that runs on every peer and handles all communication between computers. This service (shown in Figure 13-1) loads at startup and runs transparently in the background. It acts as a container for all the peer-to-peer services.

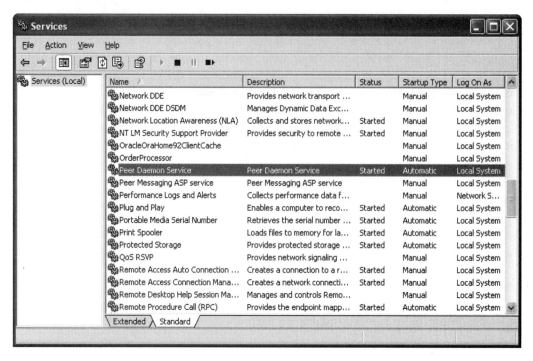

Figure 13-1. The Intel Peer-to-Peer daemon service

The peer service performs the following tasks:

- It listens for incoming messages and then delivers them to the appropriate application object (in conjunction with the .NET Remoting infrastructure). This is its most important responsibility.

- It coordinates peer discovery. It automatically submits peer information to the configured discovery service so that a particular application doesn't need to call a Register() or Login() method.

- When delivering messages, it looks up peer location information from the discovery service as required. It also maintains a local cache of peer location information (much as in the Chapter 10 example).

- It encrypts and decrypts messages in secure sessions.

- It stores messages for later delivery if store-and-forward is enabled.

- It sets up a connection with a configured relay server and uses it to avoid firewall or NAT problems. In addition, if configured as a relay server, it routes messages between peers that cannot communicate directly.

- It tracks the list of published files (much as in the Chapter 9 example).

Figure 13-2 shows the how the architecture works in a typical application scenario.

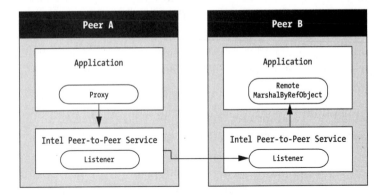

Figure 13-2. Sending a message from one peer to another

> **NOTE** *You can configure the behavior of the peer service by modifying the settings in its configuration file. We'll cover this topic in detail later in this chapter.*

Peer-to-Peer URLs and Remoting

The peer service works by mapping peer URLs to Remoting endpoints. In other words, your application works in terms of abstract peer-to-peer endpoints. These endpoints include information about the remote computer and the remote object and indicate additional information such as whether or not the message should be encrypted before it's sent. The peer-to-peer service translates the peer-to-peer endpoint into that actual Remoting endpoint, and it handles the additional steps that may be required to bypass a firewall or create a secure session, and so on.

So far, you've become well-acquainted with the URL format used by .NET Remoting. It starts with the prefix *tcp* or *http* (depending on the protocol used for communication) and indicates the remote application and object. Here's an example:

```
tcp://localhost:8000/RemoteObject
```

URLs with the Intel Peer-to-Peer Accelerator look quite a bit different. They start with the prefix *peer*, which indicates that the message must be handled by the Intel messaging enhancements. The peer URL format is shown here:

```
peer://[PeerName]/[Application]/[Object]?[Parameters]
```

The peer name is a dynamic GUID that's generated at install time and uniquely identifies the computer (regardless of the application). The application and object have the same meaning as they do in an ordinary Remoting scenario. Finally, the URL also allows a query string portion that specifies additional parameters. There are currently three parameters you can use:

- PeerSecure=True specifies that the communication must be encrypted in an SSL session.

- If you've enabled store-and-forward, PeerExpire=<Time> and PeerLive=<Seconds> can set how long a message is retained if the peer is offline.

When using these options, you won't need to modify the URL manually. Instead, you can use the methods provided by the Intel Peer-to-Peer Accelerator Kit classes.

Remember, the underlying transport mechanism is still an HTTP transfer over Remoting. The peer prefix indicates a *virtual* transportation specification. The peer service translates peer URLs into the actual endpoints, as shown in Figure 13-3.

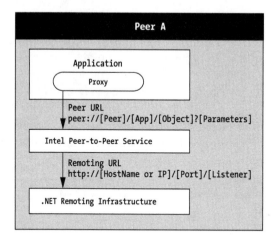

Figure 13-3. How the Intel Peer-to-Peer Accelerator Kit maps peer URLs

The Discovery Service

The discovery service is implemented as a web service that exposes three methods: SetPeer() for adding peer information or updating it, RemovePeer() for removing peer registration, and lookup() for retrieving peer URLs. The peer service handles interaction with the discovery service transparently and caches recently looked-up information to optimize performance.

Every directory service contains information about the peer, its URL, and a timestamp. This data is stored and transmitted as an XML fragment.

```
<PeerInformation>

  <PeerName>pCDA296F7E06511D1BFD300C04FB12345.peer</PeerName>
  <URL>http://10.1.1.26:4375</URL>
  <URL secure="true">https://10.1.1.26:4376</URL>
  <EntryTime>2001-09-28 18:12:19Z</EntryTime>

</PeerInformation>
```

The timestamp is used to determine which entry to use if multiple registrations are found. When retrieving the peer-connectivity information, the peer service can choose to submit a minimum date, in which case all peer information older than this date will be ignored. The peer service uses this feature intrinsically to retrieve updated information if a message delivery attempt fails.

Intel Peer-to-Peer Drawbacks

Despite its promise, the Intel Peer-to-Peer Accelerator Kit isn't without some limitations. For example, when you examine the peer-to-peer messaging application developed later in this chapter, you'll notice that response times are slower than in the original version. Part of this is due to the need to forward all messages through the peer service. Another consideration is the fact that the Intel Peer-to-Peer Accelerator Kit only supports the HTTP Protocol for exchanging data with the relatively verbose SOAP messages, rather than leaner binary messages over TCP. In addition, the revamped application requires some additional considerations that weren't necessary in earlier implementations, and therefore complicate the code.

Another limitation is the reliance on a discovery service. Intel follows the same approach as the examples in this book by using a separate web service to map peer names to connectivity information. However, this means that you need to include a server in your peer-to-peer system as well as a configuration file that tells all peers where to access it. Though an early beta of the Intel Peer-to-Peer Accelerator Kit experimented with broadcasting, it isn't supported in the release version, and hence there's no way to create fully decentralized peer-to-peer applications (although you can configure multiple discovery servers and thereby reduce the burden on a single computer). It's also important to note that the Intel solution for firewall traversal, while useful, is still more rudimentary than that offered by more mature (and far more complex) peer-to-peer applications such as most Gnutella clients. It requires you to provide an available relay and tell the peer where to find it—additional configuration steps that can only complicate life.

Finally, one other potential problem is the way that the Intel Peer-to-Peer Accelerator Kit generates URLs. As you've seen, these don't use fixed endpoints with the machine name or IP address. Instead, they use a GUID. In order for a peer to connect to another, it must know which GUID to use in constructing the URL. Fortunately, the GUID is machine-specific, so you can distribute the GUID for a server endpoint in a client configuration file, much as you would with .NET Remoting. However, this also means that if you want multiple peers to interact (for example, in a chat application), you'll almost certainly need some sort of central component that allows peers to retrieve the URLs of other peers on the system. This component is in addition to the peer-to-peer discovery service, which isn't application-specific. The server component might map user names or e-mail addresses to GUID values, while the discovery service maps these to the required peer-connectivity information.

Installing the Intel Peer-to-Peer Accelerator Kit

You can download the Intel Peer-to-Peer Accelerator Kit at the companion site for this book: http://www.prosetech.com. This site will also post any update links for the Intel Peer-to-Peer Accelerator Kit if they become available. (Unfortunately, at the time of this writing, the Intel Peer-to-Peer Accelerator Kit is no longer available on the Microsoft-supported http://www.gotdotnet.com site).

The Intel Peer-to-Peer Accelerator Kit download is in the form of a ZIP file with two setup applications. One allows you to install the peer-to-peer name server (used for discovery), while the other includes the Peer-to-Peer Accelerator Kit, which includes the required assemblies, documentation, and optionally, several sample applications and the source code for the toolkit (see Figure 13-4).

> **TIP** *Intel also provides white papers and a rudimentary peer-to-peer case study at* http://www.intel.com/ids/p2p.

The peer-to-peer name server installs the discovery web service and discovery database. It can only be installed on a server version of Windows, such as Windows 2000 Server or Windows Server 2003. However, if you want to test on a single computer, you only need to install the Peer-to-Peer Accelerator Kit.

The Peer-to-Peer Accelerator Kit setup installs files into the *[InstallDir]\Intel\ P2P\v1.0* directory. (By default, the root installation directory is *C:\Program Files.*) In this path are the following subdirectories:

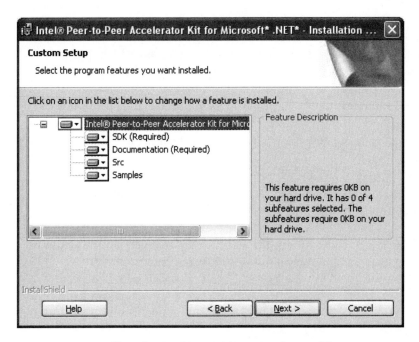

Figure 13-4. Installing the Intel Peer-to-Peer Accelerator Kit

- *Bin* contains the compiled Intel Peer-to-Peer Accelerator Kit assemblies, which you'll need to reference in your peer-to-peer applications.

- *Config* contains two files that define machine-specific configuration settings, such as peer service.

- *Docs* contains a white paper specification and an HTML Help file that acts as a basic namespace reference. This namespace reference only includes the subset of the Peer-to-Peer Accelerator Kit classes that you'll need to use directly.

- *Samples* contains several sample applications. Some of these have associate Visual Studio .NET project files, but most simply include the source code. All samples are in C# syntax.

- *Src* includes the complete source C# code for the toolkit, organized by namespace. You can use this to learn about the operation of the toolkit or integrate some of its techniques into your own code. Some of the code, such as the code that's required to implement SSL secure channels, is unmanaged C++ code.

The core namespaces and classes are as follows:

- Intel.Peer.Messaging includes the PeerChannel class, which works with Remoting and the peer service to allow peer-to-peer communication.

- Intel.Peer.Security.CertificateManagement includes the PeerCertificate Management utility class, which contains a small set of methods that can be used to create, remove, and check for peer certificates and key pairs.

- Intel.Peer.File.FileCopy includes the PeerFileCopy and PeerFileURI Collection classes, which allow you to easily integrate file-transfer functionality into your peer-to-peer applications.

- Intel.Peer.Messaging.Utility includes the PeerWebRequestUtility class, which allows you to use peer-to-peer communication with the WebRequest class. We won't consider this approach in this chapter.

Configuring the Peer Service

You won't need to perform any additional configuration to test the Intel Peer-to-Peer Accelerator Kit. The peer service is automatically installed and configured to run on startup as part of the installation process. However, when testing peer-to-peer applications in distributed environments, you'll have to specify the discovery service to use and optionally configure a relay service.

Both of these details are configured by editing the *Intel.Peer.Common. Dameon.config* XML configuration file, which is found in the *InstallDir]\Intel\ P2P\v1.0\Config* directory.

Here's the basic outline of the configuration file sections:

```
<?xml version="1.0" encoding="utf-8" ?>
<PeerConfiguration>

  <!-- Entry for the ListenerPort and LoggingLevel -->

  <!-- Entry for the Listener -->

  <!-- Entry for the Peer Name System -->

  <!-- Entry for the Secure Listener -->

  <!-- Entry for the Relay -->

  <!-- Entry for Tunnel -->
```

```
<!-- Entry for Port Mapped data -->

<!-- Entry for Store and Forward service -->

<!-- Entry for FileCopyService -->

</PeerConfiguration>
```

The first section allows you to configure the port that the peer service uses to listen for incoming requests. You can also configure the client certificate to use when creating secure sessions as well as a proxy address and port.

```
<Messaging LoggingLevel="0">

  <ListenerPort>8080</ListenerPort>

  <ClientCertificate>C:\Program Files\Intel\P2P\v1.0\data\Security\Client.cer
  </ClientCertificate>

  <HttpProxyHost></HttpProxyHost>
  <HttpProxyPort>1</HttpProxyPort>

</Messaging>
```

You can also set a logging level from 0 to 5, where 0 indicates no logging and 5 indicates the maximum number of log messages. The log messages are written to a Windows event log named PeerServices.

The secure listener entry configures the server certificate as well as the port to use for SSL communication.

```
<Module Name="SecureListener" Assembly="...Intel.Peer.Messaging.Services.dll"
  TypeName="Intel.Peer.Security.SecureListener.SecureListenerInitializer"
  Load="true" Essential="true">

  <ListenerPort>8443</ListenerPort>
  <ServerCertificate>
    <Name>MyCert</Name>
  </ServerCertificate>

</Module>
```

The peer-name system entry is where you configure the discovery service. You can use the <Cache> element to configure how many peer entries will be retained in local memory or on disk. The peer name system entry also specifies the <URL>

element with the HTTP path to the *.asmx* web service that performs the discovery. The server name is the only part of this URL that you should need to modify, because the discovery service is installed by default as *peernameservice.asmx* in a virtual directory named *peernameservice*.

```
<Module Name="PeerNameSystem" Assembly="...Intel.Peer.Messaging.Services.dll"
  TypeName="Intel.Peer.Messaging.NameService.PeerNameSystem"
  Load="true" Essential="true">

  <DataStore Assembly="...Intel.Peer.Messaging.Services.dll"
    TypeName="Intel.Peer.Messaging.NameService.PnsXmlStore">
    <Cache>
      <OnDisk>
        <MaxEntries>1000</MaxEntries>
        <Path>C:\Program Files\Intel\P2P\v1.0\Data\NameServiceCache</Path>
      </OnDisk>
      <InMemory>
        <MaxEntries>100</MaxEntries>
      </InMemory>
    </Cache>
  </DataStore>

  <ServerInformation>
    <URL>http://{server_name}/peernameservice/peernameservice.asmx</URL>
  </ServerInformation>

</Module>
```

Optionally, you can specify several server URLs. In this case, the peer will pass its information to every server whenever an update is performed. On lookup calls the peer will try the servers in order until a response is returned.

In addition, you can also configure the store-and-forward entry to configure how much space is allocated for messages (in megabytes) that are queued for attempted retransmission. You can set where they should be stored, how often delivery should be reattempted (in seconds), and the maximum life span a message is allowed to have (in days). The defaults allocate 10 MB of space, retry message delivery every ten minutes, and allow stored messages to last a full week on the peer.

```
<Module Name="StoreAndForward" Assembly="...Intel.Peer.Messaging.Services.dll"
  TypeName="Intel.Peer.Messaging.StoreAndForward.PeerStoreAndForwardService"
  Load="true" Essential="true">
```

```
<StorageSpace>10</StorageSpace>
<StoragePath>C:\Program Files\Intel\P2P\v1.0\Data\StoreForward</StoragePath>
<MaxLive>7</MaxLive>
<DeliveryInterval>600</DeliveryInterval>
```

```
</Module>
```

Finally, the relay and tunnel elements allow you to set up firewall traversal solutions. The relay element allows you to configure a peer to act as a relay server (or "super peer") that takes additional responsibility for transmitting messages between peers that could not otherwise communicate, as shown in Figure 13-5.

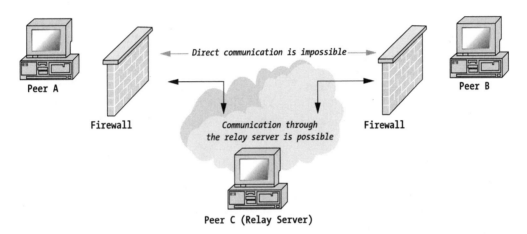

Figure 13-5. The role of a relay server

In Figure 13-5, Peer A is unable to open a connection to Peer B. However, it can contain the relay server hosted by Peer C. If Peer B is also using Peer C, all communication can be routed through subconnections in Peer C. These are called tunneled connections, and they use the BEEP Protocol.

This is how it works, step-by-step:

1. During startup, the listener on Peer A makes a connection to the relay service on Peer C and opens a channel using BEEP. It identifies itself to the relay using its peer name.

2. The relay returns one or two new URLs that can be used to contact Peer B through the relay on Peer C. These URLs are also returned by the tunnel to the peer service on Peer B.

3. When a message is sent through the relay service, it examines the path, determines which peer it's for, and then opens a channel on the peer's tunnel and relays the data.

4. The relay continues to operate this way until the tunneling connection from the peer is closed or lost.

To configure a peer to act as a relay server, specify a port to use for receiving requests and one for tunneling connections. You must also modify the <Module> tag and set Load to true (which isn't the default).

```
<Module Name="Relay" Assembly="...Intel.Peer.Messaging.Services.dll"
  TypeName="Intel.Peer.Messaging.NetworkConnectivity.RelayService.Configuration.
  RelayInitializer" Load="true" Essential="false">

  <TunnelIdPath>C:\Program Files\Intel\P2P\v1.0\Data\TunnelIDs.ser</TunnelIdPath>
  <RelayPort>100</RelayPort>
  <TunnelPort>200</TunnelPort>
  <UsesBEEPTunnel>true</UsesBEEPTunnel>
  <HttpCallPorts>1024..1054</HttpCallPorts>

</Module>
```

Once you have a relay server, you can make use of it in other peers by configuring the tunnel entry. Once again, you must set Load to true. You must also set the tunnel endpoint to the host name where the relay service is running.

```
<Module Name="Tunnel" Assembly="...Intel.Peer.Messaging.Services.dll"
  TypeName="Intel.Peer.Messaging.NetworkConnectivity.Tunnel.Configuration.
  TunnelInitializer" Load="true" Essential="false">

  <TunnelEndpoint>{relay_host_name}:200</TunnelEndpoint>
  <BEEPUsage>
    <UsesBEEPTunnel>true</UsesBEEPTunnel>
    <BEEPProxy>
      <Endpoint>{beepproxy_host_name:port}</Endpoint>
      <EndPoint>{second_beep_proxy_host_name:port}</EndPoint>
    </BEEPProxy>
  </BEEPUsage>

</Module>
```

Clearly, the manual configuration steps that are involved make this a less-than-perfect solution. Other firewall traversal mechanisms are defined in the Intel Peer-to-Peer Accelerator Kit architecture specification but not implemented.

Creating a Messenger that Uses Intel Peer-to-Peer

To get a better understanding of how the Intel Peer-to-Peer Accelerator Kit works in a peer-to-peer application you might design, this chapter modifies the peer messaging application (first presented in Chapter 4) to use the toolkit. This gives the added benefit of firewall traversal and integrated security, but it also requires some unexpected code changes.

The next three sections present the basic changes that are required to the interfaces, server, and client. After reviewing these, you can continue with the last section to easily add enhanced security.

Changes to the Talk Component

The first step is to redefine the interfaces used in the system. In a peer-to-peer application developed with the Intel toolkit, you don't use the ObjRef directly. Instead, when a peer wants to communicate with another peer, it constructs a new Peer URL and uses the System.Activator object to retrieve a proxy.

To support this approach, the signature of the ITalkServer.AddUser() method needs to be modified slightly so that it accepts a peer URL instead of a ITalkClient.

```
Public Interface ITalkServer

    ' These methods allow users to be registered and unregistered
    ' with the server.
    Sub AddUser(ByVal [alias] As String, ByVal peerUrl As String)
    Sub RemoveUser(ByVal [alias] As String)

    ' This returns a collection of currently logged-in user names.
    Function GetUsers() As ICollection

    ' The client calls this to send a message to the server.
    Sub SendMessage(ByVal senderAlias As String, _
        ByVal recipientAlias As String, ByVal message As String)

End Interface
```

This example is using the centralized version of the Talk .NET application. If it was the decentralized version, you would also need to modify the GetUser() method to return a peer URL instead of an ITalkClient reference.

Changes to the TalkServer

Even though the Intel Peer-to-Peer Accelerator Kit includes a discovery service, a coordinator component is still required to help online peers discover one another for messaging purposes. Before modifying the TalkServer, you need to add a reference to the *Intel.Peer.Messaging.dll* assembly and import the following namespace:

```
Import Intel.Peer.Messaging
```

The first change is how the TalkServer coordinator object is registered. Instead of using the configuration file and the RemotingConfiguration.Configure() method, the registration must be performed programmatically (although you could store some of this information in application settings in a configuration file to allow easy modification).

The registration consists of three steps: defining an application name, registering a new channel, and registering a new well-known Singleton object that clients can call. At the end of these steps, the server displays the URL of the Talk .NET server coordinator object in the trace display (see Figure 13-6).

```
' Set the application name. This information is used to create the complete URL.
RemotingConfiguration.ApplicationName = "TalkServer"

' Create and register the channel for peer-to-peer communication.
Dim Channel As New PeerChannel()
ChannelServices.RegisterChannel(Channel)

' Register the ServerProcess object as a Singleton so clients can call it.
Dim Uri As String = "ServerObject"
Dim ServiceEntry As New WellKnownServiceTypeEntry(GetType(ServerProcess), Uri, _
    WellKnownObjectMode.Singleton)
RemotingConfiguration.RegisterWellKnownServiceType(ServiceEntry)

' Retrieve the complete URL and display it.
Dim Url As String = PeerChannel.GetUrl(Uri)
Trace.WriteLine(Url)
```

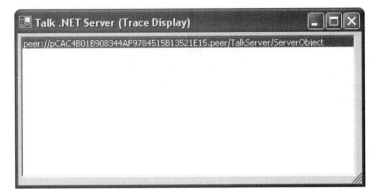

Figure 13-6. The server object URL

The TalkServer requires very few additional changes. The new AddUser()
method must be modified so that it stores a collection of Peer URLs instead of
ITalkClient references:

```
Public Sub AddUser(ByVal [alias] As String, ByVal peerUrl As String) _
  Implements TalkComponent.ITalkServer.AddUser

    Trace.Write("Added user '" & [alias] & "'")
    SyncLock _ActiveUsers
        _ActiveUsers([alias]) = peerUrl
    End SyncLock

    MessageDelivery.UpdateUsers(_ActiveUsers.Clone())

End Sub
```

The message delivery code must also take this change into account. Before it
can contact a peer, it must convert the URL into a proxy. Here's the abbreviated
code from the MessageDelivery class:

```
' Deliver the message.
Dim Recipient As ITalkClient
Dim PeerUrl As String
Dim Sender, MessageBody As String

SyncLock RegisteredUsers
    If RegisteredUsers.ContainsKey(NextMessage.RecipientAlias) Then
        PeerUrl = RegisteredUsers(NextMessage.RecipientAlias)
        MessageBody = NextMessage.MessageBody
        Sender = NextMessage.SenderAlias
```

```
        Else
            ' User wasn't found. Try to find the sender.
            If RegisteredUsers.ContainsKey(NextMessage.SenderAlias) Then
                PeerUrl = RegisteredUsers(NextMessage.SenderAlias)
                MessageBody = "'" & NextMessage.MessageBody & _
                    "' could not be delivered."
                Sender = "Talk .NET"
            Else
                ' Both sender and recipient weren't found.
                ' Ignore this message.
            End If
        End If
End SyncLock

If PeerUrl <> "" Then
    Recipient = CType(Activator.GetObject(GetType(ITalkClient), PeerUrl), _
        ITalkClient)
    Recipient.ReceiveMessage(MessageBody, Sender)
End If
```

Optionally, the server can also enable store-and-forward to ensure that message delivery is reattempted periodically if the peer cannot be contacted immediately. In order to support this feature, the server must be calling a method that's marked with the <OneWay> attribute, because there's no way for it to be sure that the method has actually executed. The ReceiveMessage() already uses this attribute. The only other step is to add the parameters to the peer URL that instructs the peer service to cache the message if needed. You do this by using the shared PeerChannel.EnableStoreAndForward() method and by specifying an absolute expiration date as a DateTime object or a number of seconds to live. The following example caches a message for up to 120 seconds.

```
If PeerUrl <> "" Then
    PeerUrl = PeerChannel.EnableStoreAndForward(PeerUrl, 120)
    Recipient = CType(Activator.GetObject(GetType(ITalkClient), PeerUrl), _
        ITalkClient)
    Recipient.ReceiveMessage(MessageBody, Sender)
End If
```

The peer clients can use the same approach to cache messages sent to the server (although this would be less useful) or to cache messages sent to other peers.

Changes to the Talk Client

As with the TalkServer, you need to add a reference to the *Intel.Peer.Messaging.dll* assembly and import the Intel.Peer.Messaging namespace on the client. The client also needs to register its peer channel and the ClientProcess Singleton programmatically. The first step is to define the channel and a unique application name. In this case, the user alias is used as the application name. This allows you to run multiple clients on the same computer without creating a conflict.

```
RemotingConfiguration.ApplicationName = [Alias]
Dim Channel As New PeerChannel()
ChannelServices.RegisterChannel(Channel)
```

The next step is to register the remotable ClientProcess object so that the server can contact the peer:

```
Dim Uri As String = "TalkClient"
Dim ServiceEntry As New WellKnownServiceTypeEntry(GetType(ClientProcess), _
  Uri, WellKnownObjectMode.Singleton)
RemotingConfiguration.RegisterWellKnownServiceType(ServiceEntry)
```

Now the peer can create a proxy object for talking to the server using the server's URL. In this case, the URL is constructed by using the defined application and object name, along with the machine-specific peer identifier. Remember, to avoid hard-coding these values, you can read them from the application settings section in a configuration file.

```
Dim Peer As String = "pCAC4B01B908344AF9784515B13521E15.peer"
Dim App As String = "TalkServer"
Dim Obj As String = "ServerObject"
Dim Url As String = "peer://" & Peer & "/" & App & "/" & Obj

' Create the proxy.
Server = CType(Activator.GetObject(GetType(ITalkServer), Url), ITalkServer)
```

The final step is to register with the server using the local peer URL. All this code takes place in the ClientProcess.Login() method.

```
Dim PeerUrl As String = PeerChannel.GetUrl(Uri)
Server.AddUser(_Alias, PeerUrl)
```

In the original Talk .NET application, the client application registers the ClientProcess object and then creates a new ClientProcess instance to start sending messages to the server. When the server calls back to the client, no new object is created. Instead, the existing ClientProcess instance is used. However, with the Intel Peer-to-Peer Accelerator Kit, this behavior changes. If you use the exact same approach, you'll actually end up with two ClientProcess objects: the one you created manually and the one created by the Remoting infrastructure to handle the server callbacks. This creates a significant problem. Namely, the Talk form will no longer receive the ClientProcess.MessageReceived event, because it will occur in a different object than the one it's using.

The recommended way to solve this problem is to use some sort of shared location to store a callback. Emulating the design pattern used in Intel's own Messenger sample, you can make three changes:

- Make all the members and methods of the ClientProcess class shared, *except* for the ITalkClient methods such as ReceiveMessage(). Change the other parts of the application so they use these shared methods and don't try to create a ClientProcess instance.

- Use a callback instead of an event to contact the Talk form.

- In the ReceiveMessage() method, check the shared callback delegate. If it's initialized, raise the callback.

Here's the abbreviated ClientProcess code:

```
Public Class ClientProcess
    Inherits MarshalByRefObject
    Implements ITalkClient

    ' This callback is used to transfer the message from the remotable
    ' ClientProcess object to the Talk form.
    Public Shared MessageReceivedCallback As ReceiveMessageCallback

    ' The reference to the server object.
    Private Shared Server As ITalkServer

    Private Shared _Alias As String
    Public Shared Property [Alias]() As String
        Get
            Return _Alias
        End Get
        Set(ByVal Value As String)
            _Alias = Value
        End Set
    End Property
```

```
Public Shared Sub Login()
    ' (Code omitted.)
End Sub

Public Shared Sub LogOut()
    ' (Code omitted.)
End Sub

Public Shared Sub SendMessage(ByVal recipientAlias As String, _
  ByVal message As String)
    ' (Code omitted.)
End Sub

' This is the only nonshared method.
<System.Runtime.Remoting.Messaging.OneWay()> _
Private Sub ReceiveMessage(ByVal message As String, _
  ByVal senderAlias As String) Implements ITalkClient.ReceiveMessage

    If Not ClientProcess.MessageReceivedCallback Is Nothing Then
        MessageReceivedCallback(message, senderAlias)
    End If

End Sub

Public Shared Function GetUsers() As ICollection
    Return Server.GetUsers
End Function

End Class
```

With these changes, the Talk .NET application becomes fully functional. Another recommended change is to reduce the frequency that the client retrieves new users from the server by increasing the tmrRefreshUsers timer interval. This is useful because the communication latency is noticeably greater than it was with the pure Remoting solution.

Adding Security

In order to communicate using secure encryption, you simply need to instruct the peer service by adding the PeerSecure option to the end of the peer URL. This can be accomplished using the shared PeerChannel.MakeSecure() method.

```
Dim Peer As String = "pCAC4B01B908344AF9784515B13521E15.peer"
Dim App As String = "TalkServer"
Dim Obj As String = "ServerObject"
Dim Url As String = "peer://" & Peer & "/" & App & "/" & Obj

Url = PeerChannel.MakeSecure(Url)
Server = CType(Activator.GetObject(GetType(ITalkServer), Url), ITalkServer)
```

In addition, you can configure a service to require secure sessions and reject requests that don't use them. In this case, you use the shared PeerChannel .SecureWellKnownServiceType() method. This can be called for both the ClientProcess and the ServerProcess objects before they're registered with the Remoting infrastructure.

```
Dim Uri As String = "ServerObject"
Dim ServiceEntry As New WellKnownServiceTypeEntry(GetType(ServerProcess), _
  Uri, WellKnownObjectMode.Singleton)

PeerChannel.SecureWellKnownServiceType(ServiceEntry)
RemotingConfiguration.RegisterWellKnownServiceType(ServiceEntry)
```

> **TIP** *You cannot use the store-and-forward capability in conjunction with secure messages.*

Unfortunately, life isn't nearly this simple. In order to create a secure SSL session, the peers must be able to authenticate one another using certificates. That means that you must create a certificate for every peer and store it in the local certificate store. You must also configure the trusted roots on both peers so that certificates signed by this peer are trusted implicitly. (A better and more secure alternative is to sign the peer certificates using a trusted third party, such as a local Windows server or certificate authority. However, the Intel Peer-to-Peer Accelerator Kit API doesn't support this functionality directly.)

This process can be accomplished programmatically using the PeerCertificate Management class, which is demonstrated in the CertificateManagementUI sample application (see Figure 13-7). Essentially, this application calls the PeerCertificateManagement.CreateKeyAndSelfSignedCertificate() method to generate a new certificate (with a 512-bit RSA asymmetric key pair), sign it, and add it to the local personal certificate store.

Figure 13-7. The CertificateManagementUI utility

Figure 13-8 shows the CertificateManagementUI utility.

Figure 13-8. Creating a new certificate

Once a certificate is created, you still have several additional steps to complete. First, run the makecert.exe utility included with the .NET Framework, and find the certificate in the Personal store (see Figure 13-9). You must then perform three additional tasks:

- Export this certificate to a *.cer* file stored on your hard drive (typically in the *Intel Peer-to-Peer Accelerator Kit* directory).

- Import this certificate into the Trusted Root store for the current user.

- Import this certificate into the Trusted Root store for the peer you want to communicate with securely.

All of these tasks are described in more detail, along with the basics of client certificates, in a lengthy HTML file called *CertificateManagement Education and Help.html,* which can be found in the *CertificateManagementUI* directory. A detailed discussion is beyond the scope of this chapter.

Figure 13-9. The makecert.exe utility

Finally, you need to modify the configuration file to use this new certificate. To configure the certificate for incoming connections, you modify the <ServerCertificate> tag to use the certificate name:

```
<Module Name="SecureListener" Assembly="...Intel.Peer.Messaging.Services.dll"
 TypeName="Intel.Peer.Security.SecureListener.SecureListenerInitializer"
 Load="true" Essential="true">

  <ListenerPort>8443</ListenerPort>
  <ServerCertificate>
    <Name>P2PUser1</Name>
  </ServerCertificate>

</Module>
```

You must also configure the certificate in order to use it for outgoing connections. In this case, you need to reference the exported certificate file instead of the certificate name, because the certificate information will be read from the disk, not from the local store. This quirk is related to a limitation in .NET's support for retrieving certificate information.

```
<Messaging LoggingLevel="0">

  <ListenerPort>8080</ListenerPort>
  <ClientCertificate>C:\MyDir\P2PUser1.cer</ClientCertificate>
  <HttpProxyHost></HttpProxyHost>
  <HttpProxyPort>1</HttpProxyPort>

</Messaging>
```

Finally, you must restart the peer service using the Computer Management utility in the Control Panel.

Clearly, the configuration steps involved in setting up SSL authentication and encryption are far from minor. If you need a more flexible, dynamic form of authentication and validation, refer instead to the custom examples developed in Chapter 11.

> **NOTE** *With encrypted communication, the peer service performs the encryption and decryption. Thus, an unencrypted message could be sent if an attacker could determine the underlying Remoting address and contact it directly. For that reason, you should not rely on SSL sessions for encryption, unless your computer is behind a firewall that makes port-scanning attacks impossible.*

Dissecting the Samples

To learn more about the Intel Peer-to-Peer Accelerator Kit, you can explore the samples (and if you're somewhat more ambitious, the source code for the toolkit itself). Unfortunately, the samples are only provided in C# syntax. However, as you no doubt already know, almost all C# code can be converted to VB .NET code on a line-by-line basis. This means that once you acclimatize yourself to the altered syntax, case sensitivity, and preponderance of curly braces, you should be able to determine exactly how the code samples work.

The next few sections introduce each of the sample applications and briefly describe the underlying operation and design decisions. You can also refer to the *readme.htm* file that's provided in each sample directory, which supplies limited information about how to test the example.

FileCopy

The Intel Peer-to-Peer Accelerator Kit also provides basic functionality for transferring files and monitoring their progress. The underlying operation of the file copy feature is fairly similar to the custom approach developed in Chapter 4. Files become available when they're "advertised," at which point they're dynamically associated with a unique GUID. If a peer wants to download the file, it uses the GUID in its request. Unlike our custom solution, the use of a peer service allows shared files to persist between application sessions. To remove a file from the available pool, its advertisement must be specifically cancelled. If a physical file is moved or deleted, the advertisement will still remain and an error will occur if another peer tries to download the file.

The FileCopy example is a console application that allows you to transfer a file between two peers. This functionality does not include any way to associate application-specific metadata (such as MP3 song information) with a file, so you still need to add these features to a central coordinator or lookup service if you need them.

Messenger

This Messenger example is a Windows application that allows instant messaging, similar to the Talk .NET application. It uses a global session concept, whereby all registered peers become a part of the same chat room. Messages are sent to every peer, which means that the system won't scale well to extremely large networks.

The Messenger is similar to the decentralized version of Talk .NET because the central coordinator (called the listener) is used for storing registered user URLs. It doesn't perform the actual message delivery. The central coordinator uses a "push" model. Whenever a new user joins the system, the new user list is sent to each registered peer. When sending a message, the peer goes through each entry in the local copy of the user list and contacts each peer separately.

The peer clients aren't configured with any information about the location of the listener. When launching a peer client, you must supply a command-line parameter that indicates the peer ID for the machine where the server is running. The listener displays this information in a console window when it first starts. (See Figure 13-10.)

> **NOTE** *One significant limitation in the design of the Messenger application is the fact that it doesn't use interfaces. This means that the shared assembly (ListenerObject.dll) must contain the complete code for both the server and peer remotable objects. In fact, this DLL even includes the Windows form code, which means that the server must be updated if you want to change any aspect of the peer UI.*

Figure 13-10. The Intel Peer-to-Peer Messenger

Scribble

The Scribble example is a collaborative Windows Forms application that allows multiple peers to share a single whiteboard. Whatever one peer draws on the whiteboard will be replicated to all registered users.

The Scribble example uses the same design as the Messenger. It's composed of two components: a Scribble server application and a Scribble client application. The Scribble server component records a list of registered users and provides the user list to all peers that connect with the system. The peers, however, communicate directly.

> **TIP** *The* readme.htm *file included with the Scribble example shows the logic in detailed pseudocode so that you can understand the operation of the application without needing to dive into the C# source code.*

SharedCyclesP2P

SharedCyclesP2P (see Figure 13-11) is a Windows application that demonstrates one way to build a distributed task manager. SharedCyclesP2P uses a foreman application, which divides a computer-intensive graphic into a user-defined number of smaller jobs and a large number of worker peers that perform the actual work. The foreman assigns job portions to the pool of workers and combines the results. One of the most interesting aspects of the SharedCyclesP2P application is that it tackles a relatively practical example (rendering a ray trace drawing), rather than the more rudimentary prime number search that's used to demonstrate distributed computing in Chapter 6. Figure 13-11 shows a partially complete rendering job displayed in the foreman.

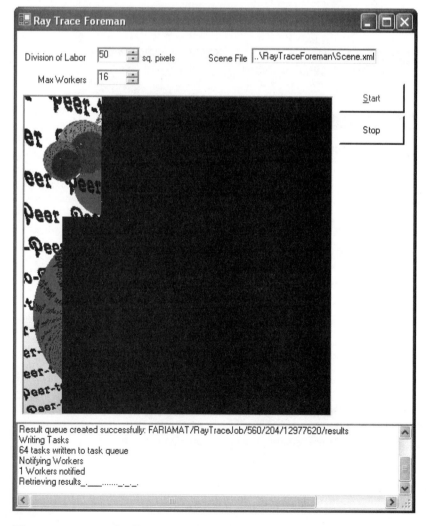

Figure 13-11. A partially complete SharedCyclesP2P job

The *readme.htm* file included with SharedCyclesP2P includes detailed information for testing the example. The most significant limitation in SharedCyclesP2P is that it doesn't provide a discovery mechanism for locating worker peers. Instead, you need to take the peer ID, which is displayed in the console window, and paste it into a text file. The foreman reads this text file to locate available workers. Clearly, you would need to replace this mechanism with some type of registration mechanism or an application-specific discovery service before making this into a production application.

ShareBaby2

ShareBaby2 (see Figure 13-12) is a file-sharing Windows application that works somewhat like the example presented in Chapter 9. It makes use of a discovery service and database for sharing file keyword information and uses multiple threads to manage concurrent uploads and downloads. However, it doesn't offer the same features for file-progress monitoring. It doesn't use the simple FileCopy API included with the Intel Peer-to-Peer Accelerator Kit.

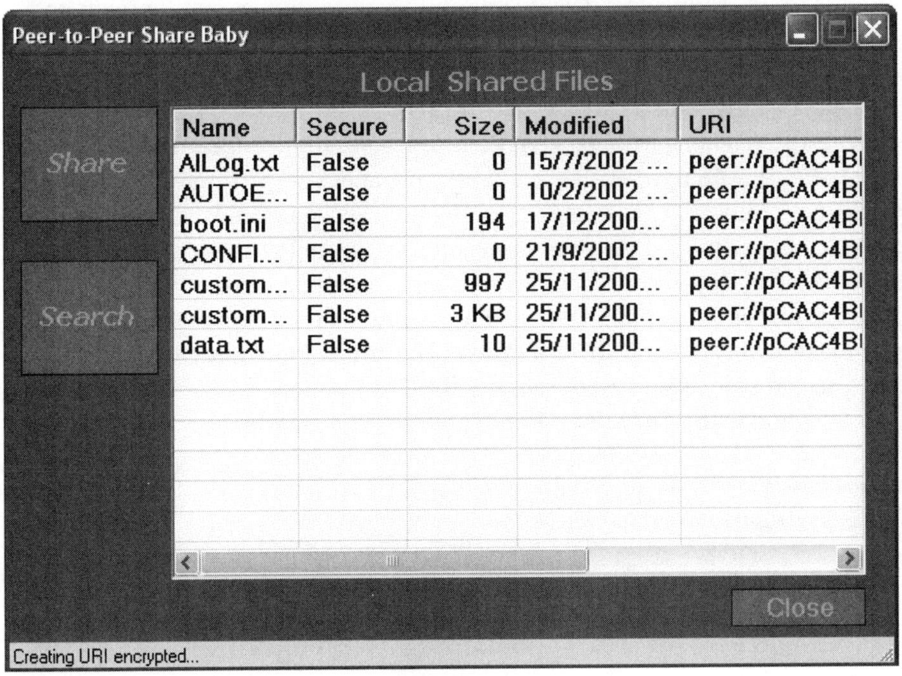

Figure 13-12. The Intel Peer-to-Peer ShareBaby2

Peer ASP Host

The peer ASP host is a console application that shows how you can host an ASP.NET web service inside a peer-to-peer application. In order to perform this feat, the ASP.NET process is actually hosted inside a custom host application instead of the Internet Information Server (IIS). It's a thought-provoking example of how you might want to combine these two technologies, but it does introduce an additional layer of customization that could make it difficult to upgrade your application to future .NET Framework releases and adopt new features.

The Last Word

Intel's Peer-to-Peer Accelerator Kit is an excellent example of how extensible the .NET Framework really is, and how it can lend itself to a new programming paradigm such as peer-to-peer. It's still too early to decide whether Intel's Peer-to-Peer Accelerator Kit will live up to its promise or become another interesting sidebar in the history of programming. Presumably, Intel is committed to peer-to-peer technology today because they hope it will drive the adoption of their hardware in the future, and despite investing in peer-to-peer development and belonging to peer-to-peer working groups, Intel's interest could waver.

Unfortunately, the fact that the toolkit is written as a proprietary component (rather than a traditional open-source project) doesn't encourage confidence. Unlike most emerging technologies, there's no supporting developer community or hub on the website where you can find news about ongoing developments or plans. But whatever the ultimate fate of the Intel Peer-to-Peer Accelerator Kit, you can still learn enough about peer-to-peer development to make it worthwhile to examine it closely and experiment with some of the samples. Comparing this code to some of the samples in this book will also help you understand the trade-offs and design decisions inherent in any peer-to-peer programming project. In fact, you can even review, modify, or use the C# source code, which is installed with the setup in the *[InstallDir]\Intel\P2P\v1.0\src* directory.

Index